ROSS AND THE NEW YORKER

New York Herald Tribune, Don Rice, photographer

HAROLD WALLACE ROSS

ROSS AND THE NEW YORKER

by

DALE KRAMER

Harold Ross died in 1952, R.I.P.

LONDON
VICTOR GOLLANCZ LTD
1952

The untitled poem by Ogden Nash is copyrighted 1934 by Ogden Nash.

The verses by Dorothy Parker are reprinted by permission of Methuen & Co., Ltd. and the Viking Press, Inc.

"Villanelle of Horatio Street, Manhattan," by James Thurber, copyright 1927, the F-R Pub. Corp.

"A Box to Hide In," by James Thurber, copyright 1931, is reprinted by permission of Hamish Hamilton Ltd. and of the F-R Pub. Corp.

The article by E. B. White, on p. 149, copyright 1925, the F-R Pub. Corp.

All of the above material first appeared in *The New Yorker* magazine.

Printed in Great Britain by
Lowe and Brydone (Printers) Limited, London, N.W.10

TO

MY PARENTS

Contents

1 UNLIKELY . . . STILL . . . 1
2 RISE AND FALL OF A PROMISING HOBO 5
3 PVT.-GEN. ROSS 19
4 CON MAN 35
5 FAILURE 57
6 FRANTIC SEARCH 73
7 BEDLAM 97
8 GLEAMS IN THE FORMULA 113
9 THE ARTISTS 125
10 BIG FOURSOME: ANGELL—WHITE—THURBER—GIBBS 139
11 THE EDITORIAL WARS 167
12 THE FORMULA SHINES 185
13 COASTING UPHILL 211
14 THE JOURNALISTIC FRYING PAN 245
15 "I AM SORELY PRESSED. . . ." 259
16 PLUSH-LINED RUT? 277
INDEX 299

ROSS AND THE NEW YORKER

Unlikely . . . Still . . . 1

IT HAS BEEN RUMORED that there is no Harold Wallace Ross. Despite a few frenetic appearances by Ross on the public scene, there are some who still claim that he is a literary hoax. A man who looks and acts like Harold Ross couldn't possibly, they argue, be editor of the nation's smartest magazine.

It is certainly true that a more implausible candidate for the role of Mr. Sophistication could hardly be found. One naturally imagines the editor of the New Yorker to be an up-to-date version of the delicate-featured, top-hatted gentleman who appears every February on the cover of the anniversary issue. In the mind's eye this aesthete, a Homburg placed jauntily on his aristocratic brow and an ironic smile playing on his lips, strolls about the city in search of material. His sensitive ear is attuned to the sounds of the metropolis. When he returns to his Proustian cork-lined room he edits the magazine with a gentle but occasionally sardonic hand.

Ross does not quite fit this description. When the New Yorker began publication in 1925 his outstanding physical characteristic was a shock of coarse brown hair that stood straight up to a commanding height of three inches. This, with his big-toothed mouth, unorganized features, and rawboned figure, gave him the look of a backwoodsman. He had a lusty, raucous voice and a taste for earthy epithets. His restless hazel eyes were those of a hell-raiser. Today his appearance has changed, to be sure. His hair has wilted. It lies flat, a lusterless mouse color. He has begun to stoop and to lean to the right. But he still looks like a backwoodsman, a retired one, perhaps, who has returned to town to polish the loafer's bench before the general store.

On the job and off he fails to behave in a manner befitting the editor of a sophisticated magazine. Readers expect the offices of the New Yorker to reflect its rich, aloof tone. The corridors, lined with cell-like cubbyholes, have been compared by staff members to the slum area of a rabbit warren. Behind the magazine's decorous façade has been a nerve-shattering editorial uproar unsurpassed in publishing circles.

Ross never puts on his battered felt hat, much less a Homburg, for relaxed strolls about the metropolis. For one thing, he hates crowds, especially where vehicular traffic is present. Mingling with strangers makes all kinds of trouble for his ulcers. This, in turn, brings grief to waiters. One, indignant and slightly nauseated by Ross's request for a stewed orange, declared testily that he had never heard of such a thing. "Go," Ross shouted, "and stew one!"

The fragile, chaste bouquet of the New Yorker's prose could be manufactured, most readers assume, only under the direction of one who delights in fine conversation. Ross grunts, mutters, explodes, rarely finishes a sentence, and rides off in half-a-dozen directions. A conversation dealing with abstract theories is considered by him to be silly, if not actually damaging to the mental and physical health of participants. Cosmic thinking, he has said, is pretty sure to lead to insanity or worse if indulged in regularly.

Ross was born in a town whose population would not

have filled a block of New York's larger apartment houses. Although he became a newspaperman at an early age, he never worked in the book or drama departments where he might have learned how to edit a magazine famous for the impeccability of its grammar and the subtlety of its prose. He was usually a leg man, telephoning his information to the office. He studiously avoided the sophisticated end of newspaper work, and shouted "fancy pants" or worse at those who dealt with the arts. He was a dedicated tramp, a skillful freight hopper, a man little bothered by a dirty shirt or a cheap lodging. He was Roughhouse Ross, picture snatcher, water-front skulker, loudest man at the poker table. His contempt for "Eastern dudes" was monumental.

As a soldier in World War I, Buck Private Ross was noted for uncouthness of garb and ungainliness of figure. In Paris, while on *Stars and Stripes*, he met Alexander Woollcott and Franklin P. Adams. After the war Ross intended to go to the South Seas to become a lotus-eater, but he decided to pause briefly in New York. When Edna Ferber first saw him, shooting craps down on the floor at F. P. A.'s house, she thought he was someone picked up overseas by Woollcott and Adams for laughs. Ross stayed on in New York and for several years edited a veteran's magazine whose chief editorial policy was "Pay your dues."

As a young man, Ross thoroughly enjoyed a good pratfall. His many years as editor of the genteel New Yorker have not robbed him of his taste for slapstick. Not long ago a faithful reader, chancing to meet him at a fishing camp, was invited to a lodge he was sharing with some buddies. There was a well-stocked bar and the guest accepted a drink. When he touched his glass a bell rang, lights flashed, an electric shock swept through him, and he fell through a trapdoor.

Despite this mass of contradictions, Ross alone could

have produced the New Yorker. He is probably the greatest editor of his time. And the man and his career are twice as preposterous as even the legend makers—and countless legends cluster around the New Yorker—have dared to suggest.

Rise and Fall of a Promising Hobo 2

George ross, a mining technician, was a large, florid man of a usually genial disposition but resolute convictions. A Scotch-Irishman from northern Ireland, where the feeling against religious dogma was strong, he was not merely opposed to tightly organized religion—he loved to argue against it. In the silver-mining town of Aspen, Colorado, where his son Harold Wallace was born on November 6, 1892, there was no issue to wholly test his forensic powers. But in Salt Lake City, where he moved when Harold was seven, he had a foe worthy of his mettle. Mormonism, he was convinced, ought to go.

He was not, however, a fanatical hater. He enjoyed his theological battles, and to get the most out of them he naturally had to know what he was talking about. He therefore made himself as familiar with the Mormon religion as a church dignitary. Nothing pleased young Harold more than to be present when his father and a Mormon friend placed a Book of Mormon and a Bible between them and went to work on each other. Ridicule was George Ross's basic weapon, and he was a gifted satirist.

As Harold grew up he fought with his father and more than once ran away from home. "They were too much alike," a family friend said later. "Each wanted his own way and wouldn't give in to anyone else." But Harold always credited his father with bequeathing a sense of humor to him.

The religion of his mother, Ida Ross, was Scotch Presbyterian, a sect obsessed by sin. She was a strong, simple, practical woman and a good teacher. To her can probably be traced Ross's high moral sense, which he translated into his magazine. He is squeamish about off-color things in print and a dirty word uttered in the presence of ladies offends him. His own use of earthy epithets was explained by a friend: "When Ross comes out with a big round poolroom oath he thinks he's been a real naughty boy, so he feels good for quite a while." Others have noticed that he sometimes uses profanity as a gap-filler while searching for a word he wants, or merely for trailing off a sentence.

His childhood was far from isolated. Any suggestion that he is countrified—and it is a suggestion that has been made thousands of times—irritates him. In mining camps there is always a big turnover of children who have grown worldly-wise in their travels. Salt Lake City contained a large non-Mormon element. It was, in fact, one of the more wide-open cities of the Rocky Mountain region.

Like other boys of the day, Ross read dime novels and the other routine adventure thrillers. But he also carefully followed reports of real adventure in the newspapers and wherever else he could. One thing he doted on was wars. When he was twelve the Russo-Japanese conflict was raging, to his intense satisfaction, and he read every line he could find about it. One of the great war correspondents of the time, Frederick Palmer, became his hero. Although gallant soldiers were quite approved of by Ross, his favorite was always the war correspondent. He decided to become a newspaperman. That was romantic enough in itself, and when a war came he would be ready for it.

As a freshman at West Side High School he made the staff of the school paper, the *Red and Black*. One of his acquaintances was John Held, Jr., later a celebrated artist, who was also on the school paper and who drew a regular cartoon for the Salt Lake City *Tribune*. Since he was now in the trade, Ross began hanging around the offices of the Salt Lake City *Telegram* and the *Tribune*, which were issued from the same plant. He was quiet, almost diffident, as he watched the office poker games and listened to conversations of the seasoned newspapermen.

No one ever fell more overwhelmingly and faithfully in love with a profession. Whenever the opportunity presented itself Ross jumped a fire engine or joined the cops on a mission. Finally he was given a part-time job running errands for the *Telegram's* sports editor. In Salt Lake City in those days, when an editor wanted to talk with a prize fighter, he sent for him. One of Ross's duties was to go into the Stockade, an area of the city filled with saloons and bawdy houses, and rout out whatever fighter his boss wanted. He was familiar with the district from having delivered ice cream sodas to the bawdy houses while working for a drugstore. Professors of literature do not habitually recommend student employment in a red-light district. Yet in a sheltered boy the contrast, the shattering wonder, may help to develop a sense of objectivity.

Ross wanted to become independent, largely because he was having more trouble than ever with his father. George Ross had gone into the demolition business, and sometimes his son worked for him as a timekeeper. But the more they were together the more they got on each other's nerves. During one departure from home Ross got as far as Colorado Springs, where an uncle lived. Another time he set off for California with an older boy, who abandoned him in Albuquerque. He hiked most of the way back home.

Instead of reporting for the junior year of high school Ross went to work full time on the *Tribune*. Afterward he was skeptical of high school graduates, and his scorn of college men was monumental.

Pay for newspapermen was low, but jobs were plentiful and the turnover rapid. A man who quit or was fired went across the street to another newspaper and hung up his hat and went to work. Or he moved on to another town.

It was the heyday of the tramp newspapermen. The term was not one of derogation. They were a proud, even haughty race, and they set themselves apart. Freedom was their watchword, authority their mortal enemy. A boss thought hard before speaking harshly to one of these aristocrats of the road, especially if he was shorthanded. For the tramp would immediately be up and away, sometimes after launching a paste pot at his traducer. When the whim was upon a tramp he moved without direct cause.

Ross met dozens of these gentlemen of the road as they boomed through on the way to California and back. Tramp reporters, copy editors, and printers were among the first great boosters of the California climate. Many refused to winter anywhere else. Most were excellent raconteurs, with a thousand tales of Chi and Frisco and Cincy and New Orleans and the Big Town. Many were deep readers—Shakespearean scholars, followers of Adam Smith, Henry George, Plato, Karl Marx, Schopenhauer.

Book learning, though, rated lower than other items in the tramps' code. At the top of the list stood Integrity. The tramps could not be bought and sold or made to do anything against their will. No fiercer non-conformers were to be found anywhere. Above book learning also stood Experience. The clansmen were contemptuous of the man who stayed in one place, wasting his life away. To learn about life you had to live, and that meant travel. To know about newspapers you had to work on scores of them up and down and across the land.

Ross was eighteen when, in the summer of 1910, the wanderlust overpowered him. He had grown to above medium height. With a muscular, graceless body and aggressive shoulders, he looked able to take care of himself, and was. Occasional short rations did not distress him greatly, a dirty shirt bothered him hardly at all, and he could enjoy a bed despite bedbugs. He hopped freights and in the direst emergencies went afoot.

A great many years later Ross covered a stretch of the Union Pacific in a private car that had belonged to E. H. Harriman, railroad magnate. Ross reminisced to his host, W. Averell Harriman, the magnate's son, of the days when he had walked the U.P. ties. As a memento Harriman gave him the car's name plate.

Ross's exact itinerary as a tramp newspaperman was soon lost to the memory of even himself. Now and again he would go home, but restlessness always hurried him away again. To his bosses, Ross was a happy-go-lucky, poker-playing, hard-swearing youth who was unlikely to rise far in the bourgeois journalistic world. He was competent, but his work was not outstanding even on those occasions when he took an assignment seriously. His dress-up attire was often dominated by a pair of screaming yellow shoes. His hair flopped in all directions two minutes after he had combed it, which was not very often. It wasn't until quite a while later that he adopted the stand-up horse brush of hair. A point of honor with tramp newspapermen—and a good share of the stationary ones—was an occasional long binge, referred to generally in the West as a "run." Ross had a noble respect for the code though he was not really a hard drinker.

He was always convivial, whether drinking or not, but there was a widely held belief among his close companions that his horseplay and explosive talk were cover-ups for shyness and uncertainty. Since an uncommonly large part of his time was spent at the poker table others believed that his noise was designed to disguise his strategy. Yet in a curious, inexplicable way Ross's buckshot conversation could be very convincing. And despite his lack of a commanding figure, leadership in any group gravitated to him—usually leadership in hell-raising of some kind. All of these qualities were demonstrated at the time of his first arrest.

Late in 1911 he had gone to work on the Sacramento *Union,* which had once harbored another roving journalist, Mark Twain. It had a bright Sunday supplement in which members of the large and capable staff were allowed to indulge journalistic flights. The "canned" feature section was not yet known.

One day Kenneth Adams, the city editor, suggested to Ross that he hop a Southern Pacific freight and beat his way over the summit of the Sierra Nevada to Truckee. Out of this ought to come, Adams thought, a two-page illustrated piece. As soon as he had left the office Adams ordered another reporter to follow him and see what freight car he boarded. Ross failed to detect his tail, who went back with the number of the train and the car.

Adams telephoned to the sheriff of Placer County, an old friend, and asked him to meet the train with all available peace officers, yank Ross off, and jug him without stating a charge. A little while after midnight in the town of Auburn a party including the sheriff, several deputies, and the town marshal deployed before Ross's car, flashed their lights in, and ordered him to come out with hands reaching for the sky. When he emerged, blinking and swearing, they hauled him onto a buckboard and rushed him to the local calaboose. The prisoner's story that he was really a reporter for the Sacramento *Union* was greeted with tight-lipped laughter.

Ross's noisemaking abilities brought the sheriff's reluctant agreement, after an hour or so, to put in a call to the *Union*. Adams said to tell Ross that he was not known on the paper. Ross was standing at the cell-block door, hands gripping the bars, when the sheriff delivered the message. He knew now that a joke was being played on him.

Resignedly he turned to his fellow inmates, mostly petty offenders. "Well," he said, "it was a pretty good story and it might have worked."

The sheriff went home to bed. Next day he inquired of the jailer how Ross was faring.

"He's got them convinced," the jailer replied, "that he's wanted in Salt Lake City for three murders. He's also judge of the kangaroo court. He's ruling with a pretty high hand."

After his release Ross filled two pages of the *Union's* supplement with a humorous account of his experiences. From that point forward he was Hobo Ross.

Many years later when Alva Johnston, the chief developer of the New Yorker's profile form, was visiting his home town of Sacramento he mentioned to a group of newspapermen that he was in the employ of Harold Ross, who might be remembered by some of them. Old-timers stared in amazement.

"What," one of them demanded finally, "could you possibly be doing for Hobo Ross?"

Ross demonstrated in Sacramento that he was just as

footloose as any other member of his clan. One day he disappeared. Ken Adams, thinking he was off on a "run," continued him on the pay roll, collecting his check every week for four weeks. He was getting worried when Ross reported in—by letter, from Panama City.

"I came down here," he wrote, "to find out if there might be a grain of truth among those lies you told me about Panama City."

A year or two earlier Adams had been on a roving assignment to Central and South America, and sometimes he had told Ross stories about the Panama City dives in which Central American revolutions were hatched. Ross, an admirer of the banana nations stories of O. Henry, had found the temptation to see for himself irresistible.

Back in the United States, Ross went to work in New Orleans on the *Item*. In those days the clansmen traveled what they called the Southern Circuit, being sure to hit New Orleans and Atlanta. Ross covered the courts for the *Item*. That meant sitting in the continuous poker game, cutting out occasionally to make a round of the news sources.

A young reporter on the *Item*, Bess Rowland, who later married Marquis James, the biographer, remembers Ross as a competent but not outstanding reporter who was in love with the tramp newspaperman tradition. She also recalls his yellow high-button shoes and peg trousers. His wardrobe did not appear to be large.

Ross's bosom companion in New Orleans was six-foot-two, rawboned Bill Ryan. Ross walked worshipfully at Ryan's heels, for Ryan stood high in the rovers' clan. He could turn out a top-notch story, which made him welcome on any paper, and he had a reputation as a magnificent drinker and a student of philosophy. Later on Ryan mysteriously dropped out of sight. For years, even after he was successful in New York, Ross hoped to locate Ryan, but the closest he ever came was word from a man who thought he had seen him in the Middle West.

Twice Ross penetrated to the outskirts of the Big Town and laid siege. In the tramp's handbook only the great Manhattan dailies were Big Town papers. It was the custom of clan members to camp outside and launch forays against their objectives. Ross's outposts were Hoboken and Brooklyn. None of his attacks on Manhattan was successful. The Big Town sent him scurrying back West, cursing the smart-aleck Eastern dudes harder than ever.

Nearly everyone in the tribe selected a great author or philosopher as a kind of patron saint. The philosophy of Herbert Spencer, the English positivist, suited Ross down to the ground. Spencer might have been a member of the clan. He had little formal education, never had a single grammar lesson, and boasted of his lack of formal knowledge of syntax. He read little, but his curiosity was highly developed, and by close observation he picked up such information as he needed. Spencer was a powerful advocate of individual freedom and a bitter enemy of encroachment by the state or other organized forces. Thus he, too, hated authority. His perfect man stood free, strong, proud, four-square, valuing his integrity above everything else, and Spencer himself was noted for inflexible sincerity. Ross had always liked the integrity part of the rovers' code. The philosopher went against the code, true enough, by being sedentary and ascetic. He swore but once in his lifetime—a fact bound to sadden Ross. But these shortcomings could be overlooked. It was by the Spencerian, or haphazard, system of picking up knowledge that Ross ran across a piece of writing which he immediately pronounced to be the proper textbook for editors and writers. Next to Spencer, Ross's favorite authors were rovers Joseph Conrad, Mark Twain, and O. Henry. His new bible was an article by Twain, "Fenimore Cooper's Literary Offenses."

The chief weapons selected by Twain for his assault on Cooper were a series of rules for writing a story. The author must "say what he is proposing to say, not merely come near it; use the right word, not its second cousin; eschew surplusage; not omit necessary details; avoid slovenliness of form; use good grammar; employ a simple and straightforward style." Other rules were longer, but the one with which Twain beat Cooper the hardest was the requirement of plausibility. By a close analysis of *The Deerslayer* and other tales Twain showed Cooper blundering foolishly about in the forest, rather than appearing as a believable master of woodcraft.

Mark Twain's solid piece of work was the foundation on which Ross later built the New Yorker. It held up remarkably well, especially after he had reinforced it with H. W. Fowler's *Dictionary of Modern English Usage*.

When Ross blew into San Francisco in 1916 he had, at twenty-three, been four years on the road. He had picked up another tramp and together they solicited work at the newspaper city rooms. At the *Call and Post* there was a single job, which the city editor said they could either draw straws for or split into shifts between them. The division would be fifteen dollars for one, ten for the other. They decided in favor of the split. On the flip of a coin Ross got the ten-dollar portion. But it was coffee money, and that was what he needed more than anything else at the moment.

Ross was put to work on the water front and the assignment was soon increased to full time. The fog and Ross complemented each other. Hunching along the shadowy piers in his battered raincoat, an old felt hat pulled over his searching eyes, casually rolling a Bull Durham cigarette, he was picturesque enough to have served as the pattern for Hollywood's devil-may-care reporter. His roaring, exuberant coverage of the water front became legendary.

He took slightly more interest in his work than before and began to get a reputation as a hound for facts. A reporter who is able to keep people talking gets more information than the one who simply demands answers to questions. Ross's scattered shots brought the facts showering down. The custom was to set up a partnership with another ship's reporter for mutual coverage protection. Ross joined with Gene Cohn of the *Bulletin*. Despite Ross's seemingly windy conversation he never violated a confidence.

The hobo's time for moving came. But Ross stayed on. Though he did not exactly feel settled, he liked San Francisco. The Barbary Coast had long since disappeared, but an atmosphere of adventure remained. Hospitable saloons ranged from Pisco John's, home of the famed Pisco Punch, to roistering water-front dives where sailors from all over the world gathered. San Francisco's restaurants were among the best in the world. There was even a literary bohemia. At the Bohemian Club such flamboyant characters as the poet George Sterling and novelist-adventurer Jack London could frequently be found. Ross admired London, although he did not approve of his socialism: he was convinced, along with Spencer, that Marxism was synonymous with regimentation. When London committed suicide Ross felt that too much thinking about socialism was responsible.

Ross customarily addressed people brusquely by their last names and usually he was plain "Ross"—unless a topical nickname was current. But in San Francisco he was called Hal by his friends. Sometimes around the Press Club it was extended to Roughhouse Hal or Roughhouse Ross. Once when the club needed furniture he led a naval expedition to the Panama-Pacific Exposition and commandeered wicker chairs and settees from the Danish exhibit. Fortunately the exhibition was over.

As a cribbage player Ross was fierce, loud, profane, and magnificent. He often ate off his cribbage winnings. At poker he was not considered so good. He disagreed, and regularly backed his view with his pay. That he was the most tireless player in San Francisco, and maybe the world, everybody agreed. On the rare nights when no game was available he could often be found lying in bed in his cheap hotel, reading Herbert Spencer.

His close associates noticed, however, that after a year in San Francisco he was breaking some really serious rules of the rovers' clan. A member in the best of standing rarely sought relaxation anywhere but in the saloons, the bawdy houses, or at the gaming tables. Word began to seep around that Ross, in a sly way, was becoming something of a ladies' man. Worse still, one of courtly behavior. It was established beyond quibble that he had sent gifts of candy and flowers to the telephone girl at his rattletrap hotel. There was good reason to believe that he had favored others in like manner. As compensation for what was widely regarded as an unhandsome countenance this was forgivable. But evidence mounted that the ladies found him attractive. Whether the cause was his reckless attitude toward life, contrasted with his courtliness, or some charm even more difficult to explain, no one knew.

Local patriots thought of San Francisco as a cultural, cosmopolitan city. Because of this attitude it was fashionable for lawyers, bankers, and other solid men to rub shoulders with the literati at the Bohemian Club and elsewhere. A "character" was regarded highly. Roughhouse Hal, the hobo newspaperman, qualified. Many of the more substantial citizens viewed themselves as masters at the cribbage board. A tussle with Ross sweated them, and his grapeshot fusillades of conversation were intriguing. He was sometimes a guest in the big houses.

Observers noted, along with the breaking of the hobo code, a sign or two that Ross was not entirely satisfied with his acomplishments to date. Though still under twenty-five, he would not tell his age. He even tried to give the impression that he was younger than he really was.

Ross had followed the European war with fascination and he hungered to see and report it. But because of his youth and lack of professional standing he stood little chance of a war correspondent's assignment. His interest in the conflict was more than journalistic. Spencer had written bitterly against military states, holding that only after war is outlawed can the shackles be struck from the individual man. Germany, in Spencer's opinion, was the worst military state of all, and Ross agreed with him.

A few days after the United States declared war on Germany in the spring of 1917, Ross was hustling along the water front when a sign halted him.

Recruiting Headquarters
18th ENGINEERS (RY.) REGIMENT
"First to France; First to Fight"

That sounded right. Ross made inquiries and then rushed to the *Call and Post*. His enthusiasm was catching. From there he went to the Press Club. Before long he had recruited half a dozen journalists, including Roy Kirk, his current roommate. It was almost a squad.

The recruiting people intimated that Ross would become

a corporal right away. Did Ross throw up his hands in horror at this offer of command? He did not. He was willing to *be* Authority. The incident had a profound effect on him and probably on American culture. The desire for pomp and power was one more crack in the rovers' code, and it was too big for mending.

Ross had made a fine, even magnificent, effort to be a hobo. He simply did not have what it took.

Pvt.-Gen. Ross 3

THE 18th Engineers moved up to Fort Lewis, Washington, for training, and the matter of the corporalcy was dropped. The journalists recruited by Ross enthusiastically launched a regimental publication. Ross had brought along an old portable typewriter, with one set of keys for capital letters, another for lower case. The typewriter was his sole contribution to the newspaper. As if trying to repair the crack in his hobo's armor, he plunged into poker and the pursuit of love more vigorously than ever.

The regiment's prediction of "first to France" was fairly accurate, since it arrived among the first 25,000 troops. The "first to fight" boast proved, however, to have been an idle one. Made over into a construction unit, the regiment was sent to Bordeaux. Part of the work was the construction of ditches. The men were a rough, hard-boiled lot, difficult to handle. The average age was twenty-eight—old for soldiers. They were railroad bullheads, cow hands, hoggers, international tramps. Many were drunks. All had been hungry often and most of them had been in jail at least once. The hard physical labor under discipline embittered them. The harassed officers, wanting to get amenable kids from the draft, began transferring the old hands to other outfits.

Ross was not a brawling tough, but he was dangerous in

his way. As a convincing talker and a natural rebel (and he did not like to dig ditches any better than anybody else) he was a troublemaker. His company commander was a rough-spoken man of the old school who especially did not want anyone around who was smarter than he was. He had Ross trundled off to an officers' training camp.

From the first Ross questioned his ability to withstand the camp's discipline and, if he managed it, his capacity to move completely over to the other side as a giver of orders. The freezing cold at Langres in the foothills of the Vosges Mountains, where the camp was located, brought out the old tramp in him. He had to have heat if a summer climate was not available. After a while he saw in one of the English-language dailies published in Paris a notice that soldiers with journalistic experience were wanted for a contemplated troop newspaper. The layers of discipline which the Army had so laboriously applied now slipped to the ground.

"So," a buddy later said reverently, "without saying good-by, go to hell, or anything else to the commandant, he caught a truck for Paris."

The first issue of *Stars and Stripes* (dated February 8, 1918) was already off the press when Ross arrived at its offices in the big, gloomy Hotel Sainte Anne, not far from the Palais-Royal and the Louvre. The entire editorial staff, consisting of one person, sat at a cast-iron, marble-topped café table, editing copy. This was Hudson Hawley, a former editor of the *Yale Record*. He still looked faintly like a college grind despite a figure that definitely set off the khaki wool blanket blouse, trousers, and wrap leggings of the enlisted men's uniform. Ross did not look military. His big trench shoes had never been shined. His blouse was unbuttoned and his leggings spiraled haphazardly. An overseas cap sat sideways on his head.

Ross inquired of Hawley the whereabouts of the officer in charge, and was directed to Lieutenant Guy T. Viskniskki, who sat in a small room by himself. Like nearly everyone who was to have anything to do with *Stars and Stripes,* Viskniskki was a man of considerable parts: In a more or less perverse way he left a mark on the military traditions of the United States. He was not merely an officer in charge of getting out a publication: he looked upon himself as a kind of field commander, and behaved as such. He would unhesitatingly place staff members under arrest for editorial slothfulness or insubordination.

A tall, gaunt, ascetic man, he would have looked like a monk even if the balding of his head had not left a tonsure. In the Spanish-American War he had been a sergeant and afterward had worked for a newspaper syndicate. A fierce patriot and even fiercer militarist, he had been among the first to rush to the colors and had arrived in France early, attached to the censorship staff. When he was put in charge of *Stars and Stripes* the A.E.F. command believed vaguely that a soldier publication might be good for morale. Viskniskki was given a little money and granted authority to collect a staff. He set off at breakneck speed. (Eventually *Stars and Stripes* paid over to the United States Treasury the original cash advance and a good deal more.)

Visk (the enlisted men called him Visk only behind his back) handed Ross a fistful of copy and told him to get it ready for the paper. He would work out the transfer problem later. Ross sat down at one of the little marble-topped café tables and went to work. Another enlisted man, Albian A. Wallgren, had reported for editorial duty but, not wanting to get off on the wrong foot, had immediately gone AWOL. Wallgren was a big, handsome Marine who liked his cup of wine. Hawley thought he was probably in the brig at the moment—a correct guess, as it turned out. But Wallgren never stayed in for long, for he was as popular with the Marines as his cartoons became with *Stars and Stripes* readers.

Arriving a couple of hours after Ross was John T. Winterich, alumnus of Brown University, who had been a copy editor on the Springfield (Massachusetts) *Republican*. The unathletic and slightly myopic Winterich was an even less likely soldier than Ross. That he looked more like one was a tribute to the disreputableness of Ross's uniform.

Ross's bad-dressing championship was seriously challenged a week later with the arrival of Alexander Woollcott. (The all-around title for worst-dressed at the war was held by Heywood Broun, but he was a civilian correspondent and anyhow had gone home before Ross arrived in Paris and struck his best form.) Knowledge of Woollcott's approach, heralded from afar, had filled Ross with disgust. There were already too many college men. He and Winterich had taken a room together at the YMCA and he liked the others all right. But he wondered how many college men a newspaper, especially a spokesman of the troops, could stand. Far more horrifying, Woollcott had been a drama critic—a New York critic to boot. There could be no more of a fancy-pants dude than that!

Seated at the little marble-topped tables when Woollcott arrived were, as he later put it, "three of the strangest-looking and, by strictly military standards, the least alarming soldiers I ever saw before or since." They were Ross, Winterich, and Hawley. By the same strict military standards Woollcott added nothing to the ferocity of the group. He was short and pudgy and his beaked round face would have been owly without the help of his thick-lensed spectacles. He had a magnificent physique for contesting the title of worst-dressed soldier, but he lacked heart, being congenitally rather neat.

"Where'd you work?" Ross inquired solicitously.

"The New York *Times*," answered Woollcott, with only slight condescension.

Ross threw back his head and laughed in a manner which Woollcott regarded as demoniacal. Finally Ross had to be helped out of the room.

Woollcott was not, Ross discovered quickly, an easy man to rib. Though not inclined to physical horseplay, Woollcott was strictly a roughhouse type—one of the roughest to appear in United States literary circles during the last few generations. He always carried a sharp knife for skinning friend, foe, or innocent bystander. Ross's profanity seemed wooden compared with Woollcott's obscenity. In contests of personal insult Woollcott was often able to reduce his opponents to tears. He himself was impervious to insult, at least in open battle.

To most of the others Ross appeared, as he had in his hobo days, happy-go-lucky and fairly competent. Some of them called him "Buddy." Woollcott thought he saw more in Ross. They were drawn to each other, in a cutthroat sort of way.

The sixth enlisted man to join the staff was artist C. LeRoy Baldridge, a former cheerleader at Chicago University. He was described by Woollcott as faintly resembling the Goddess of Liberty. Baldridge was, as a matter of fact, a practicing liberal who had written for the sometimes pacifist *New Republic,* which caused Visk, the fanatical patriot, to suspect him of being a German spy.

These six became the editorial board of control and remained so after dozens of others had joined the staff. This appointment was made by themselves, without Visk's knowledge. It was deemed unwise to let the commander know directly that he was being superseded.

The inevitable turmoil was hazardous but enormous fun for the control board members. When one undertook to relate an encounter with Visk, the others were quaking with laughter before half a dozen words were out. Though not very strict about shined shoes and buttoned buttons, Visk lined up everybody in the mornings for calisthenics. Even officers were required to exercise. Captain Franklin P. Adams, who wrote a column, was once caught by Visk standing behind a post, merely flopping an arm into view occasionally. Discipline was also strict in editorial matters. Visk wouldn't hesitate a second to issue a flat order about the use of a comma or the wording of a headline. Failure to comply might mean arrest.

When battles were at their hottest the board members fell back, particularly if under arrest, on frigid military subordination. "Will the lieutenant allow the private the privilege of stating an opinion?" was a likely question. The tactic could be effective as well as exasperating, as Ross demonstrated.

Each week as the press deadline approached, Visk set out to paste up a dummy for the front page. Just as regularly he needed help from either Ross or Winterich. One time when Winterich was away on leave Visk and Ross had a brisk exchange about the use of a comma, which ended with Ross under arrest. Evening and the deadline approached together. Visk worked desperately with paste pot and scissors under a single light, while Ross sat silently at one of the little tables in the outer gloom. No one else was around. Visk passed close to Ross many times on unnecessary little errands.

Finally Ross asked with a great show of humility, "May the private have the lieutenant's permission to go to the can?"

Visk did his best to look startled. "Why, Harold, I thought you had gone! How in the world are you, my boy?"

"The private is under office arrest and therefore is not permitted to leave," Ross replied courteously.

Visk appeared stunned at the very thought of such a calamity. "Why, Harold, whatever put such a thought into your head?"

Ross relented, for the good of the service, and made up the paper.

Stars and Stripes hurtled to enormous popularity with the troops. A box in the upper left-hand corner declared, "The official Newspaper of the A.E.F." On the other side of the page stood the slogan, "By and for the Soldiers of the A.E.F." Under a three-column picture of General Pershing in the first issue had been a message from him to his troops: "The paper, written by the men in the service, should speak the thoughts of the new American Army and the American people from whom the Army has been drawn. It is your paper. Good luck to it."

In its pages were news from home, information which the command wanted to get across to the troops, stories from the front, cartoons by Wallgren, and drawings by Baldridge. There were reams of poetry. The Kaiser, reading *Stars and Stripes*, might have dismissed the American Army as a gang of poets.

Wartime propaganda was like boiling syrup, and some of it gurgled in *Stars and Stripes*. A typical kettleful was a poem entitled "What We're Fighting For." It was illustrated by Baldridge's drawing of a woman holding two small children in her lap, a boy reading a book and a girl smiling contentedly. A typical stanza:

This is what we're fighting for—
That the girl on mother's knee
May not know the scourge of war,
Shock on land and shock on sea;
That the little boy may read
On and on of Fairyland
Undistraught by Teuton greed,
Safe from blow of Teuton hand.

Most soldiers were convinced that destruction of the Hun would make the world safe for democracy, as advertised. Ross was as caught up emotionally in the crusade as anybody. When Winterich, an art and book lover, remarked that in addition to participation in the war he had welcomed a chance to see the cultural riches of Paris and to brush up his French, Ross was shocked that thoughts other than of downing the Kaiser had entered anyone's mind. Even Woollcott floundered happily along the front, sending back stories in every paragraph of which the flag waved freely.

It was Visk, though, who stood forth as the greatest—and certainly the most humorless—patriot of them all. One day he called in Ross, Winterich, and Woollcott and ordered them to interview a congressman newly arrived from the States.

"Why three of us?" someone inquired.

Visk made an impatient gesture. "For a good reason, naturally," he said. "I want you to interview him, and after that I want you to beat him up. He's a pacifist."

The strong-arm squad, once outside, broke into uncontrollable laughter. Since Ross more closely resembled a rough-and-tumble fighter than the others, he was assigned to handle the beating. Later they reported to Visk that the congressman was too big to tackle, and besides, had a formidable bodyguard. Charles A. Lindbergh, Sr., of Minnesota, the congressman, was a large and rangy man, but a genial one, and the interview had gone off pleasantly.

Control board members had their fun, but they worked hard. Ross was completely serious about a job for the first time in his life. Winterich noticed that in their room at the YMCA Ross was generally without the foggiest notion where his razor was, and did not hesitate to tear up the room in a hunt for it. On the job everything had to be in perfect order. He was generous in loaning money—and a snarling skinflint about loaning his scissors.

Ross was surprised that he liked being editor. Or, to be more accurate, he was surprised that he *was* an editor. One of *Stars and Stripes*' popular features resulted directly from Ross's new-found editorial initiative. The plight of French children orphaned by the war appealed to Ross's sentimentality. The possibility of a newspaper campaign to help them excited Ross the journalist. He originated a plan whereby the orphans were to be cared for by American troops. A unit would raise money for the "adoption" of a child, insuring care of it for a year. The response was tremendous. More than four million francs (nearly a million dollars at the current rate of exchange) were raised.

In a roundabout way Ross was the originator of Father's Day. Growing tired of the Army slogan, "Write to Your Mother," he started a small campaign urging an occasional letter to Father. It was the period of the beginning of the "days" for people and things, and the momentum of "writing to Father" was influential in establishing Father's Day.

Fun off duty equaled that of warring with Visk. Not entirely unofficial, but always pleasant, were Visk's orders to locate Wally Wallgren, the footloose Marine. Wally's regard for deadlines remained at a low point, but the popularity of his cartoons prevented Visk from firing him. Constant office arrest, while a tantalizing prospect to Visk, would have been demoralizing. Anyhow, Wallgren took the irritating position that a prisoner should not be asked to do creative work. Three or four of the board would be sent to retrieve him from some bistro. Since they knew Wally's favorite haunts they could arrange the time of search to suit their convenience.

Favorite off-duty rendezvous of Ross and his cronies was Nini's, a tiny restaurant in the narrow Place du Tertre (Street of the Turtle) on top of Montmartre. Because of its considerable distance from the *Stars and Stripes*, they usually gathered there on Saturdays, making a day and a night of it. Few Americans penetrated to Nini's unless guided by one of the set. Habitués included Captain Franklin P. Adams, Lieutenant Grantland Rice, correspondent Richard Oulahan of the New York *Times*, George Boas, later head of the Philosophy Department at Johns Hopkins University, George T. Bye, who was working for a civilian news service but contributed to *Stars and Stripes*, Walter Duranty, and many others.

There was great drinking and talking, some eating, and considerable gaming at the small tables. The usual contest was craps, but sometimes it was poker, and so Nini's was to go down as the birthplace of the celebrated Thanatopsis Literary and Inside Straight Poker Club, even though it was not christened until after its transfer to New York. Ross and Woollcott engaged in a few loud and insult-filled games of cribbage, but the group atmosphere usually precluded individual combat.

A special guest at Nini's, brought first by Woollcott, was pretty, dark-haired Jane Grant. She had beat her way to the war as a member of a movie-showing outfit, after failing to wangle a correspondent's assignment. Some years before she had emigrated from Joplin, Missouri, to New York and become a member of the small but fierce band of lady journalists battering down the male chauvinism of newspaper city rooms. She had been the first of her sex on the New York *Times* to get an even break with male reporters on assignments.

Woollcott and Jane Grant had conducted a mild off-and-on romance while he was also a *Times* reporter. But it was dead now, and Woollcott, an able matchmaker, concluded that Ross and Jane would make a good pair. He had decided, for one thing, that Ross ought to settle in New York. Several board members had commenced to talk of descending in a body on the United States metropolis after the war, perhaps to start a tabloid newspaper patterned after *Stars and Stripes.*

Ross's personal intention, he claimed, was to return to San Francisco, outfit a boat, and go to the South Seas. The life of a lotus-eater appealed to him. But sometimes he entered into the daydreams of a publication edited by the board. He liked the idea of a high-class tabloid. Occasionally there was talk of a magazine that would report a city in somewhat the manner they were trying to report the war. There would be humor and personalities and straight descriptive writing, all aimed at an intelligent audience. Woollcott once told Baldridge that he could picture the rise of Ross to the very top of the New York editorial heap.

At the end of Jane Grant's first visit to Nini's, Woollcott

commanded Ross: "See the lady home." Ross already had that project in mind. Woollcott's judgment was good: Ross and Jane soon began keeping regular company.

When the war ended, *Stars and Stripes* was asked to assume an even greater morale task. Soldiers were bored, which caused an AWOL problem, and they were angered by delay in their shipment home. Board members were willing to oblige. But with wartime discipline relaxed they stepped up resistance to Visk's authority. At the same time Visk was weakening his position in battles with his superiors. In one of these he himself was arrested.

Philip Von Blon, a staff member, had written, and Wallgren had illustrated, a story about a new uniform which the Quartermaster Department had in the works. The commanding general of the District of Paris didn't like the story and undertook to jump down Visk's throat. Visk was at once the Spartan. He took full responsibility, declaring that he had written the story and even drawn the picture. The general had him arrested and confined to quarters, but after a couple of days the restriction was lifted.

Finally the control board members, chafed to the limit by Visk's captious rule, wrote out statements accusing him of various misdemeanors and demanded his removal. No one in authority showed much interest until Hudson Hawley conceived the notion of carrying the documents to Major General James G. Harbord, commanding general of Services of Supply, whom he had met while writing stories about him. It was felt that Harbord had enough of the civilian in him (he later became chairman of the board of the Radio Corporation of America) to view their case with sympathy. An audience was arranged through the general's aide, Captain R. Norris Williams, a famous tennis player, and the board members presented their case.

At first General Harbord read with good-humored disregard of what he supposed were typical enlisted men's gripes. But gradually he became interested, and at the end made some telephone calls. The result was Visk's transfer, though board members thought the action less a direct result of their statements than a culmination of Visk's other troubles.

After the war *Stars and Stripes* alumni conceded that the paper might never have come into being except for Visk's single-purpose drive. And there is little doubt that his conflict with the self-appointed control board had much to do with establishing the principle, carried over to *Yank* magazine and the *Stars and Stripes* newspapers of World War II, that enlisted men themselves ought to edit Army publications directed to the rank and file. In the heat of struggle the board members had sworn to refuse commissions in case, as rumored, they were offered. They never got a chance to complete their noble gesture.

Ross became boss of *Stars and Stripes* after Visk's departure, subject to dismissal by the other board members. Visk's titular successor, Major Mark Watson, a seasoned newspaperman, told the enlisted men to go ahead and get out the newspaper according to their best judgment. After talking over the situation, board members decided that a chairman, or managing editor, was essential. Ross's candidate was Winterich, whom he considered the best copy man he had ever encountered. But Winterich, of a retiring disposition, declined. Ross thereupon was tendered the post on the strength of his demonstrated initiative. He laid down one proviso—that his decisions would be absolutely final up to a designated period each week, when the board could fire him. Woollcott maintained afterward that before each meeting Ross hurried him on an out-of-town assignment. From this "chairman of the board" post arose the not wholly accurate story that Ross was the editorial genius of *Stars and Stripes.*

Whether Ross the hobo would have worked two minutes for Ross the editor is debatable. The rise to managing editor brought no improvement in his appearance and failed to diminish his love of horseplay. Yet he was a demanding taskmaster. His goal was perfection, and anyone failing to match his pace he looked on as a traitor to *Stars and Stripes.*

One surprised observer of the metamorphosis was Ken Adams, who had started the nickname "Hobo" back in Sacramento. When reporting for duty to *Stars and Stripes,* Adams came upon Ross sitting at a desk talking with a meticulously dressed colonel who had come to complain about a story. Ross's trench shoes were on the desk, his blouse was unbuttoned, his wrinkled overseas cap sat on the back of his head, and a Bull Durham sack dangled from his teeth as he rolled a cigarette. He was not entirely lacking in courtesy, however. The colonel had been permitted to sit down.

"Now, Colonel," Ross was saying tolerantly as Adams approached, "we have a job to do here." He ran his tongue along the edge of the cigarette paper, finished shaping the cigarette, and struck a match on his shoe. "Why don't you go back and do whatever it is *you're* supposed to do?"

Then, seeing Adams, Ross broke out his infectious grin and jumped to his feet.

The colonel and apoplexy struggled briefly, the colonel won, and he got up and stalked out. Adams discovered later that he rushed directly to General Pershing's headquarters, gained an audience, and demanded that Ross be court-martialed. Pershing replied that Ross and the others were doing an excellent job and would be let alone.

One day a representative of Butterick, one of the big

United States publishers, showed up at *Stars and Stripes* and expressed a desire to talk about carrying the newspaper over into civilian life as a magazine for returned veterans. Eyes bugged at the mention of possible salaries—a hundred dollars a week, maybe more. Woollcott's future was assured on the *Times*, but the others had come into the Army from low-paid jobs. By going with the new venture they would make three or four times more than they ever had. The dream of the tabloid was for the moment blacked out.

Because of his position as managing editor Ross signed the contract with Butterick. Then he signed individual contracts with Woollcott, Winterich, Wallgren, Hawley, and Baldridge. They were impressed that Ross made a clinching payment not in francs but in American dollars which he had gone to considerable trouble to dig up.

Now that he was on the entrepreneur track, Ross roared ahead at an alarming speed. As part of his editorial duties he read the publications of Army units, all of which carried jokes. A booklet filled with the jokes, he thought, ought to sell widely enough at a franc apiece to net a reasonable profit for both the compiler and a publisher. He offered the publisher's role to Winterich, who was mildly shocked at the idea of a couple of buck privates selling the Army its own jokes. But Winterich did suggest a title, *Yank Talk*, which Ross filed away in his mind.

Two *Stars and Stripes* circulation men, Melvin Ryder and Stewart Carroll, were more amenable, and Ross graciously allowed them to finance the venture. While the publishers hunted up a printer and a usable French civilian address, Ross whacked up his joke files and pasted his choices into copy. Wallgren was induced to draw a cover showing a couple of helmeted Yanks, one sucking a pipe, and both looking properly relaxed.

The Red Cross immediately bought 50,000 copies, startling the two publishers, if not Ross. Other sales were heavy. For a new edition, *More Yank Talk*, Private Ross, man of affairs, hired Winterich at five hundred francs as clipper and paster. Though a careful worker, Winterich was able to finish in a couple of nights, making his pay something like fifty dollars an hour.

News of the sensational publishing success naturally brought a rush of others anxious to get into the act. Woollcott hurriedly got up *Château-Thierry: A Guide to the Battlefields*, on which publishers Ryder and Carroll lost money, including Woollcott's five-hundred-franc advance. Baldridge illustrated a book of verses by Hilmar Baukhage (who later dropped both versifying and first name for radio broadcasting). It was a flop too.

One afternoon Ross was sitting on the terrace of the Café Napolitaine totting up his profits and talking with Walter Duranty. Duranty was never without gloomy news, which he always dispensed with relish. This particular afternoon he was on the subject of the value of the franc: he expected it to break disastrously at any moment. While the new entrepreneur fidgeted Duranty went on and on with inexorable logic.

Suddenly Ross jumped up and rushed away. He went and got his profits—three thousand dollars in franc notes—and hurried to the post office, intending to convert his funds into dollars by taking out a money order. There was, he found, a limit of a hundred dollars on each. Ink splattered wildly as he filled out thirty forms. Duranty had been right—the franc broke badly shortly afterward.

Con Man 4

"The successful launching of a magazine from scratch," an admirer of Ross once said, "requires, in addition to editorial talent, the confidence man's gift of tongue, his gambling instinct, and his ability to lose himself in his task. Ross has them all. As a convincer he differs from the grifter in that he believes in what he says and his words hit the listener like hail in a high wind."

When Ross arrived in the United States in May 1919 he was not yet ready for his big push. The metamorphosis from hobo newspaperman to editor was not yet complete. The success of *Stars and Stripes* had been due, in large part, to the simple fact that the troops had little or nothing else to read. He needed experience before tackling the city dudes. Though his ambition was beginning to burn, he had not decided exactly what he would set on fire.

Ross settled with Winterich in an apartment on West Eleventh Street and went to work on plans for the vets' magazine. The name *Stars and Stripes* belonged to the Army, but the Butterick Publishing Company was not reluctant to capitalize on the wartime careers of staff members. When the magazine appeared in September 1919 it carried the masthead:

THE HOME SECTOR
A Weekly for the New Civilian
Conducted by the former Council of
The Stars & Stripes

Ross was editor and Winterich managing editor, while the rest of the "big six"—Baldridge, Wallgren, Woollcott, and Hawley—were listed as editorial staff members. Hawley had stayed abroad as European correspondent. Woollcott was back as the *Times's* dramatic critic, but he participated wholeheartedly in the new venture. The staff also contained Ross's old San Francisco roommate, Roy Kirk, and *Stars and Stripes* veterans Philip Von Blon, J. W. Rixey Smith, Tyler H. Bliss, George Boas, and Edwin G. Burrows.

The introductory editorial began: "By the same bunch, for the same bunch, in the same spirit." It ended: "Does an audience made up of red-chevron men seem a limited audience to address? It is merely to surround a soap-box with the healthy manhood of this country."

The early issues indicated that the editors were not quite sure what to say from their soapbox. A buddy-buddy cartoon depicted a clean-cut youth who had halted his chauffeur-driven car to reminisce with an equally clean-cut young street sweeper. "And remember the night Fritz dropped a big one over . . . ?" A Baldridge drawing showed the troops returning home to Terrorism, High Cost of Living, Toryism, and American Prussianism. At the same time *Home Sector* was vigorously boosting the American Legion, many units of which were engaging in more than a little terrorism. The old clipper-paster of *Yank Talk* had plenty of jokes. Example:

BATTLE BROKEN

"That Argonne mule of yours seems to be a hard-working animal."

"He is, but we have to fire off a barrage every morning before he feels enough at home to do anything."

There was a report of a projected congressional investigation of "Hardboiled" Smith, an officer accused of brutality to American soldiers in a wartime prison which he had commanded. Campaigns were launched for veterans' legislation and reports made on facilities for care of the disabled.

Ross had one campaign that caused occasional twinges of alarm among staff members. W. O. McGeehan, a sports columnist, was commissioned to write a piece reiterating the popular wartime charge that Jack Dempsey had ducked the draft. It was illustrated with a photograph of French heavyweight fighter Georges Carpentier in uniform and one of Dempsey wearing a derby hat and a fur-collared overcoat. Ross had known Dempsey slightly in Salt Lake City just as the heavyweight was beginning his career. After the McGeehan piece, Ross found other ways of badgering Dempsey. For one thing he wanted to prevent him from making public appearances. Office staffers, nervously expecting an invasion at any moment, prepared to sell their lives dearly.

One day Woollcott showed up at the *Home Sector* with a business card on which he had had printed Dempsey's name. A receptionist agreed to deliver the card to Ross without revealing its real bearer. Woollcott followed close behind and peeked through the door. Afterward he swore that Ross blanched and his knees shook when he looked at the card.

Home Sector was thrown off stride by a printers' strike

that caused suspension of eight issues between the fifth and sixth numbers. It was a blow from which a new magazine had little chance of recovering. Besides, advertisements had not arrived in expected quantity. Red-chevron men were fairly anxious to hear about themselves, but the general public did not crowd the soapbox. The owners gave the staff the choice of heavy retrenchments or suspension.

At this moment a proposal arrived from outside. The American Legion, growing by leaps and bounds, was in a financial position to afford something more auspicious than the small weekly that a young Oklahoman, Marquis James, had been getting out almost singlehanded. *Home Sector* staff men were offered a chance to shift to it. The others left the decision to Ross, and he decided to move. The editors put together the last issue of *Home Sector*, dated April 17, 1920, and quietly departed.

The prospect of editing a house organ did not fascinate Ross, but there were other considerations. As an engagement present he gave Jane Grant his Legion contract. It called for ten thousand dollars a year—a considerable jump from the ten dollars a week for which he had gone to work on the San Francisco *Call and Post* barely four years earlier.

Jane Grant had gone back to the *Times* after the war and she kept her job after her marriage to Ross, to save money and because, a staunch feminist, she believed that a woman ought to have a career of her own. She did not, as a matter of fact, care for the title "Mrs. Harold Ross," any more than her friend and newspaper colleague Ruth Hale had accepted "Mrs. Heywood Broun" after marrying the rising *Tribune* columnist three years earlier.

As, in a left-handed way, Ross had sponsored Father's Day, he now unwittingly promoted a militant women's organization. Because of the housing shortage the newlyweds moved in with Heywood Broun and Ruth Hale. Among the two blazing feminists and a sympathetic Broun there was much talk of women's rights. Ross was not really interested in the struggle. Herbert Spencer had, after all, stated that women's participation in state affairs would lead, because of their maternal instincts, to increased control of the individual. If women wanted to hang onto their maiden names it was all right with Ross. But he wanted less noise about it around the house. They ought, he said bitterly, to hire a hall. They did. The Lucy Stone League was founded, with Ruth Hale as president and Jane Grant as secretary. (Lucy Stone was a feminist who had also kept her maiden name.) Among the members was social worker Frances Perkins. Many years later, when she was Secretary of Labor Perkins, she ran into Ross at a Washington party and greeted him warmly.

"She remembered me from the old Lucy Stone days," Ross, awe-struck, told friends in New York later.

Woollcott busied himself with introducing Ross into the circle which later became fabled as the Algonquin Round Table.[1] Soon after the war Murdock Pemberton and John Peter Toohey, theatrical press agents, growing tired of Woollcott's ceaseless paeans of glory, many of them to himself, had called a few of their mutual literary friends to lunch at the Algonquin Hotel for the purpose of satirizing him. Woollcott brought Ross along.

The Round Table set (so named because of the shape of

[1]Much has been written about the Round Table. Frank Case, the Algonquin host, reminisced about it in his two books. His daughter, Margaret Case Harriman, devoted a volume to it. Samuel Hopkins Adams dealt with it in his biography of Alexander Woollcott. So did I in my biography of Heywood Broun. The Round Table story is sketched briefly here because, as will be seen, it had a profound influence on Ross and what became known as "New Yorker humor."

the table eventually furnished for its exclusive luncheon use) soon became the aristocracy of New York sophistication. Not many of the habitués were original New Yorkers. The polish of prep and finishing schools was rarely seen. The parents of Heywood Broun were, true enough, in the Social Register; but Broun himself had been dropped after his marriage to Ruth Hale, who had been raised on a Tennessee farm. And Broun, far from respecting the silk-stocking tradition, now and then appeared in public without any socks at all.

New Englander Robert Benchley had graduated from Harvard, and then had worked as a personnel director. One of his duties was to organize clambakes. George S. Kaufman, a former ribbon salesman, and Marc Connelly had come from Pennsylvania. Edna Ferber had lived in Ottumwa, Iowa, and other outposts. The Pemberton brothers, Brock and Murdock, were natives of Kansas. Franklin P. Adams hailed from Chicago. Alexander Woollcott had been born in a former communal settlement in New Jersey. Dorothy Parker also came from New Jersey.

It was a journalistic bohemia, given to uninhibited horseplay and ribald wit. That Ross, a mere house-organ editor, was granted a place among the columnists, critics, and rising dramatists was a tribute to his personal charm and to his ability to hold his own in repartee despite his scattered talk. Ross claimed responsibility for having revived the Round Table's poker auxiliary, the Thanatopsis Literary and Inside Straight Club, out of the remnants of the games at Nini's in Paris. He and Winterich had started a weekly game in their Greenwich Village apartment. At the Thanatopsis he was happier than at the Round Table—though he felt the Easterners were hardly fast and rough enough for a son of the Old West.

Chief celebrator of the Round Table and Thanatopsis was Franklin P. Adams in his "The Conning Tower" column in the *World*. In Adams' "Diary of a Modern Samuel Pepys" which appeared in his column. He glanced from time to time at Ross.

To J. Toohey's in the evening, and played at cards till late, and won a small sum, albeit H. Ross taunted me with my inability to win, saying he could play better than I, albeit he lost what it would have taken him six months in the army to get.

Home, where I find E. Ferber and Janet [sic] Grant and Miss Rosalind Fuller; and A. Woollcott, very grand in a silk hat, and H. Ross; and we had a frugal supper, and all left before eleven.

Thence to J. Toohey's, and found H. Ross there, back from California. Well, quoth he, I shall have to win at cards this evening, forasmuch as my trip was costly and I had some unforeseen expenses. Oh, said I, a couple of tips, hey? All greeted this sally with laughter, yet the thrust was false, sithen there is nought niggardly about Ross.

And to H. Ross's and we talked about the low state periodical comick literature is sunk into.

H. Ross and Janet come to dinner, and we talked about the time newspaper men had blundered into successes, and most of the blunders were owing to inebriety. . . .

To J. Toohey's, for a short and silly game of cards, which I ought not waste my time at, and nobody gaining aught but H. Ross, by stupid good luck, too, albeit he prates over his skill and acumen.

And thence to O. Pain's, and great talk of bookshelves, and H. Ross, with great vainglory, said he was an old woodsman and volunteered to build them all the bookshelves they wanted, which I doubt he can do, having trouble enough when he essays to build eights at casino. But he is reluctant to admit there is aught he faileth to excel in.

With the Tablers it was sometimes hard to tell where juvenility left off and sophistication began. Ross had a set of letterheads printed with the top line: "Harold W. Ross—Man About Town." In one corner was an item from F.P.A.'s column, listing H. Ross as among those present one night at Benchley's house. In a show put on by the Tablers, Ross played the part of Lemuel Pip, an old taxi driver. Lemuel Pip never came on stage and wasn't heard. He waited outside in his cab.

Though having compromised himself by staying in New York rather than setting off for the South Seas, Ross did what he could to escape a charge of dudery. His stand-up brush of hair was believed by his friends to be a protest against big-city ways. His clothes were better than in the old hobo days, but hardly any neater than his Army uniform had been.

But behind his appearance was an ever more intense ambition. He hated being the editor of a house organ and was biding his time only until he could launch a venture of his own. The high-class tabloid talked about in the Paris days was still in his mind. But Jane Grant talked with Carr Van Anda, the *Times's* famous managing editor, who said the project would take millions. That was out of the question. Ever since his water-front days Ross had toyed with the idea of a shipping paper which would give the news of ship movements and other technical knowledge of the trade. He formulated plans and was promised backing. But his heart wasn't in it any more.

That left the magazine of reporting and humor they had talked about in Paris—the magazine that would cover a big city as they had tried to cover the war. He talked about it endlessly. But no one paid much attention—not even Woollcott, who had been disillusioned by *Home Sector*. There existed, however, no better school for a magazine of American wit and sophistication than the Round Table and Thanatopsis.

Before the war many of the Round Tablers had been affected by the revolt of Greenwich Village against Puritanism and the self-satisfaction of the bourgeoisie. Now the postwar generation was looking on these mores as ridiculous. The Tablers, having found their audience, were attaining great popularity. No matter where their birthplaces, they were now city wits. Because of the time spent in New Orleans, San Francisco, and Paris, Ross claimed that he was as cosmopolitan as anyone. He belonged also to Mark Twain's vital West and the open road of tramp newspapermen. He had in him the best of the two worlds.

The two leading mediums of wit and sophistication were F.P.A.'s column and *Vanity Fair*, the glossy-paper monthly. Adams had been a successful columnist for a decade. For many years he had been publishing the quips, poems, and sketches of Dorothy Parker, Kaufman, Benchley, Donald Ogden Stewart, Newman Levy, Marc Connelly, Ring Lardner, Irvin S. Cobb, Edna Ferber, Alice Duer Miller, and scores of others who were already famous, were to become famous, or were to miss by a narrow margin. Many were discoveries of his. To "make" F.P.A.'s column was an honor. He was interested in building the reputation of no one. Contributions of his friends were rejected as readily as any others. He printed only what he considered worthy, and he addressed a highly intelligent audience.

At the Round Table, F.P.A., a dour, dark, cigar-champing man with a dry, cutting wit, was the elder statesman. This was so by virtue of his greater years and his ability to milk the fabulous sum of twenty-five thousand dollars a year out of wit and humor. Ross admired F.P.A. as a stickler for proper grammar, and especially as a talent scout. Round Table conversations were fast and stinging. Important opinions were usually disguised with satire or at least cynicism. But had Ross been a student taking notes, Adams's off-the-cuff lectures would have filled many notebooks.

Proof that America contained enough well-heeled sophisticates, or those who considered themselves sophisticates, to support a magazine edited strictly for them was provided by *Vanity Fair*. The expensively vivid caricatures which graced its covers so far departed from the usual romanticized cover illustrations that the intelligentsia knew that they were for them alone. The average number contained more than a hundred large, glossy pages, most of them filled with advertisements for Pierce-Arrows, imported perfumes, and other luxury items. There were departments for sports, bridge, and "The Well-Dressed Man." Books, theater, painting, and allied arts were covered in signed essays. Satirical pieces, generally parodies, set off the gorgeous reproductions of photographs and painting.

Three of *Vanity Fair's* staff members sat regularly at the early Round Table. Robert Benchley was managing editor and a leading contributor of "nonsense" humor (for example, his "The Social Life of the Newt"). Ross had printed Benchley in *Home Sector*, which indicated that he was broadening, for Benchley had been a pacifist during the war. A gentle man, Benchley rarely used the whiplash of satire. His side-kick, small, pretty, dark-eyed Dorothy Parker, *Vanity Fair's* drama critic, employed it regularly. Her lethal conversational striking power was partly camouflaged by demureness, but her blows landed naked in print. Robert Sherwood did editorial chores and occasional satirical pieces. Round Tablers Heywood Broun and Alexander Woollcott were regular contributors, and others appeared from time to time.

Ross soon met *Vanity Fair's* editor, Frank Crowninshield, a delicately handsome, Old World gallant who fancied brocaded white waistcoats, excellent food, and wines of choice vintage. At any rate he liked to *write* of exquisite wines as if he had savored them. His acquaintances were aware that he never used alcohol, and the fact that his little deception was never held against him was due to the esteem in which he was held. "Crownie's" graciousness was famous. He sometimes rejected a "perfectly marvelous" piece of work on the ground that "everything else in the magazine will seem inferior." When an author was taken by Crownie to a lavish luncheon, he knew that rewriting would be asked.

Yet at bottom Crownie was a shrewd, hard-bitten Yankee who viewed sophistication as a business. Americans, especially the rich, still looked abroad for culture. This fact was reflected in *Vanity Fair*. While not unsympathetic to Sinclair Lewis, F. Scott Fitzgerald, John Dos Passos, Sherwood Anderson, and other bright stars of the American literary renaissance, Crownie's predilection for European culture caused him to give preference to such writers as Thomas Burke, G. K. Chesterton, Hugh Walpole, and Arthur Schnitzler. A page of photographs of American playwrights would be carefully labeled as such. The celebrated "We Nominate for the Hall of Fame" page usually included as many foreign as American names. Crownie went in for reproductions of European, usually French, paintings. He sometimes bought the originals and held them for a market pushed up by their appearance in *Vanity Fair*.

Crownie was in his roundabout way a strong editor, but in the final analysis Condé Nast, the publisher, was the policy maker. From this fact Ross learned a valuable lesson. Nast was a dilettante famed for his lavish and novel parties, usually garnished with celebrities from abroad. *Vanity Fair's* greatest value to him was enhancement of his prestige; *Vogue* was his big money-maker. Several of Nast's theatrical producer friends complained to him about the lambastings Dorothy Parker administered in *Vanity Fair* to their productions. They also disapproved of her ardent support of the actor's cause in the bitterly fought Equity strike.

When she was dismissed by *Vanity Fair*, Benchley and Sherwood gave notice. During the two weeks between notice and departure the trio did their best to turn the chic offices of the Nast publications into a shambles. In off-duty hours they marched up and down the street outside, displaying *Vanity Fair* discharge chevrons.

There were torrential discussions at the Round Table about the affair. Ross was convinced that a major tenet of editorial freedom was freedom from decision by the business office. In his judgment a man was either the editor or not the editor.

Also aimed at the sophisticated set was the monthly *Smart Set*. According to a notation on the cover, it was "A Magazine of Cleverness." The slogan was changed, after a while, simply to "Edited by George Jean Nathan and H. L. Mencken," which was doubtless intended to mean the same thing. The cover usually displayed a man with a monocle paying close attention to a pretty girl. Nathan and Mencken had a joint department in which they kidded absurdities of American life. In his book reviews Mencken was well into his attack on Puritanism and cant in American letters. F. Scott Fitzgerald, Thyra Samter Winslow, and other "modern" writers were appearing in *Smart Set's* pages.

The humor weekly, *Judge*, was filled with he-she jokes and short anecdotes ranging from 100 to 300 words. There were a few longer pieces by "nonsense" humorists Stephen Leacock, Oliver Herford, Gelett Burgess, and Walt Mason.

The other national humor weekly, *Life*, worked in serious comment, including political cartoons. Many depicted bearded Bolsheviks, bombs in hand, enticing American workingmen or engaging in some other deviltry. *Life* ran criticisms of books and drama, as well as a "confidential guide" to the theater. Benchley became drama critic not long after the *Vanity Fair* battle. Sherwood moved over too. *Life's* jokes were also of the he-she variety. Short nonsense articles and biteless satirical pieces were common.

Life and *Judge* were basically "family" magazines aimed at a nationwide circulation. This meant that the editors sought a fairly low common denominator of intelligence and sophistication. Drawings were romanticized. An illustration of a nice old lady would make a cover. Or a comic valentine would do. The bright caricatures of *Vanity Fair* would have seemed outlandish to most readers of *Judge* and *Life*.

Ross developed a theory after studying the humor and sophistication magazines. It seemed to him that much local New York City advertising revenue was missed because of the national editorial policies. Why should a smart New York store, restaurant, theater, or the manufacturer of a luxury item spend money for an advertisement that would be wasted on a reader in Dubuque, Iowa? *Vanity Fair* made out better than *Life* and *Judge* because most of its readers lived in urban areas (chiefly New York City and environs).

As added proof Ross cited the rotogravure sections of the metropolitan papers, which got fat advertising.

The rest of Ross's theory grew out of his newspaper experiences. The humor in *Life* and *Judge* was stale, he concluded, for the simple reason that editors could not get it to their readers fast enough. When they did print a timely cartoon or joke the big spread between deadline and delivery insured its death before arrival. A weekly magazine of wit ought, he thought, to be produced as fast as a weekly newspaper, with a spread between editor and reader of only a few days. He was a believer, also, in humor with a local flavor. F.P.A.'s stuff, for example, would not be relished by New York readers if he aimed also at readers in Dubuque.

No one took Ross's theories very seriously in those first years after the war. Even for himself and Jane Grant the starting of a magazine was a far-off dream. He settled into his unimaginative job on the Legion paper. Usually it was thirty pages of cheap paper, with a cover line such as "DUES ARE OVERDUE." A typical story was "What's Become of the Army? Legislative Parsimony Has Reduced Its Substance to a Shadow and Its Morale to Zero" written by "An Officer Who Got Out." The "Bursts and Duds" department had a plentiful supply of items like this:

YOU CAN'T BEAT LOGIC

Demon Reformer: "Don't you know tobacco shortens lives?"

Smoker: "I've smoked for 65 years and I'm 80 years old now."

D. R.: "Well, if you hadn't smoked you would probably be 90 now."

A few non-house-organ touches were managed, but only a few. Ross sometimes bought John Held, Jr.'s drawings of knobby flappers and their beaux for the cover. He got slick-magazine writer Hugh Wiley and others, including Round

Tablers, to contribute. Ross's old war correspondent hero, Frederick Palmer, was given a page to fill every week. Marquis James produced two closely documented series, "Who Got the Money" and "The Profiteer Hunt."

"When you work for Ross," one employee of the period has said, "you work hard." The staff toiled in an old loft building on West Forty-third Street between Eleventh and Twelfth avenues. Freight trains clattered up and down Eleventh Avenue all day, and in the summertime the stench from nearby slaughterhouses was all but overwhelming. Staffers were nevertheless pretty certain that if a letter was not answered on time, or any detail was overlooked, the ceiling would come down.

Ross chafed under the restrictions of high Legion officials. Sometimes he took home articles they insisted that he print and read them aloud for their unconscious humor. He would be allowed to make only a few changes before putting them in the magazine. Only his burning ambition to someday make a mark in his own right kept him on the job.

Admirers of the old Hobo Ross would have been shocked, despite the slight improvement in his attire, by his idea of the home life he now wanted. For a permanent residence Ross and Jane Grant, in company with Hawley Truax, a former roommate of Woollcott's at Hamilton College, planned something rather elegant. Truax had given up his law studies to manage the estate of his father, a successful New York lawyer. Though shy and erudite, a reader of Greek for pleasure, Truax was a passionate cribbage fan and often played with Ross and Jane. They talked of renovating a property owned by Truax and turning it into a communal house with separate apartments.

There was one major obstacle: Woollcott. They all liked him, but they all knew his passion for dominating everything around him. They decided to go ahead surreptitiously.

The plot failed miserably, for Woollcott was not the kind from whom secrets are kept. He showed, however, no resentment over the idea of keeping him out and plunged happily, and very ably, into the arrangements. Shortly after one of his fingers was in, all of him, plus the seeds of doom, entered. Woollcott secured two other tenants, Kate Oglebay, a childhood friend of his, and William Powell, a public relations man.

Two narrow houses far over on West Forty-seventh Street were thrown together. In the basement were the kitchen, a communal dining room, and a room for the Thanatopsis cardplayers. It was agreed that any tenant could, with due notice, use the basement facilities for private parties. The rest of the house was divided into apartments. Ross and Jane Grant had the parlor floor. Woollcott and Truax each had an apartment on the second floor. The apartments of Powell and Kate Oglebay were on the top floor. The establishment was usually called Chinaman's Chance because of the Chinese servants with whom Jane staffed it. But oriental ways were not confined to the menials. Once an old newspaper crony of Ross's, arriving for dinner, was badly shaken by Hobo Ross's appearance in a magnificent oriental robe.

Friction developed quickly. Exchanges between Ross and Woollcott since the war had taken on real bitterness. Woollcott enjoyed the role of benefactor because of his delight in directing other people's lives and his deep affection for Ross. But he fought duels with all his friends and was a master with the sword. When he got into a fight over the card table with a Round Tabler who happened to be the wife of another Tabler, he remarked, "The trouble with you, my dear, is that you are married to a cuckold." The subtlety of the charge was appreciated by the Tablers, but they thought she did right by throwing her drink in his face.

Ross was not cut out to be a protégé to begin with. But friends of both were convinced that he was scared of Woollcott, and that he fought him regularly to prove to himself that he wasn't. A story which Marc Connelly tells illustrates the point. One night he ran into Ross and they had dinner at the Algonquin. Ross explained that later he was to meet Woollcott, who was taking him to a play opening. He gave Connelly the play's name.

"Too bad," Connelly said, shaking his head sadly. "It'll be an awful turkey. Woollcott knows it will be."

Ross was indignant. "God damn him, he's only invited me to one other and it was terrible. When there's a good play he takes somebody else. I'll be damned if I meet him."

They sat on. Just before theater time Woollcott, wearing a cape and silk hat, appeared in the doorway. He stared at them for a moment, drew his cape around him, wheeled, and strode off.

Ross began to fidget. "Connelly," he said, "you've got to help me figure a way out of this."

Being among the number convinced that Woollcott had Ross buffaloed, Connelly was enjoying himself, but he vowed to help. They loafed around Times Square for a while, went to the flea circus, and at an amusement arcade had some pencils made up with Woollcott's name on them as an appeasement gift. Then Ross had an idea that a conciliatory telegram would be a good thing. He asked Connelly to write it. In a moment Connelly had a draft ready.

DEAR ALECK: I'M IN A BIT OF A JAM. IF ANYBODY ASKS WHERE I WAS TONIGHT WILL YOU SAY I WAS WITH YOU.

ROSS

Ross began to quake violently, according to Connelly's later account, at thought of the addition the telegram would make to Woollcott's rage. Then he began to laugh. In the end the fun of sending the message outweighed the terror, and they dispatched it.

Ross and Woollcott charged each other with cheating at cribbage. Friends thought that, for the hell of it, *both* cheated. Woollcott was a notoriously poor loser, unwilling to quit while behind, always ready to retire while winning. They could get a fight out of that or nearly anything else.

The communal dining room caused irritation for everybody. Ross was developing his first ulcer. Truax's stomach was bad too. They ate soups, toast, and special health dishes. Often Woollcott refused to come to the table while the "slop" was being served. He wanted heavy meat dishes and rich desserts. But most of the household disputes arose from Woollcott's love of company and his contempt for the privacy of others. Ross often brought work home from his office or put his mind to one or another of his contemplated projects. Jane Grant, besides managing the house and filling her *Times* job, was writing for the *Saturday Evening Post*. Woollcott rose late, dined, went to the theater, composed his review, and was ready for a few hours of pleasure. Often he decided on conversation with, or to, Ross and Jane. And he would not hesitate to wake them up for the purpose.

When others entertained guests Woollcott would barge in uninvited and play the role of life of the party. Or, better yet, he would carry the prize guests off to his private quarters. When his presence was desired he would play hard to get. Once when he arrived home and was invited to join a gathering he stood in the doorway and said haughtily, "I would rather go and lie face down in a pail of Italian garbage."

Ross lost sleep, curiously, because of the new freedom that was agitating the sophisticated set. Ruth Hale felt deeply that Heywood Broun ought to go out on dates, and sometimes she insisted on it. Agreeable by nature, Broun would set forth, but usually he ended by joining Woollcott and going to his apartment to talk. Because of the speed with which Broun did his work, he was never pressed for time. Ross, trying to sleep, would hear their droning voices, and he grew bitter against the newfangled marital theories.

The first big household fight came one night when Woollcott brought home a large party of theatrical friends to celebrate the return from Europe of his favorite actress, Mrs. Minnie Maddern Fiske. They came late and the revelry ran high. Finally in desperation Ross and Jane asked them to pipe down. In a towering rage, Woollcott took his guests from the communal portion of the house to his own quarters, locked the door, and stepped up the noise.

The incident was smoothed over, but Ross, fed up, wanted to dissolve the partnership. Jane Grant was willing but she felt that Ross ought to be the one to broach the subject to Woollcott. Though a sound man in a quarrel, Ross dreaded starting one. He talked of writing a letter, but was slow getting to it, and the household rocked along.

Although living on a fairly high scale, Ross and Jane Grant had been salting money into the bank against their venture into publishing. Before they were quite ready Ross got a chance, in 1924, which he thought might obviate the need for starting something new. He was offered the co-editorship of *Judge*. In a publishing shake-up the firm which handled printing for both *Judge* and the Legion magazine took financial interest in *Judge*. Ross's reputation as a hard worker was well known, and the firm's officials chose him as the man to protect their investment. Physically, Ross moved about eight feet to his new office. John Winterich became editor of the Legion magazine.

Ross's experience at *Judge* confirmed his theories about the value of topical, localized humor and local advertising. Sometimes he walked into the mailing department and gloomily surveyed the huge bundles of magazines returned from all over the country. Advertising was skimpy. He argued loud and long with Norman Anthony, his co-editor, for a trial of his ideas. Neither Anthony nor the owners agreed with him. *Judge* had changed only for the worse since 1920. In seeking readers on ever lower planes it was buying "Krazy Kracks" from readers at five dollars a krack and printing "Funnybones" jokes inside boxes shaped like Fido bones. The format had deteriorated. Ross pleased contributors by doing his best to pay on acceptance rather than on publication or later. But the benefit to the magazine was not apparent enough to impress anyone.

The situation was hopeless and Ross began casting around. At thirty-two, he was ready to stake everything—time, talent, savings—on a grand plunge. That was the gambler in him. Experts had appraised him of the enormous cost of starting a new publication. But he was confident that if ever he got a humor magazine going he would be able to drive it to success by sheer hard work.

Far more funds would be needed than he and Jane had between them. Potential angels were within range now, for the fame of the Round Table set was such that men and women of wealth had come into it. Logically, Woollcott would have been the one to scout for backers. But his experience with *Home Sector* had disillusioned him and anyhow his protégé was insubordinate. As a house-organ editor, Ross was no social lion. But the rich blades who sat at the Round Table and Thanatopsis were at least available for conning. Ross made up a dummy, which soon became worn from flipping in and out of his pocket. He didn't have a name in mind, for he thought *Life* was the only good one. He would work that out after he got the money.

The best prospect was well-groomed, good-looking Raoul Fleischmann. Fleischmann was vaguely dissatisfied with his life. His family's baking business interested him hardly at all. He was drawn to creative people but was not artistically bent himself. While enjoying chichi society, he was not rich enough for the yacht and polo set. The prospect of publishing a magazine of wit and sophistication caught his interest, especially when Ross said that the outlay of cash would be small. Fifty thousand dollars, Ross estimated, would be enough. Ross's own and Jane Grant's savings would account for nearly half of that. He would plow back his salary in return for stock. Jane would help out at nights.

To Fleischmann, whose fortune was in the neighborhood of three quarters of a million, an investment of twenty-five thousand dollars did not sound like an excessive gamble. He did not realize—nor did Ross—that he was roped as tight as ever a con man roped a mark.

Failure 5

A SMALL, jetsam-furnished suite of offices was taken late in the summer of 1924 in a building at 25 West Forty-fifth Street which Fleischmann's family owned. Ross set violently to work on preparations for the first issue. He frantically studied about stock issues, typography, subscription rates, copyrights, and the thousands of other big and little things that have to be known to get out a magazine. Usually there are a dozen experts to handle such matters. Despite his capacity for quick learning, he was a confused and harassed man, and he looked it. He hunched nervously about the shabby offices. One story told at the Round Table was that a servant at Chinaman's Chance made sure every morning that coins for jingling purposes were in his pocket. This was not true. He had a big bunch of keys that he jingled.

Ross's big problems were backbreaking. But once he had his own magazine, he paid equal attention to details. The office tone was set one afternoon when he was striding about with more preoccupation than usual. Tyler (Tip) Bliss, a veteran of *Stars and Stripes* and *Home Sector*, now Ross's editorial assistant, looked on worriedly, sure that some major crisis had developed.

Finally Ross plowed to a halt. "God damn it," he shouted, "we've got to get a water cooler in here!"

Bliss, a Harvard man who looked like an ex-pug, was a specialist in the he-she jokes of the *Judge* and *Life* school. He was the only regular editorial staff member. Ross's secretary was Helen Mears, a small, intense girl who had applied for the job in the hope of worming herself in as a writer for the magazine. She did write for it, too, but not until a decade or so later. The fact that she didn't know how to take shorthand added nothing to the smoothness of office routine.

As a combination public relations man, copy boy, poet, and office duster, Ross had a handsome gazelle-eyed youth named Philip Wylie. Wylie had applied to do publicity work as soon as he had heard about the magazine. Ross didn't want a publicity man. He probably would have refused an interim free offer, when it was made, had he not listened to the young applicant's life story. Wylie, son of a well-known New Jersey minister, had recently been the accused in a paternity suit. Although he had fought and won it, the notoriety had ruined a small public relations business he had been conducting. Ross told him, all right then, try some publicity. Wylie got some, and Ross later put him on a small salary and set him to doing other jobs. Wylie concluded that Ross had sympathized with a fight against injustice.

Those were the only regular prepublication staff members except for a switchboard girl and an advertising salesman and his secretary. In most offices of a like number of workers a switchboard girl would have been superfluous but Ross had a mania about telephones, as about other mechanical details. He changed the interoffice hookup from one moment to another, so that the girl earned her pay.

The advertising salesman and his secretary were not considered bona fide parts of the establishment. Ross intended to treat the business department as beneath the notice of the editorial personnel, and the best time to start was before there was any business.

There was some part-time help. Raoul Fleischmann dropped in for consultation, but he knew even less than Ross about starting a magazine. Ross was president of the F-R Publishing Company, established to get out the magazine, and Fleischmann was vice-president. The one real professional around was Rea Irvin, a handsome, pleasant, wavy-haired former art editor of *Life.* He came in one day a week to go over the art offerings. As the writer for a department to be called "The Talk of the Town," Ross had hired the part-time services of James Kevin McGuinness, a young black Irishman who was a sports columnist and contributor to the humor magazines. For a department of silhouettes of important people, McGuinness suggested the title "Profiles," which Ross accepted without enthusiasm. McGuinness also argued that the magazine should take a superior tone in its movie criticism. Ross agreed with that too. McGuinness regretted this later when he became a Hollywood producer.

Others were hired for odds and ends. Howard Brubaker, a newspaperman who had sold humorous paragraphs to Ross at *Judge,* was asked to get up material for a section to be titled "Of All Things." An about-town young man named Charles Baskerville, who later became a well-known portrait painter, was appointed to write about night life. Herman J. Mankiewicz, an effervescent, sometimes belligerent, young wit of the town, served as a kind of general utilities writer. Marquis James pitched in here and there.

Other assistants were the foreign humor publications.

Ross had the London *Punch* and the German *Simplicissimus* and French humor magazines laid out on a table. He searched them and pounded them before the faces of whatever writers and artists would listen. America was far behind Europe in humor publications, he said, and it was time something was done about it. He enlisted some aid from the Round Tablers, paying them chiefly in stock, when at all. They regarded the stock, along with Ross as editor of a magazine of wit and sophistication, as a fairly good joke. But there was a strong herd loyalty, and they pitched in heartily. One of them furnished a magazine's most important accoutrement: a name.

Fleischmann and Ross had decided to give a share of stock to whoever suggested the most fitting name, and several Tablers, fond of guessing games anyhow, were sitting around making tries. All, that is, except John Peter Toohey, who was eating. Toohey was a large, stolid, literal man.

"What kind of magazine," he finally inquired, "is this supposed to be?"

"A metropolitan magazine," someone answered.

"What metropolis?" Toohey persisted.

"New York."

"Then call it the New Yorker," Toohey said shortly, and turned back to his food.

F.P.A. tried to reduce Ross's jitteriness by spending long hours playing cassino with him, talking about humor. Though not certain that Ross was the man for the job he was undertaking, Adams agreed to come one day a week to select the poetry. Woollcott blew hot and cold, one moment saying he didn't wish to be associated with a flop, the next offering advice and help. Jane Grant, who was spending nights working up a circulation department, thought that Woollcott's total effect was to undermine confidence. Marc

Connelly was more enthusiastic than others, and he worked hard in the office. In the hurly-burly he irritated Philip Wylie by treating him as an average office boy. Wylie said nothing, but years later, when Connelly sent him a congratulatory note on something he had written, he shot back a sharp reminder of the indignity. Connelly, not having connected the office worker with the author, was amazed.

Dorothy Parker was one of the few who got any money for her efforts, but she was not a dependable clock-puncher. Besides, she was flippant. One day Ross found her in a speakeasy at a time he thought she was working at the office.

"Someone was using the pencil," she explained.

This was unfair, as the office had two typewriters. There was even a movement afoot to get a straight-backed chair or two for the tiny waiting room.

Despite confusion, harassment, and ridicule, Ross managed to put his dream on paper in a prospectus which for conciseness and prophecy has probably never been equaled in editorial manifestoes.

It came from his typewriter, as follows:

THE NEW YORKER will be a reflection in word and picture of metropolitan life. It will be human. Its general tenor will be one of gaiety, wit and satire, but it will be more than a jester. It will not be what is commonly called sophisticated, in that it will assume a reasonable degree of enlightenment on the part of its readers. It will hate bunk.

As compared to the newspaper, THE NEW YORKER will be interpretive rather than stenographic. It will print facts that it will have to go behind the scenes to get, but it will not deal in scandal for the sake of scandal nor sensation for the sake of sensation. Its integrity will be above suspicion. It hopes to be so entertaining and informative as to be a necessity for the person who knows his way about or wants to.

THE NEW YORKER will devote several pages a week to a covering of contemporary events and people of interest. This will be done by writers capable of appreciating the elements of a situation and, in setting them down, of indicating their importance and significance. THE NEW YORKER will present the truth and the whole truth without fear and without favor, but will not be iconoclastic.

Amusements and the arts will be thoroughly covered by departments which will present, in addition to criticism, the personality, the anecdote, the color and chat of the various subdivisions of this sphere. THE NEW YORKER's conscientious guide will list each week all current amusement offerings worth-while —theaters, motion pictures, musical events, art exhibitions, sport and miscellaneous entertainment—providing an ever-ready answer to the prevalent query, "What shall we do this evening?" Through THE NEW YORKER's Mr. Bibber III, readers will be kept apprised of what is going on in the public and semi-public smart gathering places—the clubs, hotels, cafés, supper clubs, cabarets and other resorts.

Judgment will be passed on new books of consequence, and THE NEW YORKER will carry a list of the season's books which it considers worth reading.

There will be a page of editorial paragraphs, commenting on the week's events in a manner not too serious.

There will be a personal mention column—a jotting down in the small-town newspaper style of the comings, goings and doings in the village of New York. This will contain some josh and some news value.

THE NEW YORKER will carry each week several pages of prose and verse, short and long, humorous, satirical and miscellaneous.

THE NEW YORKER expects to be distinguished for its illustrations, which will include caricatures, sketches, cartoons and humorous and satirical drawings in keeping with its purpose.

THE NEW YORKER will be the magazine which is not edited for the old lady in Dubuque. It will not be concerned in what she is thinking about. This is not meant in disrespect, but THE

New Yorker is a magazine avowedly published for a metropolitan audience and thereby will escape an influence which hampers most national publications. It expects a considerable national circulation, but this will come from persons who have a metropolitan interest.

For such a document the signature, "H. W. Ross, Editor," was a good deal less than awe-inspiring. Fleischmann suggested that Ross go out and drum up some "advisory editors" from among the Round Table set. Ross did it well. He has since declared sadly, "It's the only dishonest thing I ever did."

Of the Table regulars, Ross signed up Heywood Broun, Marc Connelly, Edna Ferber, George S. Kaufman, Alice Duer Miller, Dorothy Parker, and Alexander Woollcott. In addition he got the signatures of artists Rea Irvin, Ralph Barton, a leading caricaturist, and Laurence Stallings, who with Maxwell Anderson had written the smash hit *What Price Glory?* Other Tablers whose names would have helped, such as F.P.A., did not come in because of other contracts which they had signed. Broun had to withdraw because of contract difficulties before the advisory editors appeared in the magazine. Stallings dropped out because he went to Hollywood and could give no assistance. Edna Ferber felt it unwise to devote time, energy, and thought to a magazine whose success under the auspices of Ross was doubtful. Though she was very fond of him as a person, she withdrew. Sherwood and Benchley, still on *Life*, could hardly have been expected to donate their editorial prestige to a rival.

When the first issue of the New Yorker, dated February 21, 1925, appeared, the advisory editors were listed conspicuously on the first text page with nothing to indicate whom they were advising. (Ross had a high regard for *Punch* and its editor was never listed.) The advisers had reason to wish they had remained anonymous too. Most of the magazine's purchasers—there were fifteen thousand of them at fifteen cents a head—thought of themselves as squanderers.

The most inviting feature of the first issue came about by accident. Ross had wanted for the cover a picture of a theatrical curtain rising over New York City's bright lights. The artist had failed to put much life into his sketch. At the last moment Ross had asked Rea Irvin to provide something he thought would better symbolize the magazine's attitude. Irvin had already designed a type face for the cover and headings. He had also created an aristocratic gentleman to garnish the top of the first text page. For the cover he drew a portrait of the same figure contentedly inspecting a butterfly through his monocle. The gentleman seemed superior to everything that came under his gaze. Though wearing an old-fashioned high choker collar, wavy side whiskers, and curl-brimmed high hat, he might have been a modern aesthete at the horse show. He fitted a satisfied, unworried era. The model might, as a matter of fact, have been Frank Crowninshield of *Vanity Fair*.

Ross was never quite able to make up his mind about the cover. After repeating it on the anniversary number for a decade, he suddenly accused Irvin of having been too frivolous.

Inside the magazine, Ross rarely caught up with his prospectus. Leading off was "Of All Things," signed "the New Yorker." It ran two pages and contained short items meant to reflect metropolitan life. Whether the tenor was gay, witty, and satirical was open to debate. Sample:

It turned out, after a New York jury had got down to business, that the foreman didn't understand English, so the judge excused him and told the remaining eleven to reach a verdict of their own. We don't get the point. Readers of the *Daily News* doubtless don't understand English but they ought to be experts on crime.

"Of All Things" was modeled closely on *Punch's* "Charivaria." Another feature of *Punch* had been expropriated. For a long time humorists had been taking advantage of typographical errors. There was, for example, the "Bad Breaks" department in *Judge*. *Punch* had developed an editorial comment that followed a stupid, unfortunately composed, or typographically unhappy item. These appeared as fillers at the bottom of columns.

A contemporary issue of *Punch* had this end-item:

The Comtesse —— wore a light gray crepe frock with a curious "fish tail" panel in the back, and a gray hat with a brim on the sides and front only. The Princess ——, whose horse had won one of the big races of the week, wore a delightful smile—FASHION PAPER.

A tacit but crushing rebuke to her overdressed friend.

The New Yorker's imitation matched up badly:

CHAUFFEUR HELD AS BANDIT
—Headline in the *Herald Tribune*.

The start of a long-needed crusade.

After "Of All Things" came "The Talk of the Town," which contained items up to 1000 words. Here the first person singular was employed, and the section was signed "Van Bibber III." This mythical gentleman traveled, the reader was assured, in exclusive circles and reported from behind the scenes.

The news of the winter has frequently referred to White House breakfasts, but I haven't yet seen any recording the breakfast service. When I had breakfast there recently I made note for my constituents' elevation that the service was of white porcelain with a thin gold border. The American eagle is emblazoned—or should I say baked?—in the border. The sausages were very hot and the syrup was served in silver pitchers.

Many small legends have grown up around the early days of the New Yorker. There is the one about Ross's frantic effort to keep proofreaders and printers from changing "drop of a ha" to "drop of a hat." In one version he hangs around until the day-shift proofreaders have departed, makes sure it is still "ha," and then goes contentedly home to bed. While he sleeps a night proofreader changes it to "hat." A second narrator has Ross, in evening clothes, going to the printer's late at night, crawling under the press, and checking the form by means of a flashlight. In this version the press is later stopped and "ha" changed to "hat."

It is a good story either way, and under slightly different circumstances might have had a basis in fact. The phrase "drop of a hat" appeared in a theatrical review by Dorothy Parker (but signed "Last Night"). She had wept at a melodrama and in self-defense was explaining how easily she could be moved to tears. She mentioned the drop of a hat as one thing that would do it. Had she been making some other point and actually used "ha," Ross might have been under the press. His desire for perfection in his creation was such that a typographical error caused him physical pain.

To the aesthetic eye the magazine's typography was, however, unappealing. Department heads were cluttered with gingerbread. Vowels about one sixth the size of the consonants made the heading type outlandish. Ross, trying his own hand, had fallen into the beginner's error of overdisplay.

Only one Round Tabler, F.P.A., appeared in the body of the magazine over his own signature. Other recognizable names were those of Fairfax Downey, Ernest F. Hubbard, and Corey Ford, all contributors to the humor weeklies; A. H. Folwell, former editor of *Puck*; C. Knapp, ex-mayor of Saratoga Springs; Arthur Guiterman, the light versifier; and Etaoin Shrdlu, an old newspaper character who had traveled even more extensively than Ross. Signed to other items were such conglomerations as Con Brio for music, Froid for art, Touchstone for books, Will Hays, Jr., for movies, Quid for Washington Notes, Sawdust for a spoof called "The Story of Manhattankind," and Golly-wogg for "Profiles." Golly-wogg was Gilbert Gabriel, the critic, and his subject was Giulio Gatti-Casazza, opera impresario. Profile was apt, for the sketch ran a mere 1200 words.

To kid the old-style humor magazines, Ross had stuck in a joke turned upside down.

Pop: A man who thinks he can make it in par.
Johnny: What is an optimist, pop?

The trouble with this jest-on-a-jest was the proximity of others, printed straight, which were little better. Under a cartoon showing two people near a poster advertising a movie titled *Wages of Sin* was the caption:

Uncle: Poor girls, so few get their wages.
Flapper: So few get their sin, darn it.

Another showed a drunk lying on the floor of a police station.

"What's the drunk's name, Reilly?"
"Dunno, Sergeant. He claims he's a unidentified body."

The caricatures and cartoons which depended on draftsmanship and intrinsic ideas came off better. Old hand

Ralph Barton had a page caricaturing actors Pauline Lord, Louis Wolheim, Lenore Ulric, and Alfred Lunt. Al Frueh, a veteran of the *World,* depicted a man washing a train window near a sign, "Help Keep the El and Subway Clean." It was nearest to the localized humor that Ross was after. Frueh had another, a page of panels in which a man took home a picture of the leaning tower of Pisa, which influenced his family and the furniture to lean. It might have appeared in *Life* or *Judge.*

Not many advertisers had risked capital. The magazine had 36 pages, including the cover. Six and one third of them had been bought by advertisers. The inside front cover, bought by Caron Parfums, and another page, taken by Elgin watches, represented the luxury category being aimed at. The other two full pages were taken by Haldeman-Julius' Little Blue Books and by Boni & Liveright, avant-garde of the trade book publishers. Haldeman-Julius played poker with the Thanatopsis Club. Some of the smaller ads, for bookstores and theaters, were local.

Ross had taken the trouble to make plain his editorial independence of the business office. An item in "Of All Things" called for death to any of its advertising solicitors who intimated that free publicity would accompany purchase of space.

A page of the magazine's own advertising, built around a picture of a skin-dressed nomad identified as John Peter Toohey, featured a kick line: "Disobey that impulse—send five dollars." Most readers obeyed the impulse.

Raoul Fleischmann listened closely to the comments, most of them unfavorable, which followed appearance of the magazine. They pleased him no more than the state of the treasury. Ross's estimate of expenses had been wildly under the mark. The original fifty thousand dollars was nearly gone, although Ross drew only one hundred dollars of his three-hundred-dollar-a-week salary. Art director Rea Irvin got only seventy-five dollars a week and stock. Others were paid accordingly. There was ground for suspicion that Ross did not know much about starting a magazine.

Sadly, Fleischmann stuck his hat on his head and, saying nothing to Ross, set out for the office of John Hanrahan to get some advice. Hanrahan, a small, jowly, effervescent Irishman, was a magazine consultant, or "doctor." Despite the husky whisper in which he talked, he inspired confidence and had a reputation for resourcefulness. After listening to Fleischmann's unhappy story, he agreed to a closer examination of the illness, in return mostly for stock. This was the usual arrangement, the doctor gambling that his medicine would effect a cure. Stock was one thing the New Yorker had plenty of.

If Fleischmann believed that Ross would hold still for dosage he was mistaken. Hanrahan got in only because Ross lacked power to keep him out. Some medicine was forced down Ross, just as an angry bull can sometimes be doctored. Fleischmann, his confidence shored up with Hanrahan's advice, made editorial suggestions. Ross had subordinated himself to the Legion officials for a long time, and he was able to knuckle under again. But the New Yorker was his creation, almost his life, and the interference cut deep wounds.

Ross had wanted editorial independence from the business office. But the dictum, celebrated in publishing circles, that members of the New Yorker's business staff may not come into the editorial preserves without permission was not, as is generally believed, a coldly thought-out policy agreement. It developed out of a raging warfare between Ross and

Fleischmann which had no precedent. It has resulted in the only example of a publication, dependent for its livelihood on advertising, being dominated by its editor rather than by its owners.

For the New Yorker's second issue Ross used two contributions by Dorothy Parker, one a poem in the wry beat-down-by-a-man motif she had established elsewhere, the other a prose satire of a typical clubwoman. "The Talk of the Town"—around the office it was called simply "Talk"—had been shifted to the first text page. But there was little other change.

For the third issue Woollcott contributed an unsigned profile of Carr Van Anda, of the *Times*. The old stand-by, a dim look at Jack Dempsey, was tried in a profile by McGuinness. "Talk" was shifted to page 13 (in the next issue it returned to page 1 and settled there). Into every early number went the Pop-Optimist joke.

Circulation and advertising dwindled. Ross and Jane Grant desperately sought new money. One night Ross sat up late with Marquis James drinking prohibition whisky out of coffee cups.

"Have to dig up a thousand dollars before breakfast," Ross said an hour or two after midnight, as they parted.

When James arrived at the office next morning Ross, fresh as a daisy, was hard at work. "I got it," he said, barely glancing up. He had sold a complete bound set of *Stars and Stripes* to Theodore Roosevelt, Jr., for fifteen hundred dollars.

Fleischmann wavered, but he was not a quitter and he matched the sums garnered by Ross and Jane.

Ross tried a fund-raising method that had been in his mind for a long time. His contempt for Eastern poker players over the years had not been entirely jest. His fiercest scorn was reserved for the wealthy who sat in the Thanatopsis game. If ever he opened up, went his usual threat, they would go rapidly over the jumps.

One Sunday evening at the home of one of these wealthy men a game got under way. It was fairly common now for a player to win or lose a thousand dollars, sometimes more, at a Thanatopsis sitting. Stakes at first were low, but they grew as the night wore on. Most of the old regulars, seeing where the game was headed, dropped out.

Ross stayed. For several hours he stood winner. Then he began to lose. His financial plight, including the low value of New Yorker stock, was well known. Equally well known was Ross's poker bravado. His IOUs were honored as was the custom, and some of the players relished the prospect of forcing him to admit that the company was too fast for him.

Dawn came. Ross, haggard, chagrined at his loss of prestige, played on, steadily losing. The game broke up just before noon. When Ross signed his final IOU the total came to twenty-nine thousand dollars.

There was nothing left for Ross but to throw himself desperately into his work. The advisory editors had done all they could. Because of heavy commitments elsewhere they were not able to fill his pages. Marc Connelly and Dorothy Parker continued to write for the magazine. Frank Sullivan, whose reputation as a light columnist for the *World* was high, furnished a piece about the difficulty of understanding taxicab rates. In paying Sullivan, Ross gave a hint of what he considered proper editor-author relations. He sent Sullivan a check for a sum far above the magazine's usual rate. Sullivan thought it too high under the circumstances and refused it. Ross replied that he liked the piece and would pay well for what he considered superior work.

Ring Lardner contributed a small poem and there were a few other "names" in the magazine. But the general quality remained low.

Ross put notices on newspaper bulletin boards asking for contributions, especially about life in New York. He tried to give out assignments to reporters, but he could not afford to pay much and the prestige of the New Yorker was not seductive. To fill the magazine every week was a big job in itself.

Early in May, two and a half months after the first issue, Fleischmann called the principals together. Everybody knew the magazine's future was at stake. Circulation hovered around 10,000, far below what was needed. Advertisers were indifferent. Each issue carried only three or four pages of paid copy, and there was less in sight.

Fleischmann, Hanrahan, Ross, and Hawley Truax, close adviser to Ross on business matters, gathered at the Princeton Club on the morning of May 9. They sat gloomily in a corner of the almost deserted main room. Ross wanted a definite decision that he could pass on to the staff and contributors.

Fleischmann announced regretfully that he was pulling out. When the little band of mourners filed from the club Ross was still not quite ready to give up. But he found it difficult to believe that a spark of life remained.

Frantic Search 6

Ross decided to set his worries aside long enough to watch Franklin P. Adams get married that afternoon. Nearly the whole of the Algonquin crowd gathered at the wedding. It was held at Greenwich, Connecticut, just over the New York line. Because of technicalities connected with a divorce from his first wife, F.P.A. was not allowed to marry in New York State. The happiness of the bride, Esther Root, and the groom, whose saturnine face was several times seen to crack into smiles, was catching. The day was not auspicious for death, even of a magazine.

Fleischmann felt less sure of the wisdom of his decision and suggested to Ross that they meet again and talk it over. Fleischmann never added up all the reasons why he softened his decision. Magazine doctor Hanrahan had not, it was true, quite given up the patient. Crossing a street as the little band trekked back from the Princeton Club, Fleischmann had overheard Hanrahan say, "I don't blame Raoul, but he's killing a live thing." Probably most important of all was Fleischmann's unwillingness to give up his belief that the project was basically sound. Most comments by New Yorker readers had been vaguely regretful, as if speaking of a red apple which had looked wonderfully appetizing but had turned out pulpy.

When Fleischmann, Ross, and Truax put their heads together early the next week Truax had decided to risk some of his own money. He said there was a chance that his brother-in-law, Lloyd Stryker, the attorney, would invest some. One or two men he knew in the financial district might also contribute.

Fleischmann agreed to keep the magazine afloat while the hunt for capital continued.

Truax searched mightily, and despite his retiring nature argued the case wherever he got a chance. He caught Edward L. Bernays, a young poet turned public relations counsel, in a dentist's chair. Bernays had donated his services in getting a number of celebrities to "welcome" the New Yorker's appearance. Unfortunately, the dentist's drill suggested the nerve-shattering nature of a business relationship with Ross and he declined participation. Everywhere there were obstacles.

As it turned out, only Truax and Stryker put up any money—about fifteen thousand dollars between them, most of it Truax's.[1]

It was decided that the magazine would mosey sleepily

[1]Because there have been confusing published reports of the early financial tribulations of the New Yorker, Raoul Fleischmann, in an effort to set the record straight once and for all, gave me the following figures. The sum of $225,000 went into the magazine during its first year of publication. All but $35,000 of this was furnished by Fleischmann. During the next two years (the magazine came out of the red in 1928) an additional $485,000 was put in. Thus the total investment was $710,000—quite a bit more than the $50,000 that Ross had estimated in the beginning. There was also a $40,000 loan. Fleischmann furnished $550,000 of the total capital.

There are 265,779 shares of stock outstanding. In the spring of 1951 a share sold over the counter for about $14. The stock value of the New Yorker is thus roughly three and three quarters million dollars. Fleischmann is the largest stockholder by far.

Plainly, anyone who wanted to buy the magazine would need a great deal more than three and three quarters millions. Several stockholders have judged that ten million would swing the deal handily.

through the summer. The print run would be kept down. Meanwhile Ross would work hard in his laboratory to get some kind of usable formula. The best of the manuscripts and cartoons would be put aside for a big push in the fall. But Ross could not let anything stay put away for long. Not certain that the money would hold out until fall, he had to put the best he could find on display.

Two things were clear by now: he was not going to get much new out of the writers and artists raised in the old *Judge* and *Life* humor schools; and the Algonquin set could not be depended on to fill his magazine in their spare time. New talent would have to be discovered. One of the things he decided to do immediately was hire a new managing editor. Tip Bliss was not fitted for the job. Besides, he had come out of the "he-she" school.

Among those showing up regularly with art for sale was tall, slender Joseph Moncure March. All of his drawings had been promptly rejected. His uncle, Alden March, one of the important editors of the *Times*, suggested that he apply to Ross for an editorial job. Twenty-five, with the sensitive, intense face of a poet, he had not been connected with any of the other humor magazines. He had, however, edited a house organ for the New York Telephone Company and knew how to put a magazine together. Ross hired him.

"I just want to drop a manuscript in a slot," he said cozily, "and see it come out in the magazine." An understanding of creative people, it became apparent later, was one of Ross's major assets as an editor; but he never quite got over the belief that he could invent a vast, intricate machine that would smoothly and automatically produce a brilliant, beautifully printed magazine.

March soon found himself drawn into an emotional whirlpool. Ross generated tension in those around him. Yet at the same time he communicated his own feeling of dedication. He told March to find another youth or two, with knowledge of New York's social life.

One night March ran into an acquaintance, Fillmore Hyde, at the Jumble Shop, a Greenwich Village restaurant. Hyde was the son of A. Fillmore Hyde, a noted capitalist and Master of the Hounds at fox hunts. Young Hyde had a slightly jaundiced view of his background. March suggested to Hyde that he come into the office and talk with Ross. Soon Hyde was writing "Talk" and other pieces. His work had a satirical tone that was authoritative.

Ross next hired Ralph Ingersoll, a twenty-year-old giant who had been a heavyweight champion wrestler at Yale, common laborer in Western mines, a mining engineer, and a reporter for the New York *American*. He came to Ross under the auspices of Mrs. Franklin P. Adams. Nearly everyone recommended by a member of the Algonquin set was given a trial. But Ross seemed nonplused by Ingersoll's Eastern accent, enhanced by a lisp, and his handsomely tailored light flannel suit.

He was in the midst of a story about *Stars and Stripes* when one of his wild illustrative gestures swept a pot of ink over Ingersoll's suit. Immediately Ross's capacity for kindness rose to the surface, and he blotted Ingersoll tenderly.

"Quite all right," Ingersoll said with the magnanimity of a Yale man, and the interview proceeded.

Like others, Ingersoll was impressed by Ross's enthusiasm, and he wanted to participate.

"I don't know what kind of people I want here," Ross said. "Maybe I need people out of the Social Register. A descendant, say, of this fellow Ward McAllister, who thought up the business about New York's top Four Hundred."

"It just happens," Ingersoll said, "that I am Ward McAllister's grandnephew." (He signed himself, as a matter of fact, "Ralph McAllister Ingersoll.")

Ross studied the matter for a while and then advised Ingersoll that he could go to work at forty a week. He paid the others more than that. The fancy suit and the "McAllister" probably brought Ingersoll's rate down.

As the ink-spattered new staff member departed he saw Ross run his fingers helplessly through his upright hair and heard him explode, "Jesus Christ, I hire *anybody*."

Life in the shabby offices became an endless conference. The desperate search for a pattern, or formula, that would make the magazine click continued. Ross himself preferred "formula" as the proper term and used it constantly. After a while it took on a kind of magical connotation, as if a potion would be discovered that would make the magazine's pages wonderfully fascinating. The magic formula was so much in the minds of everybody that, long before the first sparkle, Ross was expressing fears that it would freeze.

New ingredients were added, others taken away, and various combinations tried. Ross decided that New York City, for the purposes of his magazine, was divided into three major categories: Wall Street, Broadway, and Park Avenue. He abandoned the first after running a few "Wall Street Notes." But in appealing to the second he was recognizing the rise of a large class, later known as café society. In the theater, speakeasy, and cabaret sets a new aristocracy was appearing. The younger generation was breaking its bonds and swamping the places of gaiety.

Even Park Avenue youngsters were mingling in the café set. But Ross did not forget their elders. He spoke constantly of the Gold Coast, or "class," audience he was after. The most important list for circulation promotion was taken from the Social Register. This was not because Ross was a social climber. He was, true enough, easily impressed by the rich, but he knew it and placed himself on guard. Now and then he preached that a journalist ought to have no friends lest he be influenced by them. He searched for snob appeal —a term used regularly by him—because, in his concept of success, luxury advertising was required. But he did not intend to kowtow. High society would be kidded, but preferably as if from the inside.

Fleischmann was socially proper enough. Once when Ross was afraid that he was getting discouraged to the point of withdrawing (the magazine was losing five thousand dollars a week) he sent March to lunch with him. Fleischmann and March had gone to the same prep school. Ross thought that fact might at least prove he was employing the right kind of editorial help. March was pretty sure he ruined the whole effect by using the wrong fork for fish. He was corrected gently by Fleischmann.

Ross was hoping for a peak circulation of from 50,000 to 70,000. That many intelligent readers, he thought, could be found among people who had luxury money to spend. The snob appeal, he hoped, would come from genuine intellectual superiority as well as from social standing.

Choosing an audience was far simpler than discovering how to capture it. It has been said that Ross has never known what he wants, only what he does *not* want. In the beginning there was some basis for this legend. He definitely wanted to get away from the *Life* and *Judge* formula. But he could not do so entirely and manage to fill his pages. He could hardly know exactly what he wanted, for neither he nor anyone else had ever seen it. He lacked the writing —let alone drawing—talent to produce it himself.

He had no choice but to function as a true editor—to

bring the most original out of others. At his best he was a sort of editor of people. He had also a previously unrevealed intuitive judgment of the worth of a manuscript. He could spot weak places, while not always knowing what should be done to strengthen them. His chief editorial attribute has always been detachment, which comes largely from his basically satirical view of things and people. As a result he often seems to act negatively when actually being creative.

"There isn't enough good stuff written on the North American continent every week to fill a magazine," he would preach to the staff. "We'll just have to print what we dislike the least."

He was quick to see the worst in a manuscript or drawing. He never said, "This is what we want." An accolade was, "This is *in the direction* of what we want." People were viewed by him in the same way—flaws before virtues.

"When the revolution comes," said Dorothy Parker, "it will be everybody against Ross."

Endlessly in those first months Ross discussed the shifting about of departments in the magazine, the invention of new ones, and the dropping of old ones. He gathered books, art, theater, music, and the movies under one heading, "Critique." "Talk" started off too abruptly, he thought. March suggested that it might be prefaced by shorter paragraphs. Ross agreed. Perhaps editorial comments on the times would lend the proper touch. Fillmore Hyde was assigned to do the paragraphs, which carried the heading, "Notes and Comment."

Ross was available to everyone who came in with a manuscript or an idea. He readily stuck on his hat and went out after material. There were great battles with the geniuses. Already Ross's reputation as a roarer was high. March often heard the wounded cry of genius coming from his office.

Fights usually started because of his negative approach, his habit of stating unqualified dislikes without offering a logical explanation.

Actually Ross was, at this point in his career, embarrassed by office scenes. While unshakable in his refusal to print certain things, he was not unreasonably obstinate. He could be driven from a point, and a common end of a fight was his remark, "Well, all right, we'll try it." The sign of his real anger was increasing quietness accompanied by growing pallor.

The little staff worked day and night. Half the time they were on the verge of collapse. The worst of it was that they were unable to build up a backlog of usable material. Cover paintings were seized from under the artist's brush. At the last moment March and Wylie rushed copy to the printer and stood over the linotype operators until it was set. Then they read the proof hurriedly while the type was being put into the forms. This was dangerous, for an error that got through took a good deal out of Ross, and he was apt to write a stinging memo about it.

At this time another discouraging blow fell. Ross's father became critically ill in Salt Lake City.

"Keep it going if you can," Ross said wistfully to his staff, and caught a train.

Altogether he was away for several weeks. His father died and he stayed to comfort his mother.

The staff had managed to keep the magazine staggering along, and on his return he resumed the battle. There were a few moments of near triumph. At one art conference—nearly everybody on the staff sat in on them at one time or another—Wylie held up a drawing of a woman waving good-by to friends departing on an ocean liner. The liner and the friends were not in the picture, to be sure, but the woman's attitude vividly created the whole scene. She was plainly a very nice woman in comfortable circumstances, who enjoyed her dessert at meals and a chocolate or two in between. Her enthusiastic nature was demonstrated by the way she had climbed on the lower girder of the picket barrier to wave her handkerchief a little nearer to the ship. Her hunched shoulders pushed up the floppy brim of her hat.

"This comes nearer to it," Ross said.

The others were excited. The picture was drawn from life, capturing with ease and grace a whole strata of American society—the upper-middle-class housewife and clubwoman. But Ross tooted no horns. The picture was used as a simple "spot" decoration on the lead page of "Talk." The drawing was unsigned.

The artist, Helen Hokinson, a small, shy girl in her middle twenties, was called in and asked to submit work regularly. She was soon ready with enough drawings to fill a double-page spread. It displayed ladies at the beach, not all of them plump, and was headed, "Why I Dislike the Sea Though My Father Was a Sailor."

One morning a tall young man came in, wearing paint-smeared canvas pants, a turtle-neck sweater, and ragged sneakers. He left his portfolio with Wylie and departed silently. He did not expect much of the New Yorker or, for that matter, of his total efforts as an artist. He went back to his studio in Greenwich Village and prepared for the abandonment of his drawing in favor of work in a dance band. He had played the piano for Gilda Gray, the shimmy girl, and also for a small band which included Rudy Vallee.

When a check from the New Yorker arrived in Peter Arno's attic it caused him to abandon music and return to his drawing. Arno's real name was Curtis Arnoux Peters, Jr., and he was the son of a prominent judge.

His work, though it was nearly at the opposite pole from Hokinson's, also had an immediately favorable reaction at the New Yorker. And, like Hokinson's, his first contribution was used as a decorative "spot" for the first page of "Talk." It showed a tall, clean-limbed girl silhouetted in the up-and-outward sweep of a dive. Few details of the girl or the people around the pool were shown, but their smartness was somehow beyond question.

About that time Ross was considering the value of a woman's touch in the "text." It was a matter that he approached with extreme reluctance because of his old-time newspaperman's prejudice against the female journalist. A lady secretary was bad enough. Ross's heroic efforts to muffle his profanity were not always successful. With women around, you could not even spit on the floor with any peace of mind. He had temporarily fought off an attempt by Fleischmann's wife Ruth, a professional interior decorator, to get up a fancy reception room.

"What," he would sometimes demand, "will the *Stars and Stripes* boys say if they find me being run by a bunch of women and children?" To Ross, an elderly man of thirty-three, March, Wylie, and the others were hardly more than babes. He always feared that the frail Wylie would suddenly crumple.

A possible female helper suggested by Herman Mankiewicz was Lois Long, theater editor of *Vanity Fair*. She would know how to appeal to the young cabaret-speakeasy set, being a leading member of it. Ross agreed to an interview and was not disappointed by her appearance. She was twenty-two, exceptionally well constructed, tall, and dark-haired. She had striking features embellished by violet-gray eyes. Also she had energy in abundance. Her movements and her conversation were supercharged. She could have modeled for Miss Jazz Age.

Since Ross had no particular ideas in mind, Long (Ross tried to resist the encroachment of femininity by using simply her last name) suggested that she do a night-life column, while keeping her job on *Vanity Fair*. Ross was agreeable, since Baskerville was departing.

Lois Long merely went on with her dining and dancing as before, allowing her escorts to foot the expense account without being aware of it. The column's title was changed from "When Nights Were Bold" to "Tables for Two," a notable reduction in corniness. It was signed "Lipstick." Lipstick's column was the first popular feature of the magazine. After a while the author revealed her sex, but, since cabaret owners were not aware of her identity, they were constantly being bothered by imposters who wanted to freeload. She issued a warning, describing herself as "a short, squat maiden of forty who wears steel-rimmed spectacles, makes her son pay her dinner checks, and habitually carries a straw suitcase filled with Aquazone."

The gypsy atmosphere of the New Yorker office was enhanced by her appearances between midnight and 3 A.M., straight from night spots, to pound out the column before the bootleg gin or brandy had worn off. She was strong and nimble, which was fortunate, for often the key to her cubbyhole had gone astray. On those occasions she used the doorknob as a footrest and propelled herself gracefully over the partitions.

Ross decided to appeal directly to women readers and women's apparel advertisers with a fashion section. He thought Lois Long could do the job, and he assigned March to pry her completely away from *Vanity Fair*. It was not easy, for, like everyone else, she considered the New Yorker's health to be bad. Since *Vanity Fair* paid poorly, she finally agreed. The heading "Fifth Avenue" was selected for her shopping column.

"What," she inquired of Ross, "is our policy?"

Ross tore at his forelock. "Jesus," he said, "I don't know. We'll have to make one up."

A little while afterward, trying to describe a jewelry display which had not impressed her, she went to Ross.

"The stuff is terrible," she said. "What will I do about it?"

"Say it's terrible," Ross answered.

The remark nailed down, in a way, the editorial standard of the New Yorker. Willing as he was to appeal to a "class" audience and to luxury advertisers, Ross's editorial integrity —plus his natural irreverence—prevented a policy of kowtowing. He held to his conviction that if he could get out a magazine that was read by a small but select audience the advertisers would have to come in and stay in.

He set up a hard and fast rule that the business department might communicate with Lois Long only by means of memoranda routed through himself.

One of the items in "Talk of the Town" seemed to Ross to strike a properly irreverent note.

> Her Royal Highness Queen Marie of Roumania in an article in *Cosmopolitan* magazine says, "Often I have been asked how I retain that look of youth." She recommends laughter; not mincing affected little smiles, but honest laughter. Thus it is proved again that royalty is fickle. Only a little while ago we remember seeing that the only thing that would keep Her Highness' complexion young was Pond's Cold Cream.

Advertising continued to fall off, which resulted in a series of promotion pieces superior to most of the regular text. In the summer of that first year of publication ads were lacking even for the back cover and the inside front and back covers. They couldn't very well be left blank. No law forbade the use of regular text, but custom was against it. Besides, the cover had to be printed in advance of the rest of the magazine, since color was used. Ross talked with Fleischmann and Rea Irvin about the possibility of working out something. The high-hat symbol, they decided, should be employed once more.

They called in prolific young Corey Ford. He was twenty-three, under the top age limit of twenty-five that Ross seemed to have set. He was a former editor of the *Columbia Jester*, a gay and handsome youth whom one would expect to find at the big game, wearing a coonskin coat and escorting the prettiest girl in the stands. He was selling to *Life*, *Judge*, and *Vanity Fair*. Ford listened, nodded, went back to the Beekman Place apartment he shared with Frank Sullivan, and created Eustace Tilley.

Tilley was the hero of a series entitled "The Making of a Magazine," which began on the inside front cover of the issue of August 8, that first summer. He was a younger man than the figure of the original cover. His top hat was of a newer style, without the curved brim. He wore a morning coat and striped trousers. Ford borrowed Eustace Tilley's last name from an aunt—he had always considered it vaguely funny. "Eustace" was selected for euphony.

Tilley was always busy, and, in the illustrations by Johann Bull, always poised. He might be in Mexico, supervising the vast farms which grew the cactus for binding the magazine's pages together. The Punctuation Farm, where commas were grown in profusion, because Ross had developed a love of them, was naturally in a more fertile region. Tilley might be inspecting the Initial Department, where letters were sent to be capitalized. Or he might be superintending the Emphasis Department, where letters were placed in a vise and forced sideways, for the creation of italics. He would jump to the Sargasso Sea, where by insulting squids he got ink for the printing presses, which were powered by a horse turning a pole. It was told how in the great paper shortage of 1882 he had saved the magazine by getting society matrons to contribute their finery. Thereafter dresses were made at a special factory and girls employed to wear them out, after which the cloth was used for manufacturing paper.

Fleischmann, who had moved into the offices to protect his venture, gathered the series into a promotion booklet. Later Ross took a listing for Eustace Tilley in the Manhattan telephone directory. In time Eustace Tilley became confused with the gentleman of the original cover.

The popularity of the Tilley series was large only in comparison to the popularity of the rest of the magazine, and even Ross's young torchbearers realized that the flame was dimming. In Greenwich Village, which Ross did not particularly wish to penetrate, staff connection was a social asset because the magazine seemed mildly avant-garde. But the New Yorker was generally ignored or ridiculed. One noon a few staffers were in the elevator with opposite numbers of a little weekly called *Time*, which had been started a couple of years earlier by Yalemen Henry Luce and Briton Hadden. The offices of the two magazines were in the same building. A stranger was overheard saying to his companion, "You know, I don't believe there is one really interesting magazine being published." Gloom and the elevator descended together.

Ross wanted, he told March, to be able at a glance to know the exact schedule of every page of the coming issue.

March obligingly hung the page dummies (the magazine was down to 24 pages) on the walls of his office, marking them to show the material thus far selected for each.

Ross would stand before them, pulling at his hair, surveying the blank spaces for which no copy was available. Then, jingling moodily, he would walk to the water cooler, cuff it a couple of times, go to his desk, and scratch morosely among the odds and ends he was holding for further consideration.

Yet he was beginning to haul back copy as it was about to go to the printer. He would brood over it, though aware that finally he would have to let it go to fill up the pages. He rarely touched it with a pencil, partly because the writers were certain to object, and partly because he was not positive he could improve it.

Ross scoured the newspapers for craftsmanship he liked, then telephoned the writers and offered them assignments. One whose work attracted him was Morris Markey, a *World* rewrite man who occasionally signed feature stories. Markey had a talent for describing a thing with simple clarity, bringing it before the reader without the flamboyance of many feature writers. Ross telephoned him and asked him to do a piece about Mayor "Red Mike" Hylan and City Hall. Markey agreed, but, unimpressed with the magazine and its rate of pay, he was slow getting to work.

Ross telephoned Markey again. This time Markey agreed to come to the office. That was half the battle for Ross.

Markey appeared on a Sunday morning. Sunday was a little more relaxed than other days. Location of a quiet place to talk was nevertheless a problem. Ross's secretary was hammering a typewriter in his office and other staff members were at work elsewhere. Finally Ross pulled a couple of chairs into a corner.

Markey was a tall, blond, affable youth of twenty-five with a background that had much in common with Ross's. Markey's formal education was small. He had finished only the junior year of high school in his home town of Richmond, Virginia. He had served in the war. Later, after being fired out of a soap factory, he had started a career in journalism as a cub on the Atlanta *Journal* (where Ross had also worked). He had arrived on the *World* by way of the Newark *Ledger* and the New York *Globe*.

Ross immediately cast his spell. Reporters would be allowed to write for the magazine what they saw, he told Markey.

"Honesty," Ross said. "Honesty at any cost. Write exactly what you see, exactly the way you feel."

To Markey this was a novel idea. In his experience a newspaperman's copy was never allowed to show boredom, excitement, anger, or any other emotion. Ross seemed bent on developing a new and exciting form.

Markey agreed to quit his job and join the New Yorker staff. Before he could begin he had an offer from *Collier's*. Markey was aware—Ross made no bones about it—that the New Yorker was losing several thousand dollars a week and that its circulation had gone down to 7500. But the appeal of adventure, the chance of creating something new, decided Markey in favor of joining Ross.

After hunting a title for the pieces Markey was to write, Ross decided on "In the News." The title's genesis was the Chicago *Tribune's* sports column, "In the Wake of the News," which Ross had admired when it was under Ring Lardner's direction. Markey's assignment was to find trivial or important things which the newspapers had missed. Markey did not fancy himself as a scoop-type reporter, however, and in his pieces he strove chiefly for atmosphere and the revealing odds and ends which newspaper reporters usually had to ignore when covering spot news.

After a while Ross, fascinated as always by the details of journalism, suggested breaking the rhythm of Markey's pieces every few weeks with an examination of the New York newspapers. Markey accepted the chore with pleasure. In a short time Ross, who as a reporter had failed to land a job on a New York paper, and Markey, not long away from a soap factory, were master-minding the metropolitan press with confidence and relish. Ross chose "The Current Press" for a heading. The first report was a tabulation of space given by the papers to a fine that Miller Huggins had hung on Babe Ruth for getting roaring drunk.

Ross began to develop the war-of-nerves style of editing for which eventually he gained a fabulous reputation. Markey's submission of a manuscript was the opening shot of a battle. If something was not clear, Ross said so with rugged eloquence, and he was not above simulating confusion. Or he would declare flatly that a statement of fact—about which he often had no independent knowledge—was false. Markey's affability always disappeared and he counterattacked with fury. They would wear each other out. Victories were divided, but greater exactness and clarity resulted.

"The only thing I had talent for," Markey said later, "was looking at a thing and trying to tell people exactly what I saw. Ross knew that, and I suppose he was trying to sharpen it."

Ross had inspired his staff to great efforts, and had driven himself to the edge of a nervous breakdown. But his magazine seemed, after six months, once more about to die. The returned copies were stacked high. Woollcott demanded that his name be taken off the list of advisory editors. That destroyed part of what confidence there was left. Ross told the staff there was still a danger that Fleischmann would decide his losses were too steep and pull out, which doubtless would be fatal.

But Fleischmann was determined to give the venture a fair chance before the public. He had John Hanrahan, the publisher's counsel, and Arthur Samuels, an advertising man, prepare a series of full-page newspaper ads. In late September the rockets went up, each explosion accompanied by the odor of great bundles of burning currency. Later on Ross charged the business office with responsibility for the public's belief that the New Yorker claimed to be a magazine of sophistication with snobbish overtones. But he had the ability to prevent the campaign had he really wanted to.

The first of the ads inquired:

WHAT EXPLAINS THIS EXTRAORDINARY RECEPTION?

The answer bubbled like a medium grade of domestic champagne.

The New Yorker—unheralded and unpromoted—acquired almost overnight the largest metropolitan circulation of any class periodical. This was a spontaneous response from the New York public; from those thousands who are so surely forming the new aristocracy of New York, an aristocracy that recognizes distinguished mentality rather than genealogy. . . . Its nearest prototypes are perhaps the weeklies of London and Paris. . . . It is avowedly for a metropolitan audience. Devoted to persons of interest and to contemporary happenings on This Island, it treats neither them nor itself too seriously. It is gay but not smart alecky; sophisticated but not highbrow; gossipy but not scandalous; personal but not provincial. . . .

Included in the advertisement was the "Talk" item poking fun at Queen Marie's testimonial for Pond's Cold Cream—along with dead serious testimonials to the New Yorker by prominent citizens. Said Clare A. Briggs, the cartoonist: "First off, I thought the New Yorker was pretty poor stuff. . . . Today I crave it." There followed enthusiasms by the new mayor, Jimmy Walker, by Al Jolson, George Gershwin, Irving Berlin, and Lee Shubert.

A New Yorker reader, one gathered, was a superior being in taste and intellect. He belonged to the upper crust, even if an unfortunate birth had left him lower in the pie. Continued the advertisement: "The New Yorker concentrates its attention on those centers of amusement on which smart New York focuses its interest, and reports the anecdote and chat of clubs and theaters and hotels, of drawing rooms on Park Avenue and shops on Fifth, sports in vogue at night clubs—and at country clubs."

The magazine's covers, it continued, were as different from others "as caviar from cabbage." The profiles were "personalities of the people you know—or would like to know."

Stepping forward with more testimonials were "smart New Yorkers" Alma Gluck, Bernard M. Baruch, Jascha Heifetz, Robert C. Benchley ("because my folks come from Dubuque, Iowa"), W. C. Fields, Julia Hoyt, James Gleason, Florenz Ziegfeld, Grantland Rice, Sigmund Spaeth, Fontaine Fox, Deems Taylor, Leon Errol, and Richard Bennett.

Ross doubted that his magazine was hustled by the butler to the master and madam. But he was determined to make this come about.

One day he walked into March's office, the keys in his pocket jingling contentedly.

"I've got a real social gal coming in," he announced. "She's written a couple of pieces."

"Who's that?" March asked.

"Ellin Mackay."

March repeated, "Who's that?"

Ross exploded. "Damnedest unsocial-minded editor there ever was."

Ellin Mackay did come in, and she was, indeed, silk-stocking. Her father was Clarence H. Mackay, president of Postal Telegraph, whose father before him had been an Empire Builder and a Great Social Figure. Miss Mackay was a fetching twenty-two. Four years earlier she had "come out" at a grand party at the Ritz-Carlton. After traveling she had decided to Write, and she was sending her neatly hand-written manuscripts, bound in rich leather, to *Vogue*, *Vanity Fair*, the New Yorker, and other magazines.

Miss Mackay saw herself as no dilettante. She was in revolt. Rumors had even circulated that her father had packed her off to Europe in the hope that she would lose interest in "modern" notions. There were even darker rumors that she was supposed also to forget a man whose family dwelt several leagues below the Social Register.

Ross selected for the launching of Miss Mackay's literary career a piece titled "Why We Go to Cabarets," subtitled, "A Post-Debutante Explains." It was a forthright attack on the stag-line tradition of high-society parties.

Ross showed it to Ingersoll, with the by-line deleted. "Terrible," Ingersoll said. "But print it. It will get some attention."

Ross showed it to Fillmore Hyde. He rewrote it out of his own knowledge, filling in some obvious omissions. But Miss Mackay turned his draft over to an executive at the Social Register, who protested to Ross, and he went back to the original version. Readers unfamiliar with high-society functions (roughly ninety-eight per cent of the magazine's subscribers) had to get along the best they could.

The piece (issue of November 28, 1925) was a minor sensation. Wylie, in his public relations role, sent out copious releases, and the New York papers ran large pieces. The wire services piped the story straight to Dubuque.

When the article was broken into pieces and examined it was found to be really an ultra-smug attack on the dowagers. The stag boys at the parties were vapid and boring, the charge went. But why? Because—and this must have shivered the fixtures in many a drawing room—the hostesses had dragged in lads of not truly blue blood. Miss Mackay had personally noted the presence of young men who spoke familiarly of the Social Register and the exclusive Racquet Club as an obvious cover-up for their residence far up on the West Side.

And so, explained Miss Mackay, the modern aristocratic miss went to a cabaret with an escort of her own choosing. There were unpleasantries, of course. "We do not particularly like dancing shoulder to shoulder with gaudy and fat drummers." Ignoring the noisy flirtation of the Irish politician and the little blonde, or the fat boy and the flapper, was not always easy. "We go because, like our Elders, we are fastidious. We go because we prefer rubbing elbows in a cabaret to dancing at an exclusive party with all sorts and kinds of people."

The article was not brilliant or penetrating, nor did it result in any important changes. Its value to the New Yorker, aside from the publicity, was that it proved the time was ripe for launching a slightly iconoclastic "class" magazine. The thunder of the new literary, theater, and speakeasy prophets which had nurtured Ross—the Algonquin set—had reached Park Avenue.

Miss Mackay's second piece, a couple of weeks later, recorded the smashing of some more old customs. It was titled "The Declining Function," subheaded "A Post-Debutante Rejoices." The function, as represented to the people of the outer darkness, was a rather formal affair at which guests sat stuffily around on straight chairs, probably gilt, while a famous artist played a harpsichord. Nowadays, it seemed, the true artists were acting hard to get. The functions were no longer really exclusive. Hostesses were letting in famous people—not necessarily talented—who merely stood around being lionized by their social betters.

Perhaps the most important development, Miss Mackay continued, was the rebellion of the younger generation against parental authority and convention. The belle with "her winter" and "the most eligible man" had practically disappeared. Striking a high note of defiance, Miss Mackay wrote: "Modern girls are conscious of the importance of their own identity, and they marry whom they choose, satisfied to satisfy themselves. They are not so keenly aware, as were their parents, of the vast difference between a brilliant match and a mésalliance."

Whereupon Miss Mackay, proving that she belonged in the school of realists, defied her father and married a former Bowery saloon piano player named Izzy Baline.

Izzy Baline, who had grown up in poverty on the lower East Side, had changed his name to Irving Berlin and had amassed millions of his own by writing songs. But this made no difference to Clarence Mackay. The story of the marriage and the father-daughter rift was on front pages all over America.

One of the first things the bride did, reported the *Times*, was to telephone Ross from a City Hall booth. The conversation, in the words of the *Times:*

Ross: "Hello, Miss Mackay."

Mrs. Berlin: "Oh, no, it's Mrs. Berlin. I'm no Lucy Stoner. The fact is, I shan't be able to get my piece in on time. I'm leaving town in twenty minutes."

Afterward a legend sprang up that the Mackay articles, by capturing the attention of Park Avenue, were responsible for the New Yorker's success. The Park Avenue gentlemen and their ladies gave brief attention to the magazine, but they did not at once become regular customers. Fillmore Hyde, checking, found few copies in the drawing rooms. By hanging around newsstands he learned that the rank and file of the speakeasy set were the steady purchasers. The flattery of the promotion campaign had affected them. If not fascinated by the magazine, at least they found it pertinent and appealing. Circulation had begun to climb, and the Mackay furor accelerated the pace.

On the day before Christmas of the first year there appeared concrete evidence that Ross had been right in his belief that big local advertisers could be pulled into the magazine. On that day Ray Bowen, the advertising manager, got a contract with B. Altman & Company for 52 pages of advertising to appear during 1926. The retail advertising manager, John McCall, got a similar contract from Saks-Fifth Avenue.

Bedlam 7

On the morning of the first anniversary of the New Yorker, Ross prowled through the offices, mildly contented. There was, for the moment, an air of relaxation. At their typewriters sat Ralph Ingersoll and Fillmore Hyde, dressed in striped trousers, morning coats, and top hats. Ross guffawed heartily and, with the air of a stern, hard-working father allowing himself a few moments of relaxation on a Sunday, sat down and gossiped for a while.

For himself, Ross wanted no part of morning clothes or any other kind of formal dress. He refused to assume the mental attitudes and mannerisms of the class to which he wanted to appeal. He made it a point of high honor, his friends were convinced, to hold fast to the opposite extreme. It was at this time that Alexander Woollcott, ridiculing his old protégé's wooing of the upper classes, remarked that Ross looked and behaved like a dishonest Abe Lincoln. Marc Connelly claimed that Ross took undue pride in his horse brush of hair, now worn a little taller than before. But Ross had little time for visiting barbershops, and Connelly may have been influenced by his own notably unfertile stand. The general notion was that Ross selected his clothes for aesthetic shock to the well-groomed.

Old buddies from the hobo and *Stars and Stripes* days

telephoned Ross expecting, since he was trying to run a champagne-and-caviar magazine, to be awarded at the most a brief chat in a gilded reception room. They were urged to stay away from the office and invited to dinner or some other entertainment. Ross hated to think about anything except his work while at the office. The visitors would find the relaxed Ross the same as of old. Sid Bergh, in from San Francisco, was amazed when Ross stood in a ticket line, like any tourist from Dubuque, to get tickets for the theater. To pay for them Ross, having found his pockets empty, had borrowed $20 from one of the servants at the communal house, where they had dined.

Discord at the communal house had reached an alarming state. Woollcott's tastes, now that he was a celebrated New York figure blessed with a large income, had become grandiose. He filled the house with glamor equaled by clamor. Ross was chiefly interested in getting to sleep. He stormed and tore his hair, but he had trouble working up enough courage to face Woollcott with the suggestion of a demobilization, preferably with Woollcott moving to other quarters. It was a case of Ross's reluctance to open hostilities. His proposed solution was for Jane Grant to throw Woollcott out. Aware of the emotional hullabaloo that Woollcott was capable of raising, she did not relish the prospect. Anyhow, she thought it properly Ross's work. In the end, though, she suggested to Woollcott that he move. He was curiously amiable about it.

Ross's and Woollcott's friendship continued after the separation, accompanied by vigorous bouts of infighting. Sitting knee to knee at a game of cribbage, they would start off with good-natured insults and proceed by degrees to angry personal vilification. Tempers often went so high that the fights had to be continued by mail.

While Ross had found the late-at-night racket at the communal house unbearable, he apparently desired, if unconsciously, the wildest bedlam at the office. Since boyhood the clang of typewriters, the cries of shirt-sleeved editors, and the panicky rush for deadlines had been in his blood. The creation of a similar atmosphere, reasoned some coworkers, was a part of his defense against a guilt feeling for running a fancy-pants magazine. Others took the view that he simply felt at home working in a hurricane.

Ross himself believed that he loved quiet and efficiency and that current noise was a sacrifice that had to be made for future peace. If he tore down and rebuilt partitions, scrambled and rescrambled the desks, tried the water cooler one place and then another, and continually rearranged the telephone system, everything would fall into perfect order. His nerves and those of everybody else would at last grow calm.

Ross's office was shifted about as much as anyone else's. After a major reorganization, staff members would have to spend time hunting him. There were interim periods when he didn't even *have* an office.

Once a solemn memo went to staff members: always keep one corner of your desk clear, in case Ross wants to draw up a chair and do some work. Suddenly Ross and Elsie Dick, who by now was his secretary, would plop down and Ross would begin to dictate. Elsie Dick was a willowy, efficient girl who came to feel that nothing could surprise her. One of Ross's favorite places for dictation was standing at the water cooler. Staff members grew accustomed to nudging Ross and Miss Dick aside in order to get a drink.

Women on the staff continued to pain Ross. One of the things that bothered him was the location of the ladies' rest room. To get to the men's room, it had to be passed. A lady coming out might see Ross marching by, stony countenance firmly to the front. He spent hours trying to devise a way to build separate passages to the rest rooms. He never accomplished it.

The men's room was a favored spot for impromptu editorial conferences and was the scene of one of Ross's sharper journalistic comments. A brash young ex-hoofer, Walter Winchell, whose column in the *Graphic* was beginning to catch on, had reported that Ross did not wear underwear. This was hardly a proper sartorial practice, implied Winchell, for an editor who wanted to run a sophisticated magazine. Ross went to the men's room and stripped off his underdrawers. Then he wrapped them up and mailed them to Winchell. Ross and Winchell never got on well after the exchange.

The nomadic editorial life was, Ross thought, a terrible burden on him and occasionally he pursued solitude. For a while he tried a soundproofed office. When the construction men apprised him of the thickness of the soundproofing material they intended to use, he ordered them to double it. The office was quieter than Proust's cork-lined room. He was lonely and unhappy in it. At first he tried to mend matters by leaving the door open. Finally he moved out and had the soundproof walls knocked down to make way for other perfections.

At one point there materialized, as Ross had feared, a plushy reception room designed by Ruth Fleischmann. Silver paper graced the walls. The settees were astonishing. Cretonne was present by the dozens of yards. There were even some oriental touches. Though possibly suitable for the caviar taste the magazine was supposed to have, it disappeared in one of Ross's carpentry orgies.

Ross's drive for serenity was chiefly responsible for the

general chaos, but Fleischmann also had a share in it. He saw no point in renting a set of offices in a building in which he had no financial interest. Trouble arose because the available space in the building he did own was scattered. Units were at far-flung points. New Yorker staff members were always on the move to make way for outside space renters. Much time was spent hunting for misplaced desks. One day after a two-hour search Lois Long found hers at one end of a vast, empty expanse on an upper floor. Her assistant's desk was at the other end. By telephoning they managed to get some work done. As a protest they finally brought in roller skates and skimmed back and forth for conferences. Later they were moved into an abandoned ladies' rest room. Lois Long added to the note of informality she had set by occasionally, in hot weather, working in her slip.

Ross himself moved to the barren plateau during one of his searches for peace. He sat in lonely splendor, his nerves shattering under pressure of the silence. After a while he climbed back down.

The constant shifting of offices complicated the telephone service. But Ross's obsession with improvements of all kinds was responsible for the more fantastic tangles. When a carpenter was not sawing or hammering at an editor's nerves a telephone mechanic was picking at them with a screwdriver. The common switchboards, buttons, and extensions devised by the telephone company were soon exhausted. Ross tried hookups which allowed various helpers to tune in on him; he had direct wires between certain people and no communication at all between others. His decisions were based on how he felt individuals worked most creatively.

He was not the one to want several telephones on his

desk. With only two, it was possible to pick up the wrong one nearly every time. Rumors that the telephone company planned to switch to a dial system threw him into a panic. With it communication with the outside would never, he was sure, be achieved. Installation of French-style cradle telephones he regarded as a diabolical plot, and he blamed the movies for getting the public into a mood for accepting them. The wartime Paris phones had never worked properly for him.

Ross's deputy—other staffers sometimes used the Army term "dog robber"—was now, after a year, Ralph Ingersoll. Joseph March had retired to write poetry and later went to Hollywood. Ingersoll padded through the corridors, trying doors—when they were standing—to see if they were locked. Key jangler Ross liked to know that everything was locked up. He spent a good deal of time, as a matter of fact, experimenting with buzz locks on the door of his private office. There were times when he did not want to be available to anyone unless he released the door by pressing a button. The buzz locks complicated his life by failing to work at critical moments. He liked also to have a back-door escape route when possible.

"I live the life of a hunted animal," he would cry. At moments of deepest stress he would mutter, "God, how I pity me!"

Ingersoll opened doors on unsuspecting editors and writers to admit silent men carrying huge, unwanted filing cases. He helped Ross devise perfect systems, and originated some of his own. When inevitably they broke down or were cast aside in favor of new models, he was required to shoulder blame for the chaos.

Ingersoll submitted to the role of dog robber because of his belief that, weird as the operation often seemed, Ross was a fine editor with an element of greatness in him. But the indignities were ten times the size and number suffered by the average orderly. He was required, for one thing, to absorb Ross's ancient contempt for college men and Eastern dudes—exaggerated now by his pursuit of subscriptions among the upper crust. Ingersoll's Eastern accent was always under attack. In one editorial conference matters were delayed by Ross's stubborn insistence on accepting literally Ingersoll's pronunciation. Ingersoll, talking about Harry Thaw, made the last name sound like "Thor." After listening with pretended incomprehension for a while, Ross declared, "I'll have no mythical characters in this magazine."

Ingersoll was permitted his own smaller domain, and in many respects he matched or even outmatched Ross in ruling it. "If I gave Ingersoll a thousand dollars a week just to sit in an empty room," Ross once declared in a left-handed tribute, "before you knew it he'd have six people helping him." One category Ingersoll ruled was that of hypochondria. Ross's weak stomach demanded constant medication, especially since he occasionally breakfasted on mince pie and iced coffee. But Ingersoll's cache of medicine bottles and pill containers was larger, partly because his hair was thinning and he had great faith in restorers.

Ingersoll was allowed to hire. He also did most of the firing, on Ross's order. This was a major chore, since more people were fired off the New Yorker during its early years than are forcibly removed from most magazines in a couple of decades. The high point was reached when Ross caused the dismissal of a secretarial worker on Christmas Eve, though aware that she had a sick mother. He was criticized also for summarily firing a man who had seven children to support.

Ross's firing tribulations became legendary, because of

their number, the unexpectedness with which the ax fell, and the fantastic extremes to which he went in order to escape performing the executions directly. His allergy to direct action sprang, his close associates thought, partly from his reluctance to *start* a scene. There was in addition a fear of aggression stemming from memories of tramp newspapermen who threw paste pots. Finally there was an underlying sensitiveness to the pain of others. "Someone else was always called on to do the dirty work," an early New Yorker employee has said. "But when Ross was trapped or cornered, he stood up damned well."

Once having decided on a dismissal, he could not bear to have the victim in his sight. Many years later Ingersoll, after considerable dealing with important people while editor of *Fortune* and of the newspaper *PM*, and among high command levels in the armies of World War II, was able to recall only one other person with a similar attitude. That was British Field Marshall Montgomery, who, when thoroughly displeased with a subordinate, would cry, "I'll not have the man in my army."

The cause for the high ration of executions was more complicated. Ross's own training had, of course, been at the opposite extreme from security of job tenure. He believed that migration from job to job was advantageous to a journalist's growth. He stated that a fairly rapid turnover of all but key help was to the advantage of a publication. The maximum tenure he often mentioned was two years. He incorporated ruthlessness into his working philosophy. Many ingredients for his formula had, after all, to come from persons other than himself. During the search a good many people would have to be cast aside, just as a chemist excludes elements which he has tried without success.

Desperately short of money, working in near darkness, he had ruled out sentimentality.

There was no lack of fabulous events for embellishing the dismissal legend. The first of the executions was carried out by Philip Wylie. A girl whose job it was to keep a record of artists' contributions, cartoon ideas, and gag lines kept getting things snarled up. When it turned out that no one could decipher her handwriting, including herself, Ross decided that she had to go. He assigned the dismissal job to Wylie, slid on his hat, and departed. Every few minutes he telephoned to see how the girl was taking it. She was setting a bad precedent. Wylie was as gentle as he could be, but the girl broke into tears while gathering her belongings. Then, turning angry, she hurled expletives in the direction of Ross's empty office. These circumstances were duly reported to the fugitive by telephone and he was visibly shaken when he crawled back to his post.

Ross's fears were aggravated by his breakup with Herman Mankiewicz, general worker on the early issues and later theater and movie critic. He was an early Algonquin Round Tabler and, like the others in the early days, had little faith in Ross's prospects as an editor. His New Yorker connection was not vital to him and when starting to Hollywood for a writing stint he suggested that he be replaced. Ross asked him merely to take a leave of absence. In Hollywood, Mankiewicz was offered a regular job, but, debating whether to pursue Art, as represented by criticism, or Cash, as represented by Hollywood, he procrastinated. Ross hired someone else and so informed Mankiewicz by telegram.

Mankiewicz roared into New York, ready to have it out. He was not large or athletic. But he usually sported, as everybody knew, a sturdy malacca cane. He intended, he told members of the Algonquin set, to leave Ross a bleeding carcass. The Algonquin people bruited the threat happily about, with special attention to Ross himself, and awaited consequences, which they hoped would be dire. One day Ross, warned of Mankiewicz's warlike approach, and momentarily without a locked office or an escape route, hid in a cloak closet. For company he had Ingersoll hide with him. After thumping his cane on a desk, Mankiewicz departed.

In the end Mankiewicz had to be faced, and when he returned Ross took him into a partitioned office. Staff members gathered to listen. The debate was hot. Over the partition flew first Mankiewicz's collar. Then came his necktie. Although he confined the laying on of hands to himself and did not bloody his cane, the affair left Ross uneasy.

Once when Ingersoll refused to carry out a head-chopping, Ross hit on a new stratagem. He called the victim into his office.

"You're not a genius," he said accusingly.

The victim pleaded guilty.

"That being the case," Ross went on, turning nervously back to his work, "we won't be able to use you any longer."

The rapid turnover of personnel was largely responsible for Ross's most startling editorial innovation—the "Jesus," known also as the "Hub." Technically the "Jesus" was the managing editor, but the title was rarely used. The "Jesus" term was invented by staff members who claimed that Ross was constantly in search of a miracle man. Whenever Ross hired a new one he always told him that henceforward he would be the center of the magazine. Hence the firm "Hub."

Joseph March was the first "Jesus," though the term hadn't been invented before his departure. Ingersoll was only a part-time "Jesus" because of the other duties Ross laid on him.

The first to be called "Jesus" was Oliver Claxton, whose

qualifications to be the "Hub" consisted of brief experience as a bond salesman in Philadelphia. He had little interest, as a matter of fact, in a literary career, and was merely looking for work when a girl cousin of his introduced him to Ingersoll. Ingersoll's reason for getting him the job, Claxton felt pretty sure, was less for the good of the magazine than for the good will it might curry with his cousin. Claxton's parents were Social Register people, a fact which Ingersoll used in getting him on the pay roll at forty dollars a week, but it had no bearing on his selection as "Jesus." Ross thought bond salesmanship was a perfectly good background for the role.

Claxton was baffled when Ross threw a kindly arm around his shoulders and explained that he was to be the hub of the magazine. Claxton never worked out a clear notion of what his job was supposed to be. He merely sat idly until summoned by Ross for a conference. The conferences were remarkable. Ross had once said to Robert Benchley, "I don't want you to think I'm not incoherent," a line that Benchley cherished. Samuel Hoffenstein, the poet, once remarked that talking with Ross was like drinking a glass of water without the glass.

Ross spoke to "Jesus" with a vast incoherence. Claxton soon realized that he only wished to get himself started to talking. Out of this self-stimulation he somehow clarified his ideas. When, years later, Ross put in his office a wigged store dummy named Sterling Finny, it occurred to Claxton that the perfect "Jesus" had at last been found.

After Claxton, who was transferred to movie criticism, the "Jesus" stream flowed freely. But the procession was thin compared with the vast horde that went through "Talk" and other departments. Whoever hired them, it was almost always Ingersoll who fired them—when they did not quit in anger or merely wander on, like farm hands following the harvest. Most were faceless. It was not customary to introduce a newcomer, any more than a company commander or a first sergeant obliges a recruit with formal introductions to other members of his company. The newcomer bivouacked where he could, in a partitioned cell if in great luck, at his own typewriter if mildly fortunate.

Really astonishing quirks were required for gaining attention. One reporter for "Talk" could not bear to touch paper. Someone else had to turn the sheets in and out of his typewriter. This minor obsession resulted in some fairly interesting scatological speculation. One woman enlivened the atmosphere with a peculiar way of stimulating herself. She would be working along at her typewriter when suddenly she would stop, carefully remove her jewelry—she wore a lot of it—and lay it on her desk. Then she would go into another office, telephone her husband, give him a tongue-lashing, come back, replace her jewelry, and proceed contentedly with her work.

Sometimes Ross, after wandering morosely about the office, reflected to the current "Jesus" that he felt like the keeper of a zoo. But eccentricity did not really bother him. He was not concerned with how a writer managed to get a fine sentence on paper, or with the mental processes of an editor who improved it or brought forth a good suggestion. Had a good writer insisted on swinging from a chandelier while at work, Ross would have been less inclined to order him down than to suggest that other writers take a few swings on the chance that it would improve their stuff.

Staff members were, at various points, scared, amused, shocked, and wildly frustrated by Ross's obsession with office details, his insistent questions, his vagueness, his love of conferences, and the general atmosphere of tension he created. In a burlesque issue prepared for a party on Ross's birthday a little more than a year after publication began, they gave a picture of him which many considered only mildly exaggerated.

Spud Johnson, a staff member, wrote:

"We gotta be waggish," he says, scratching his head. . . .
Then he paces the hall like a wild hyena.
Returning to General Conference, he flips through
Six manuscripts, writes "Relax" on one,
"Tinker" on another and "Are you sure of your facts?" on the third.
Then on the fourth, "Relax," on the fifth "Tinker,"
And the last: "Too insidey. Flimsy on facts, anyway."
After another hour pacing the hall
And darting into various compartments in and out of doors
As though he were a movie comedian, he goes into art conference,
Lights a cigaret and excuses himself
Changes five desks, moves two secretaries
Into a sound-proof room . . .

Morris Markey took the reader for a tour of the premises:

An efficient-looking gentleman appeared from one of the many doors. In his hands was a singular contraption made of celluloid and china, with a thermometer, a barometer and a magnetic compass plainly visible. The thing bore a distinct resemblance to a cunning Christmas gift for little Eddie. Little Eddie is four.

"What is that, may I inquire?" I asked brusquely. You see, I had been caught in the spirit of the place, which was to ask questions.

"That," explained the gentleman, holding it up proudly, "is a little time-saving device that was just brought up to Mr. Ross. If he will only drop everything else and study it for the next fortnight, he will be able to save 20 minutes a day that he now uses worrying about our inefficiency."

He interrupted himself suddenly, and slunk back into a corner, whispering, "Shhhh!"

And through the steel door there stalked a most arresting figure; a tall, gaunt man with brooding eyes, who began to pace up and down the narrow corridor leading to the rear. His head was bent. He rubbed his hands together as if in some unhappy dream. And as he tramped back and forth, back and forth, a strange muttering came from his lips.

"Problems . . . problems," he said, over and over again. "Women . . . too many women. By God——" A tear splashed on the floor at his feet. "Nobody to take responsibility around here. . . ."

I felt him grasp my arm in a clutch of steel, and before I knew it I had been ushered through the sound-proof door into his private compartment. There was considerable commotion; for one set of movers was moving his furniture into the room, and another set was moving it out. But he did not seem to mind.

He pounced at once upon a handful of metallic objects that lay near a gas meter on his desk.

"Inventing—inventing!" he growled. "Spend all my time inventing things. Have to make telephone work. Little electric buttons everywhere." He shook his finger in my face angrily. "I've missed a conference today, inventing things," he muttered. "And you know what will happen if I miss any more conferences."

"I'm afraid I don't," I ventured.

"Prima Donna!" he screamed. But he did not lift his hand.

A little bell rang and he suddenly jumped to his feet, grabbing his hat and coat. Through an open door I could see hundreds of people racing through the corridors, getting into their coats, and with their hats thrown on their heads. I began to think of fire.

"Great God, man, where are you going?" I cried as he lunged past me.

He gave me a fleeting, sardonic glance. "To press, to press!" he shrieked. "We're going to press—to press——"

Ross was amused by the burlesque number, except for an item in "Talk." "This edition of the New Yorker was written, edited, printed and placed on the newsstands in seven minutes. Mr. Ross was in conference at the time." To question the magazine's dependence on his exertions was going too far.

Gleams in the Formula 8

MANY PARTITIONS had to be splintered and the nerves of some individuals had to be shattered before there was a sheen to the formula, but by the first anniversary (February 1926) there had been a few glints.

The magazine's appearance was far better than it had been during the galling early weeks. Rea Irvin's effete gentleman of the high hat and monocle was reprinted for the occasion. Much of the gingerbread had been sliced away from the department headings and some of the curious type had been thrown out, leaving the pages cleaner. The front text pages had been broken into three columns instead of two, making for easier reading.

By far the greatest improvement was an astonishing increase in advertising. The anniversary issue numbered 70 pages, compared with the 24 to which the magazine had once sunk. The luxury market had definitely been breached, proving the soundness of Ross's original theory. Included were advertisements for Pierce-Arrow, Saks-Fifth Avenue, Helena Rubenstein, I. Miller, French Line, Paul Poiret, and Myrbor (the last two of Paris).

Fleischmann himself had tramped the pavements hunting for advertisements during the dark days. At Williams College he had known George Washington Hill, later celebrated as the master "huckster," who at the time was moving to the top of the heap in the tobacco world by promoting Lucky Strikes. Hill greeted Fleischmann warmly and asked what he was doing. Fleischmann said he was trying to run a new magazine.

"I'll take twelve back covers," Hill said without further questions.

At the beginning of "Talk," Ross had permitted words of bravado and modesty. The bravado concerned circulation and advertising gains. It seemed to be a warning that all who wished to enjoy prosperity and happiness had better climb aboard. The new year was started with 1350 pages of advertisements under contract. Circulation had reached 40,000 a week, almost entirely in the city and suburbs. "This has been heretofore unheard of. We have, several times over, the largest quality circulation in this metropolitan district. . . . The New Yorker is one of the two or three new weeklies selling for more than a nickel to succeed commercially in America in two decades."

These were stouthearted words, considering the fact that Fleischmann was pumping in financial blood at the rate of several thousand dollars a week.

A note of shyness was struck in the comment on editorial developments. In fifty-two weeks the magazine had progressed, it was admitted, only to a point where it had been expected to stand at the end of ten. That was as far as the curtain of bland outward self-assurance was ever lifted. Everything was jake now, or soon would be, it was implied.

The hunt for the magic formula had been resumed more frantically than ever. The coarse specimens being produced showed, when broken down and analyzed, that three basic ingredients were being used:

1. Humor, mostly in cartoons and "Newsbreaks." There

was an occasional "funny piece" which usually fell in the *Life* and *Judge* tradition.

2. Easygoing shorts and bits, labeled "casuals" by Ross, including "Talk," poetry, and "slice of life" sketches.

3. Straight fact and opinion, including the critical departments, fashions, Morris Markey's pieces, and "Notes and Comment" which opened the "Talk" section.

Ross had long since, of course, given up hope of harnessing the Algonquin wits in a fast-running tandem to pull his magazine to victory, but they occasionally contributed. Best fitting the mood of the times was Dorothy Parker. The New Yorker had nothing to do with her development, but her appearance in its pages coincided with the bloom of her fame. Her scraps of poetry had the sweet-sinning younger generation and the bored suburban matrons in a tizzy.

These "Songs of a Markedly Personal Nature" were typical.

PROPHETIC HEART

Because your eyes are slant and slow,
Because your hair is sweet to touch,
My heart is high again; but, oh,
I doubt if this will get me much.

CONJECTURE

Into Love and out again—
So I went, and thus I go.
Spare your voice and hold your pen—
Well and bitterly I know
All the songs were ever sung,
All the words were ever said.
Can it be, when I was young,
Some one dropped me on my head?

INDIAN SUMMER

In my youth, it was a way I had
To do my best to please,
And change, with every passing lad,
To suit his theories.

But now I know the things I know,
And do the things I do;
And if you do not like me so,
To hell, my love, with you!

Though Dorothy Parker's work may not have been great literature, there was no real flippancy in it. She lived it to the last dregs of its bitterness. When she loved, she loved furiously; and when there were disappointments she suffered deep pain. She distilled her sorrow for the light quaffing of a flippant generation.

She reviewed books for the New Yorker over the pen name "Constant Reader," and her thrusts and bludgeon blows added to her fame as a wit. Of Christopher Morley she noted:

Christopher Morley goes hippetty, hoppetty
Hippetty, hippetty, hop.
Whenever I ask him politely to stop it, he
Says he can't possibly stop.

Book reviewing distressed her. It interfered, she said, with her reading. As for taking it up as a regular thing, she would "liefer adopt the career of a blood donor." Elinor Glyn's *It* forced her to abandon reading altogether for a while. Many times she hoped for a message that the New Yorker had suspended. When accused of ill-usage of grammar, she declared, "I know as well as anyone else that I should have said 'Maybe it is only I,' but conditions are such, these days, that if you use studiously correct grammar, people suspect you of homosexual tendencies." Of a book, *The Technique of the Love Affair*, she declared: "If only it had been written and placed in my hands years ago, maybe I could have been successful, instead of just successive."

Illness and suicide urges occasionally swept over her while she was reading. Fannie Hurst and Booth Tarkington gave her the rams. Sinclair Lewis' *The Man Who Knew Coolidge* distressed her to the point that she called on lightning to strike her. But the greatest physical distress was caused by A. A. Milne, especially by his *The House at Pooh Corner*. It was while reading *Pooh Corner* that "Tonstant Weader Fwowed Up."

Morris Markey's work was the first "text" material to be looked on by readers as distinctly New Yorker. As the form and style of Markey's pieces began to fall into a pattern, he and Ross decided that "Behind the News" (it had superseded "In the News") was a poor title for them. Markey had been reading *A Hind Let Loose*, a book of British newspaper reminiscences by C. E. Montague. In seeking a variation on Montague's title, Markey came up with "A Reporter at Large." That sounded all right to Ross, and it was substituted for "Behind the News."

The technique which Markey and Ross beat out between them was in time to strongly influence non-fiction writing, especially for magazines. Though "Reporter" pieces were factual, the technique of the short story was borrowed for their composition. There was a beginning and a middle and an end. Markey made a casual entrance into a description of a thing or an incident as if he had encountered it by chance.

"The basic idea," he said, "is to convey a sense of interest, of enthusiasm for the moment. I try to give the pieces immediacy without urgency, something that is happening now but not too overwhelming a thing." Above all, he tried to keep out the smell of midnight oil and the public library. Early "Reporter" subjects included the Black Bottom, the legal troubles which came to Earl Carroll because he gave a party at which a naked girl appeared in a bathtub of ginger ale, the market convulsion of 1926, New York gangs, and the Hall-Mills murder case.

Getting the facts straight was one of the four elements out of which Ross and his helpers developed a distinctiveness of writing. Later it was celebrated, by persons not on the staff, as "the New Yorker style." The editors have always insisted that the magazine has no "style" of writing, except perhaps for "Talk" pieces.

The second element was clarity. If Ross was able to understand a sentence himself he felt the reader would do so too. Mark Twain's dictum that a writer "say what he is proposing to say, not merely come near it" was, figuratively, on every wall. Ross insisted on formal usage of the English language. The book he was coming to know better than any other was Fowler's *Dictionary of Modern English Usage*. Commas were dearer to him than ever. Most of his dislike of *Time* stemmed from the circus contortions it forced the English language to perform.

The third element was casualness. "Say it casually," was one of Ross's slogans. "Try to tell it as if talking to a friend." He harangued his authors to take it easy. If an attack was to be made, he recommended the rapier over the bludgeon. Ross's emphasis on casualness was in part responsible for his office term "casual"—meaning a short, informal prose piece. The term "casual essay" had been employed earlier, of course, but it had customarily been used for something longer and more "set."

The fourth element, less easy to define but the most important, was the attitude of the New Yorker toward the big city and its way of life. It was a time of building, with the Woolworth Building, long celebrated in school textbooks as the tallest in the world, about to be reduced, relatively, to a small shaft. Big apartment houses were rising in great cliffs around Central Park and on upper Fifth, Madison, and Park avenues. Automobiles jammed the streets, creating anarchy but giving a feeling of enormous vitality.

The New Yorker adopted a mildly ironical, but paternal, attitude toward the city's growing pains and the vicissitudes of modern, mechanized existence. Gilbert Seldes hit the mark with a fun-poking article at the city's pretension to sophistication. He remarked that almost every New York building was superstitiously without a thirteenth floor, that taxicabs were slow, traffic was chaotic, windows of the big Fifth Avenue stores were as dark at night as those of any small town, and that few residences were built along the rivers where the views were attractive.

Manhattan was, the New Yorker felt sure, slowly burying itself. Proof was found in the New York Central Building, which straddled Park Avenue at Forty-second Street, forcing traffic to detour through tunnels. The magazine was threatened with a libel suit for saying a new office building looked like a grain elevator. Ross had a deathly fear of legal trouble, since the magazine was not in a strong enough position financially to fight a suit. Consequently a new touch of bedlam was added to the lives of several staff workers. They would be sent out into the streets with two photographs, one of the building in question, the other of a grain elevator. Their task was to stop people and demand that they look at the pictures and state which was the elevator. Finally a settlement was reached out of court. Proposals for an ambitious residential development between Forty-first and Forty-third streets near the East River, to be called Tudor City, brought editorial shakes of the head. There were just too many styles of Tudor architecture to expect anything good to come out of it.

On the cultural front, where H. L. Mencken's *American Mercury* was firing thunderous volleys into the calm ranks of the Babbitts, the New Yorker threw whiffs of grapeshot into the self-conscious revolters themselves. Ben Hecht made fun of the cult that was beginning to patronize Harlem. "My set has discovered something too marvelous for words. Negroes! Oodles and oodles of them. Big ones and little ones! Harlem, way this side of the zoo." Marc Connelly ran an inquiry on the subject, "Whatever Became of Flaming Youth?" "Talk's" weekly liquor report carried this item: "Pocket flasks, ½ pt., glass with metal top, curved body, 10 cents at all Woolworth stores." Dorothy Parker flayed the hide off self-satisfied young intellectuals in a piece about a bored young author who at a party shrugged off Sherwood Anderson as a has-been, Dreiser as a bad craftsman, and Ring Lardner as someone he had never heard of.

Even authors of established sophistication were not safe. Heywood Broun had been publicly autographing books, and he had spoofed himself for it. Nevertheless, it was demanded by "Comment" that all authors be placed under a Civic Annoyances Code until they mended their ways.

This mildly deprecatory, slightly jittery view of the city's and civilization's progress gave to the magazine's prose a muted tone of mingled despair and Olympian wisdom. It hoisted the reader to a superior place from which to smile benignly down at pretenders to sophistication. He was safe from ridicule, since the magazine advocated nothing.

The New Yorker's editorial quality was uneven. In "Newsbreaks"—the little items at the ends of columns—this low was reached:

Tickets to the Infants', Children's, and Junior Style Show were sold with the understanding that no liquor is to be brought to the affair either in packages or on the person.—From a notice issued by the management.

We understand, however, that a small amount was smuggled in in the nursing bottles.

A higher level was possible:

For several months I have been troubled with pains in my back. A friend says I have a vertebrae in my spine. Please tell me what kind of treatment I can take for this.—Pittsburgh *Chronicle-Telegraph.*

Our advice is, get a new friend.

The best of the poetry, as far as a distinctive style was concerned, came from the pen of Baird Leonard, a large, jolly woman who for years had been a regular contributor to *Life.* Her satirical "Metropolitan Monotypes" were regular features in the New Yorker. An example:

There is, for instance, The Expatriate.
He will tell you that he shook the dust of America from his shoes
Because of a national aesthetic deficiency which became trying to his sensibilities;
There were, to suit him, too many gum chewers, too few art lovers, too much machinery, too little personal liberty, too many flagrant billboards, too much commercial com-

petition, too many cheap periodicals, too few good servants, too many people to whom the Renaissance was not even a name;
So he sought refuge in a land where men are worldly and women sophisticated.
That may all be, but investigation of many such emigrants will prove
That a lucky turn of the market or the timely death of a rich relative had more to do with the case
Than the fact that the average American doesn't care whether Hamlet was mad or not;
For where in the United States can one rent a palace for thirty dollars a month
Or hire a house staff for a hundred dollars a year. . . .

Aside from Morris Markey's pieces and a few casuals, "Talk" was showing the greatest advancement in the journalistic departments. It was nevertheless slow to break away from humorous anecdotes about famous people.

For a while a major assignment seemed to be to get the latest story about Don Marquis, creator of archy the cockroach and mehitabel the cat in his newspaper column "The Sun Dial." Marquis, a rotund, hard-working, serious-minded humorist, was as lovable and funny away from his typewriter as he was at it. At New York's The Players, a club where artists and writers as well as players gather, the story of one of Marquis' departures from the water wagon was celebrated. A friend, discovering him at the bar having a drink, inquired the reason for the fall from grace.

"Boys," Marquis replied, "I've conquered that God damn will power of mine."

A slight altercation about a goat furnished a typical Marquis joke for "Talk."

Mr. Don Marquis, who has finally turned to philosophy in his writings, has not dismissed humor wholly from his life. He was traveling on a Long Island train lately, which stopped at the Port Washington station.

Looking out the window he saw a goat, of the Billy persuasion, standing about—but, surprisingly, it had no beard. Near the goat was an elder of the village, liberally bewhiskered. The situation was too much for the gay Don.

He opened the window near his seat and shouted: "Give that goat back his beard."

The bewhiskered elder started at this gruff command. Then, as titters among the people around grew to guffaws, he became indignant.

"Say, who are you!" he riposted.

"A friend of the goat," said Mr. Marquis, calmly.

A bit of research by Marquis during an ocean voyage furnished another story. He had set aside two hundred dollars to study card sharks at first hand. A man of virtuous appearance invited him to sit in a poker game with himself and a couple of other passengers. Marquis won for several days, as he had expected he would be allowed to do. When they sat down for the final session he prepared to drop his winnings and his two-hundred-dollar educational fund. Instead, he won again. Later, on deck, he overheard a woman say to her companion as he passed by, "There's the card shark that took Wallace for eighty-three dollars."

Yet some emphasis in "Talk" was being placed on straight reporting. Ex-engineer Ralph Ingersoll took a rule and laid out the department scientifically. In each issue there were so many long items, so many short ones. Typical New York scenes were described in the longer items: the dog and flower shows, backyard cafés, Fifth Avenue open-top busses. Changes of the metropolitan scene were noted, as when brown Fifth Avenue busses gave way to green ones. Copy was provided by the difficulty of enforcing prohibition, the price of booze, and the fantastic cocktails being invented for the inexperienced. Barney Gallant, one of the town's favorite hosts, dedicated a "Lipstick" cocktail ("sweet but with a wallop") to Lois Long. Recipe: two parts champagne, one part gin, one part orange juice, dash of grapefruit juice, and a flavoring of cherry brandy.

Attention was paid to the shifting mores. When the first advertisement directed at women smokers appeared the New Yorker commented: "The latest Chesterfield advertisement shows a young man smoking and a young lady sitting beside him, saying, 'Blow some my way.' The modern version is really 'Gimme one!' "

The editorial "we" was being used more often, and put the text pieces on a higher and more objective plane. The Eustace Tilley device was resurrected. He went on journeys and offered opinions on various topical subjects. Inevitably, the editor, too, was regarded as an elegant gentleman. It was taken for granted that he gathered material for "Talk" during quiet meanderings about the city and then returned to a lofty, paneled office to write down his impressions.

The Artists 9

Ross's FAITH in Rea Irvin plus his own curiosity and restlessness were responsible for the rapid development of the artists. Many friendly critics of the magazine believed that the artists led in setting the distinctive tone. In a way the artist's task was easier than the writer's. By faithfully drawing a New York object or scene which was reasonably familiar to readers, he won half the battle. Inept caption lines could not wholly destroy a good drawing.

The trouble was that artists were not accustomed to putting down what they saw. They drew comic valentines for *Life* and *Judge*, did stiff advertising illustrations, or were inclined to "artiness." Living in Greenwich Village, the art colonies, or in the country, they knew little that went on outside their immediate circles. Ross was aware that to get something new he would have to develop new people or else re-educate the old. Handicapped by not knowing what he wanted, or anything about art, he had no idea where to begin. The best he could do was to leaf furiously through *Punch* and the German and French humor publications and, when he found something he liked, show it to Irvin and tell him that it was the sort of thing he was after.

Punch's artists spent a good deal of time poking fun at contemporary mores. In one of a series titled "Trials of a

Lady of Fashion," for example, a woman debated whether straight or curved eyebrows would go best with her frock. Bobbed hair, short skirts, wide-legged "Oxford" trousers, and the newly-rich-who-pretend-to-culture ("Now this one is a Vandyke or a Turner—forget which—must look up the invoice") were all subjects for levity. A *Punch* series, "Our Social Outcasts," was carried almost directly into the New Yorker under the title "Social Errors." One drawing showed a man slinking out of Dunhill's, a swanky tobacconist's, after asking for a pack of Camels. Another depicted the chagrin of a man seeing his wife cut his bootlegger socially. A second *Punch* series, "Byways of Industry," was more or less translated into the New Yorker as "Our Industrial Crises."

Irvin's taste in art, fortunately for Ross, the magazine, and young artists, was catholic. He liked classic and modern art, and he was sympathetic to anything else that was new. He had a quick, accurate eye for good craftsmanship. More important, he knew what changes were necessary to make mediocre work passable and passable work better. As a former art editor of *Life* he was familiar with the going conception of American cartoon humor, but his own sense of humor was urbane and, since he was in his middle forties, mature.

The art department was without its share of bedlam, for which the magazine's poverty and Irvin's disposition were jointly responsible. For the seventy-five dollars a week paid to him, plus stock which still lacked a gilt edge, Irvin did not feel that he could afford to give more than a day each week. He had stipulated, upon taking the job, that he would not be required to work directly with the artists.

"All right," Ross had said, "you can be a snake in the grass."

And so, not being around very much, Irvin was never exposed to the full impact of Ross's nerve-shattering drive. The conferences for selecting the art, held on the day Irvin came to the office, were almost calm. Irvin was a serene man who, when a cartoon or an illustration was amusing, did not hesitate to enjoy it.

The art was too important, though, for Ross to leave its selection entirely to anyone else. He sat in on the conferences (he preferred the simpler term "meeting") along with his editors. They gathered at a big table in a bare office. Philip Wylie piled the submitted work on the table. If an artist had sent in an unusually large batch of drawings they would be set around the walls.

After everyone had arrived Wylie began holding the offerings aloft. He read the cartoon captions aloud. Sometimes a contribution was passed from hand to hand.

When a picture amused him Irvin's eyes brightened, he chuckled, and often, because none of the others understood art techniques, gave a little lecture. There would be a discussion and a decision. If the decision was to buy, a price was settled on. When a picture failed by a narrow margin the artist was given a chance to make changes and resubmit it. Irvin suggested improvements that might be made, and Wylie passed them on to the artists.

Ross deferred to Irvin's technical knowledge, but he participated vigorously in the meetings. Sometimes a joke had to be explained to him, not because he lacked a sense of humor, but owing to gaps in his general information which prevented the meaning from reaching him. The others were fairly sure, too, that he frequently feigned ignorance.

"Is it funny?" he would demand. "Is it dirty?" he demanded equally often. Fear of the double-entendre was with him even more when choosing cartoons than when editing the text columns. Had a serious off-color allusion slipped through, and had Ross been convinced that someone had understood it and remained silent, the culprit would have quickly disappeared from the office.

Ross's major contribution to "art"—the designation given to cartoons, spot drawings, illustrations, caricatures, and cover paintings—was the same curiosity and fierce demand for accuracy that was helping to bring the text into focus. He queried constantly, "Where am *I* in this picture?" The reader, he maintained, ought to be at a definite vantage point. He should be watching an action or overhearing a conversation.

Or Ross would ask, "Who's talking?" Sometimes the artist was requested to open the speaker's mouth wider. Ross was dealing, of course, with the people and the objects in the drawings, rather than with craftsmanship. By demanding that the characters be plain to him, and seen from a particular vantage point, he naturally got better craftsmanship. The artists discovered, with some reluctance since they often had to do a drawing over and over again, that Ross's demands, put into artistic sense by Irvin—along with Irvin's own suggestions—resulted in better pictures.

The constant overhauling of their work was made more palatable to the artists by Ross's genuine interest in their welfare. Most were devotees of modern art, which meant that the market for their talent was small. Occasionally *Vanity Fair* used a picture by one of them, but payment was mostly in "prestige." Ross did not pay much either, but he paid all he could. If Wylie, the contact man with the artists, reported one of them to be in desperate financial circumstances, Ross often bought work that he could not use. Or he made a loan. When an artist asked—through Wylie—for a higher rate of pay, Ross listened respectfully and, even if he didn't feel it was warranted or possible, gave some worry to the matter. This genuine respect for the work and welfare of contributors was rare enough in the trade to win respect for him.

Ross's "Where am I in this picture?" attitude was responsible, along with his detestation of the two-line joke, for the New Yorker's development of the one-line cartoon caption. It was probably the greatest contribution that humor has received during the last quarter century. The one-liner had been used occasionally for decades. In 1907, for example, *Punch* had such a caption. The drawing, by F. H. Townsend, one of *Punch's* great, showed a man on a motorbike which was pulling a padded chair. The chair was empty. Ahead lay a sharp curve. The caption: "Sit tight, Auntie. There's another sharp turn coming!" (Many years later the New Yorker chanced on an almost identical situation, with a toboggan substituted for the bike and chair.)

But as late as 1926 *Punch* often used three, four, or even more verbal exchanges between characters. The picture was almost forgotten while the reader sorted the joke out of the pile of dialogue underneath. The speakers were carefully identified in small capital letters. If a conversation between a porter and a traveler was being reported, the term "Porter" and "Traveler" appeared at the beginning of each bit of dialogue to guard against misunderstanding.

Under Ross's system, the picture was drawn in a way that made plain the porter was talking. And the remark in the caption would be worded so that it could have been only the porter making it.

The one-liners were usually subtle commentaries on the times. A girl said to her mother: "Peg's new bootlegger is simply marvelous—tall, small mustache, and just out of Harvard." A mother, handing jewelry to a young man, declared: "I shall have to ask you to confine your gifts to my daughter to the conventional cigarets, stockings, and gin." A girl remarked to another: "My dear, I definitely know that she wore galoshes before galoshes were being worn." A mother said to her teen-age daughter whose dress failed by three inches to reach her knees: "My dear, you simply *must* buy some longer stockings." A man lying in bed reading a newspaper addressed his wife: "What's this I'm reading about your trying to get a divorce from me?" A tourist in Italy said to a companion: "Oh Goody! Douglas Fairbanks is showing tonight at the Teatro Romano." A young married woman remarked to a friend: "We can't have any children, you know. The management won't let us."

General readers enjoyed the one-line caption cartoons more than the two-liners without noticing any shift from the old techniques. But experienced artists and humorists began to see that a revolution was going on. One of the best of them had in the magazine's darkest days predicted that the one-line caption would pull it through. James Kevin McGuinness, first "Talk" writer, was having lunch one day with famed artist Charles Dana Gibson, then publisher of *Life*, and Oliver Herford, British cartoonist and writer.

Gibson remarked to Herford and McGuinness that he did not think the New Yorker would last. Herford disagreed. *Punch*, he said, had succeeded with the long narrative joke below the cartoons. *Life* had succeeded by condensing the joke to the he-she formula. The New Yorker had condensed it further to the one-line joke and so, he thought, could not fail.

Had it been feasible, Ross would have gone a step further and eliminated the captions in all cartoons he published. This form had, of course, been tried before, chiefly in panels, a series of pictures carrying a character from one point to another. Frueh had used the form in the New Yorker's first issue. The first of the New Yorker's endless stream of cartoons about sculpturing, drawn by Gardner Rea, was without a caption. It showed simply a big block of stone and a sculptress, thinking deeply.

One reason Ross was pleased with a small, shabby young artist named Otto Soglow was his skill with uncaptioned cartoons. Soglow's previous art experience had mostly been painting baby rattles in a rattle factory. He showed up with hundreds of cartoons, drawn on typewriter paper. He used very simple lines, and his work was crude. At first the art deliberators were more interested in his ideas than his drawings. But he strove hard to improve his draftsmanship, and a few of his things, mostly "panels," were purchased. In one of them an unhappy butcher went to a psychoanalyst and ended, beaming and relaxed, as proprietor of a vegetable market. In another a small man followed a large man wearing a fur coat into a subway crush. The small man emerged wearing the fur coat.

The first cartoon series to catch on was not something bright and new in humor. Drawn by Peter Arno, it dealt with a couple of tipsy old harridans who would have seemed more at home in a funny paper. They wore long, old-fashioned dresses, carried muffs, and their hair was done up in knots when it was not streaming out behind them. A sample caption:

"I thought I'd DIE!"
"Oh, Lordy!"
"Yeh! She said go on an' dance with 'im, and he looked at me and he—whoops!—he says y' ain't paralyzed, are yuh! Me—paralyzed. Whoops! I thought I'd DIE!"

Arno had given up the idea of a dance-band career, at least temporarily, to concentrate on the New Yorker. One day Philip Wylie, having shown the regular offerings, took a drawing of the old girls out of a portfolio and held it up. Arno had said it was just a drawing that hadn't come off, but Wylie had insisted on bringing it along. The art deliberators took a chance on it. The public's reaction was enthusiastic (especially in England, where the characters may have been taken as typically American) and they were continued. Ross prevailed on Arno to sober them up, but they continued to step high, wide, and handsome. Hiccoughs were not uncommon. Later Arno wrote a book about them (on Wylie's typewriter, with Wylie at the keyboard). New Yorker readers generally referred to the characters as the "Whoops Sisters," but in the book they were Pansy Smiff and Mrs. Flusser.

The sporty old girls figured in a cartoon drawn by Arno for the burlesque number. The scene was laid inside the ladies' rest room. Their muffs were in the middle of the floor. Nothing of one of the girls was visible except her feet, underneath the wall of a cubicle. The other, washing her hands at a lavatory, had turned toward the glazed glass door to shout "Whoops!" at the silhouetted stony face of Ross as he marched by on his way to the men's room.

Helen Hokinson, probably the greatest of the cartoonists who appeared in the New Yorker during its first quarter century, was now turning her full attention to the magazine. She was, in a quiet way, an outstanding personality and it was reflected in her work. The combination of her small-town background and the big city had much to do with lifting her into the cartoonist ranks. She came from Mendota, Illinois. Her father was a salesman for a farm equipment manufacturer. From him, a quiet man who liked to read and play the piano in the privacy of his home, she got a reticence that was often taken for shyness.

He taught her to draw as soon as she was able to hold a pencil.

Many of the characteristics of the "Hokinson women," for whom Helen Hokinson became famous, were present in the artist's mother, Mary, the "mixer" of the family. The child artist grew up observing the club ladies of Mendota at their business and pleasure.

A year after Hoky—most of her friends called her Hoky—was out of high school she set off resolutely for Chicago, bent on an artistic career. Her parents expected her to return soon, with the art out of her system. She never came home again except for visits. Soon she was earning most of her living by drawing fashions for Marshall Field's and other stores. With a girl of her own age, Alice Harvey, she rented one of four studios in the tower of the Montgomery Ward Building. A neighbor was Edgar Lee Masters, who had scored a major literary success with his *Spoon River Anthology* and had given up his law practice to write poetry full time. Whenever his muse favored him with inspired lines he rushed in to read them to the girls.

Hoky and Alice Harvey moved on to New York. Hoky scratched up some fashion assignments and settled with other bachelor girls in the Smith College Club (non-Smiths were admitted), which occupied a former Russian monastery. After a little the two girls applied to the Hearst newspapers for art work. The New York *Mirror*, one of the string, needed cartoon strips. After showing their work to an art official or two, the girls were ushered into the presence of Arthur Brisbane, the noted columnist and Hearst's chief editor. The girls didn't know quite what it was all about, and Brisbane's mind appeared to be occupied with something else, possibly the chance of a gorilla beating a heavyweight prize fighter, which he always thought was pretty good. Finally he asked the girls how much money they wanted.

"One hundred and fifty dollars a week," they said together, by prearrangement, holding their breaths at the audacity of it.

"That's for the two of you?" Brisbane suggested.

"Apiece," they replied firmly.

Brisbane nodded absent-minded agreement and went out. In a little while Walter Howey, another Hearst executive, came in. Howey was the man on whom Ben Hecht and Charles MacArthur modeled the turbulent managing editor of their famous play, *Front Page*. Howey's sailor straw hat was pulled low over one eye and he was smoking a cigar. He sat on the corner of a desk and fixed them with his free eye. "Your audience will be gamblers," he said, and got up and went out.

In the end Hoky was assigned to a strip called "Sylvia in the Great City." It was popular at the Smith Club, where Sylvia might have been living. But Hoky watched shopgirls on the subway reading it, and when they didn't laugh she knew it wouldn't go. The *Mirror* dropped it.

Hoky's next step appeared bound to ruin her career. She enrolled in an art school and improved her technique. The greater depth she achieved threw her fashion drawings out of focus and she couldn't sell them. She tried cartoons for *Life* and *Judge* but they came out too stiff.

Hoky's girl friends began to notice patches on her underthings when she hung them up to dry, and that she never ate the big seventy-five-cent dinner at the Smith Club any more. They also noticed that she was very happy. She drew wonderfully lifelike pictures of snow shovelers, coal heavers, and women carrying home groceries. But no one wanted to buy them.

It was one day when Hoky was at a pier seeing a friend off to Europe that she had drawn the picture which sold to the New Yorker. Now her notebook was whipped out often as Ross and Rea Irvin encouraged her to depict life as she saw it. She had a capacity for obliviousness that came in handy. She hardly noticed when neighbors at the opera peeked at her notebook, trying to see what she was up to. At a turkish bath, disguised as a customer, she caused some consternation by walking around, pencil at work on limp paper, sketching the other customers knew not what. At first she signed her work "H. E. Hokinson," because her studies in numerology had convinced her that the sum of these letters was lucky. Later she changed to "Helen E. Hokinson."

The usual subjects of Hoky's drawings were women. Often she included herself—the slender girl with the bangs. She did it unconsciously, and when others called the fact to her attention she threw herself out. But after a while she would creep back in.

The fat woman for which she was later famous appeared occasionally. At an ocean travel agency a clerk said to the woman, swaying his cupped hands, "Of course they all have a *slight* motion, madame." Even when the women were not fat a bemused attitude was usually there. One, painting a lampshade, inquired of her instructor, "Now then—what color do I paint the sunset?"

As Hoky and the New Yorker were young, and the age of the flapper was still golden, many of her cartoons dealt with youth. A coonskin-coated lad asked his girl how she liked Vassar. "Well, it's just so juvenile and childish I'm almost passing out," she replied. Said a girl to another: "Poor Mama! She's so thrilled about my wedding."

Alice Harvey became an important contributor, too, during those early years. Her work had a fresh quality and she was especially good at drawing children. She has since married, had children, and put her art work in the background.

Barbara Shermund, a pretty girl not long in from California, had a firm grip on the young ladies of the Jazz Age. But Ross would not buy the flapper drawings of his old schoolmate, John Held, Jr. He said it was impossible to pick up another magazine without seeing one of Held's flappers. So for the New Yorker, Held did engravings in the old-fashioned melodramatic style. Some of them he had done, as a matter of fact, back in Salt Lake City when he and Ross were lads together.

Mary Petty contributed the only really devastating commentaries on upper-crust New York life. Nearly all of her characters were members of decadent old families whose blood but not their bank accounts had run thin. One of her early cartoons had an ancient and forbidding dowager saying to her butler, "No, no, Jones, leave the curtains open tonight. We must remember the poor people on the streets." The artist had been born in a brownstone on West End Avenue, the daughter of a professor. She was self-taught and drew very slowly and in great detail. In contrast to many cartoonists, she never used ideas and gags furnished by others.

Alan Dunn, husband of Mary Petty, felt the same way about employing the humor of other people. He maintained stoutly that he was not an illustrator. He was, however, far more prolific than his wife. By keeping on top of the news he got the kind of topicality Ross was after.

Other young artists were getting started in the New Yorker's pages. There was Garrett Price, who had been a friend of Helen Hokinson's in Chicago. Perry Barlow and Carl Rose began to contribute regularly. The caricatures of a young Mexican, Covarrubias, and the drawings of Russian-born Alajalov added shininess to the pages.

Several veterans were used regularly. Gardner Rea, a prolific gag man as well as artist, had been around for a long time. Gluyas Williams, a Bostonian, former art editor of *Youth's Companion*, had been drawing for *Life*, since 1919. The caricatures of Ralph Barton, a rather jaded man of the world, were often too savage for Ross's taste, but some of them were used. The work of Al Frueh, another great caricaturist, had less bite. He did most of the theater drawings.

Big Foursome: 10
Angell - White - Thurber - Gibbs

BECAUSE of the great impact of the New Yorker on American humor, journalism, art, and fiction there has been, inevitably, speculation on the roles played by various individuals in its creation. Apart from Ross and Rea Irvin, the persons who had the most telling influence in the formative years were E. B. White, James Thurber, Katharine Angell (later Mrs. E. B. White), and Wolcott Gibbs.

First to join the staff was Katharine Angell, an attractive, poised, reserved woman in her early thirties. Fillmore Hyde, a neighbor, brought her on the job about six months after the magazine started. She was hired as a reader of unsolicited manuscripts. At first she read only two hours a day. After a week she was asked to double the time she gave to the work, and a short while later she accepted full-time employment.

Katharine Angell was a Sergeant of Boston, daughter of an officer of the Boston Rapid Transit System. Though married to a successful lawyer, and mother of two children, she believed in holding a job and usually had since leaving college. At Bryn Mawr she had been an editor of school papers, and afterward had written for the *New Republic*, the *Atlantic Monthly*, and other magazines. But mostly she had done social work, first in a Massachusetts hospital, later in Cleveland, where she made a survey of the crippled and handicapped. During World War I she carried out factory inspections, dealing chiefly with occupational diseases, for the Consumers' League.

Ross knew from Hyde's account of Katharine Angell and her background that she possessed a cultivated taste. It was something he lacked and the magazine needed. He also realized after a short acquaintance that she was a woman of indomitable character and integrity, who knew how to make her taste show in the magazine. Her own feeling for good writing, and especially the rhythm of words, she was good at communicating to writers. She began handling verse, casuals, fiction, a few profiles, and attended the art conferences.

An early staff member summed up her role this way: "Ross's sense of humor in those days was pretty corny, even if he did know that the two-line joke and most of the rest of the *Judge* and *Life* stuff was scheduled for the ash can. Katharine Angell had a sure, cold sense of what was good, what was bad, what was in poor taste. She balanced Ross."

The reason Katharine Angell stayed with the New Yorker—it was, after all, regarded with a good deal of contempt in its first years—was her fascination with the opportunity to create something out of nothing. She was impressed with Ross's integrity and his creative brilliance. Her devotion to the magazine was, like Ross's, complete, and her existence became entwined with the big and the little things.

One of the more important of Katharine Angell's contributions was her suggestion to Ross that he hire Elwyn Brooks White, who was furnishing casuals and other small items.

"It was White," said Marc Connelly, one of the closest

followers of the rise of the New Yorker, "who brought the steel and the music to the magazine."

James Thurber said later: "No one can write a sentence like White's, or successfully imitate it."

Valuable above and beyond his writing talent was White's attitude toward life and his sensitiveness to the metropolis. He was restless, like Ross, but it was an inward-looking, searching restlessness. He registered the crashing thunder and the delicate tickings of the great city, and almost automatically, or so it seemed, his pen recorded them. But he had a clear brain and a warm heart. In his work there was both wonder and sorrow.

White was an individualist and an admirer of nature, especially of Henry Thoreau's writings. Whenever he went anywhere he packed his *Walden* as naturally as his toothbrush. But he was aware that solitude was to be found in the city too. His life had fitted him almost perfectly for the wide-eyed yet deep-felt eagerness that Ross needed.

As a boy White had been shy and introverted. He wrote later: "The future was always like a high pasture, a little frightening, full of herds of steers and of intimations of wider prospects, of trysts with fate, of vague passionate culminations and the nearness of sky and to groves, of juniper smells and sweet-fern in a broiling sun. The future was one devil of a fine place, and it was a long while on the way."

He was the son of a prosperous New York piano manufacturer whose home was in Mount Vernon, about half an hour by train from the city. Mount Vernon was big enough to have streetcars, but there was a rural stateliness about it. The Whites lived near the edge of town in a spacious house set in a lawn decorated with a cast-iron vase. A barn sheltered the horse which on Sunday afternoons pulled the family surrey. Young Elwyn blamed his runny nose and stinging eyes on the smell of the horse as they drove through the countryside. A doctor, knowing no more about hay fever than the rest of the medical world of the day, ordered the boy's head doused with cold water each morning before breakfast.

Elwyn liked the barn, especially its weathervane, at which he shot with his BB gun. He felt more at home with animals than with people, and he kept pigeons, dogs, snakes, polliwogs, turtles, rabbits, lizards, singing birds, chameleons, caterpillars, and mice. "In the spring," he wrote of himself, "he felt a sympathetic vibration with earth's renascence, and set a hen." The White family spent each August on a Maine lake, where the boy learned to paddle a canoe, catch turtles, and drink Moxie.

He was always in quest of something that had no name and no whereabouts. Part of the quest was for beauty, and an ideal of love. In his world was vast enchantment and also vast melancholy. There were good companions on his home block, but he was unhappy at school. Particularly he hated to be called on to recite, for, besides being painfully shy, he had difficulty expressing himself in speech. He kept a diary, chronicling the changes of seasons and his hopes and despairs. Occasionally he inserted a short poem celebrating love of nature.

In the autumn of 1917 White entered Cornell, more filled with doubts than ever because America had entered the war and he had guilt feelings that he was not doing his share. College was a bewildering experience and he kept much to himself, taking long walks. There was some gratification in his English class, where his work was sometimes praised.

When he returned to college for his second year he was already registered for the draft and immediately enlisted in the Students' Army Training Corps. He had written a poem strongly advising himself to get killed in action, and the line "Destiny makes no mistakes" raced through his head. But the war ended before even influenza could lay him low. He chewed licorice drops to ward off the flu.

With the gnawing sense of the war behind him, White found college more attractive. Though an unmistakable air of reserve was always present, he was not unsocial. He became "Andy" (and has always remained so to his friends) because the first president of Cornell was named Andrew D. White, and all male students named White were automatically rechristened with his first name. White joined Phi Gamma Delta fraternity and lived at its house. At the Saturday night sessions of the Manuscript Club, held at the home of Professor Martin Sampson, head of the English Department, other students, graduates (Russell Lord, Morris Bishop, Howard Cushman among them), and teachers recognized a distinctiveness about White's work. Two other teachers who took a strong interest in White's work were William Strunk, Jr., and Bristow Adams.

White's contributions to the college publications included humor, and he had a mild reputation among his friends for private wit, some of it prankish. At a meeting of the Sigma Delta Chi journalistic society he did a parody of a teacher who always went through exaggerated bodily contortions while lecturing. Discarding his usual shyness, White hung from a trapeze, perfectly deadpan, while delivering a lecture.

The editorship of the *Cornell Daily Sun* fell to him in his senior year, and he carried off an Associated Press award for the best college editorial. He was, in an unobtrusive way, a big man on the campus.

But the "one devil of a fine" future that White as a boy

had looked forward to was still quite a distance away. The job with the United Press which the college journalistic successes gained for him was lost after he missed a cemetery, where he was supposed to cover the funeral of a statesman, by roughly forty miles. He had taken a wrong train. He resigned, certain that he would never make a reporter for a wire service. His next position was with a silk mill's house organ, whose editor assigned him to read the horoscopes of the girl employees. Disaster followed his prediction that one very proper young lady would never marry and would have three children.

The heavenly bodies in charge of White's own fate next brought him in fairly close physical proximity to Ross, who was editing the *American Legion Weekly*. White worked for the Legion News Service, in the same building. He knew Ross by sight and observed him with awe as he passed by. F.P.A.'s chronicling of some of the activities of "H. Ross" made him a celebrity in White's eyes.

On the Legion job White earned enough money to buy a small automobile, whereupon, as he lightly put it, he resigned and drove away. The truth was that he considered himself a failure as a newspaperman. The Legion job was not in his opinion true journalism. He liked the work for the newspapers and wire services, and tried hard, but he was not quick or worldly enough. And more than anything else he lacked self-confidence.

"I was scared of them," he declared later.

The small car he bought was a new Model T Ford roadster. With his old schoolmate, Howard Cushman, he drove across the country, stopping at Ohio State University to visit Russell Lord, who was teaching journalism there, and at Louisville to see the Kentucky Derby. The open spaces of Montana appealed to White, and he might have settled there except for his hay fever. In Seattle he got a job on the *Times*. One of his troubles had been fitting himself to the hurrying sentences, the clichés, and the house rules of the newspapers. The *Times's* taboo on the word "mangle" rankled him. He felt handicapped, he said, by being deprived of the use of a single word. Once he wrote a story about a man who identified his wife at the city morgue. "My God, it's her!" the husband had cried, and White faithfully reported the exact words. A prim copy editor changed it to "It is she."

After a few months of general assignments White was made a columnist, which would have pleased him except for the kind of column it was. The big boss of the paper, a Colonel Blethen, went into executive session with himself and emerged with an idea that a humorous column on the classified advertisement page, set in the same type and style, would draw readers to the ads. It was called "The Personal Column." White wrote it—that is, the first draft. Colonel Blethen rewrote it. White figured the column had roughly a few dozen readers, some of whom were under the impression they were reading ordinary want ads. During White's fairly short career as column conductor Colonel Blethen, an officer in the reserves, was jumped to brigadier general. White, however, went steadily downhill and was dropped after being with the paper about a year.

He decided that he would continue his wanderings in Alaska. The San Francisco Chamber of Commerce, as it happened, had fitted out a ship named the *Buford*, filled it with members and their wives, and headed it for Alaska, where the passengers were supposed to improve the city's trade relations with the Far North. White had just enough money to buy a ticket to Skagway. At Skagway the ship's captain would be faced with a decision: throw White off or give him a job. The news of the young man's sad plight got around the ship, and its master, a Captain Lane, an old whaler who definitely would have said, "It's her," called him in and gave him a job as mess boy. In the firemen's mess, where he worked, White performed satisfactorily by managing to divert a small but steady flow of food from the main dining saloon to the less favored table of the oilers and wipers.

Before long all the passengers grew discontented. There was hardly anything to see except monotonous little Indian villages. White, who enjoyed watching his fellow men, was the only adventurer who enjoyed himself.

Late in 1923 White returned to New York. He spent the next few years getting better acquainted with the metropolis in the lonely way young creative hopefuls always do. They wander endlessly, standing quietly in the crowd around a policeman drawing a borrowed tablecloth over a woman who has died; tread unbelievingly among screaming children and creeping old men and perambulator-watching mothers of the slums, and, gasping, take a bus and a few minutes later walk boldly on the swept sidewalks of Park Avenue; roam the deserted canyons of Wall Street at night, feeling the grim clasp of finance; clamber shabbily dressed through the lower depths of the Bowery; peer into restaurant windows laden with fowl and hams and great steaks and lobsters, and go and sit over coffee in a cheap cafeteria; gaze with aching insides at lovely, laughing women, and buy a paper and go home to a furnished room—all the time wanting to put everything seen or felt into a poem or a book or a picture or to enthrall audiences from the stage with interpretations of it.

White was more perceptive than most, and he had behind him a lifetime of watching and analyzing and setting things down. He wanted most of all to be a poet, and, like all poets, he dreamed of selling enough of his works to make a small living. But he wanted to write other things too. He turned out little pieces about things he saw. From time to time he sent them to the magazines. They came back, usually with the notation, "Too sketchy," if a kindly subeditor had decided to include something more encouraging than a form rejection.

It was the golden age of the newspaper wits, when eager fingers opened the morning *World* to the columns on page-opposite-editorial and the *Sun* to "The Sun Dial." Many years later White, writing in *Holiday* magazine, explained what the mighty figures meant to him during his first years in New York.

> My personal giants were a dozen or so columnists and critics and poets whose names appeared regularly in the papers. I burned with a low steady fever just because I was on the same island with Don Marquis, Heywood Broun, Christopher Morley, Franklin P. Adams, Robert C. Benchley, Frank Sullivan, Dorothy Parker, Alexander Woollcott, Ring Lardner and Stephen Vincent Benét. I would hang around the corner of Chambers Street and Broadway, thinking: "Somewhere in that building is the typewriter that archy the cockroach jumps on at night." . . . I used to walk quickly past the house in West 13th Street between Sixth and Seventh where F.P.A. lived, and the block seemed to tremble under my feet—the way Park Avenue trembles when a train leaves Grand Central.

Of the *World*, he remembered "those tense midnights when I would approach a newsstand on Broadway and squander a nickel on the early edition to turn with secret torment of suspense to 'The Conning Tower' to discover whether some noble nubbin of poetry had achieved the decent fame I hoped it deserved."

Occasionally a nubbin was there, for in White, as in many others, F.P.A. kept literary hope alive. To earn a living White found jobs in advertising agencies, usually as a production worker of some kind. Often he was without a job at all. He lived in a small apartment on Thirteenth Street near Sixth Avenue with some fellow Cornell alumni and a rubber plant. The rubber plant he kept at a window near a small desk at which he did his writing. He had a certain camaraderie with the Sixth Avenue elevated railroad. It "swung implausibly in the air, cutting off the sun by day, wandering in and out of the bedchamber at night," as he described it later. Its sound was "forever singing, like the sea. It punctuated the morning with brisk tidings of repetitious adventure, and it accompanied the night with reassuring sounds of life going on. . . ."

When not employed, White's first thoughts on arising were likely to be concerned with a place to sit the day out.

"Wherever there was a public seat," he said later, "you were apt to find me."

Among his favorite haunts was Grand Central Station, almost a city in itself. He sat all day on the benches, in the morning watching the commuters, fresh from bed and breakfast, hurrying confidently to wrestle with the day's problems. In the evening he watched them go wearily home. He sat contentedly all day in the enormous main reading rooms of the New York Public Library, often merely watching others and speculating. He liked the zoo. On a few occasions he ushered at the Metropolitan Opera House, receiving in return freedom to listen to the music. He took long, quiet walks into all parts of the city, seeing and listening. He was well equipped physically for wandering the city. Being small and slight, he was about as anonymous as it was possible to be. No one felt a need for reticence because

White was near. Yet he could fall easily into conversation with strangers when he wanted to.

Had his writing been progressing, White would have been thoroughly happy. To him New York was marvelous and exciting. It was his city. Later he described his "moping" years as his most creative.

White bought his first copy of the New Yorker, fittingly, in Grand Central. He had been watching for its appearance. An artist of his acquaintance had told him that it might be the kind of magazine that would use poetry and other things he was writing. Sitting on a Grand Central waiting bench, leafing through the New Yorker's first number, White decided that this might be so. It was worth the risk of a few postage stamps. He went home, selected a piece from things on hand, and sent it off. Almost at once the lightning struck, leaving behind a small check.

In the issue of May 9, 1925—only a few weeks after the beginning—his "Defense of the Bronx River" appeared.

The Bronx River rises in Valhalla and flows south to Hell Gate. The people I have mentioned this to, from time to time, have always said, "What of it?" This cynical indifference is something I resent in New Yorkers, for if this town is ever going to get anywhere, it must study its heritage of natural beauty. When Pola Negri first came to New York a million people awaited her opinion of the skyline. Yet how many of these million know that the Bronx River is wider than the Hutchinson and not so wide as the Ohio?

People heard of the Bronx River for the first time about ten years ago when somebody named highway commission after it. There are only a limited number of names you can give highway commissions, and Bronx River happened to be one of them. The commission was meeting one day, to have fun, and someone suggested that they start a search and look for the river after which they were named, and so they did, and they found the Bronx all right and followed it up for several days to its source, traveling in canoes by night and eating as they went, living off the fat of the land, including Williamsbridge.

They passed through Woodlawn, West Mount Vernon, Bronxville, Tuckahoe, Scarsdale, Hartsdale, and White Plains, eager groups of natives crowding the banks to learn from the voyagers that the river was the Bronx. These natives had noticed the river, in a desultory way, since childhood, but had never thought of it as the Bronx. Even in Bronxville, only two inhabitants had thought of it as the *Bronx*, and they had kept their hunch to themselves.

The upshot of it was that the commission built a very good road and now the Bronx River goes virtually dry every Sunday afternoon from so many motorists using it to fill their radiators.

Commuters on the New Haven and Central know the Bronx, they know it of old by reputation, and of late by name. And they stand up for it. In Spring the willows along the shore turn a pleasant yellow, and the stream takes their color, and the little tributaries of the Bronx come rushing down from the hills in pipes and empty into the main stream, augmenting it and causing white rapids at Bedford Park. I have seen commuters forsake their newspaper and flatten their nose on the window as the train glided along the Bronx River. And I have seen a strange light come into their eyes, especially if there was a duck or something like that floating on the water. And here is one commuter who wouldn't trade this elegant little river, with its ducks and rapids and pipes and commissions, and willows, for the Amazon or the Snohomish or La Platte or the Danube, or the Mississippi, even though the latter does rise in Lake Itaska and flow south to the Gulf of Mexico and is wider.—*By E. B. White.*

The signature was "EBW." White had signed most of his offerings to "The Conning Tower" that way.

The Bronx River piece had its roots, like most of the early things in the New Yorker, in the little essays of *Life* and *Judge.* On the opposite page, as a matter of fact, was a piece by one of White's heroes and the current master of the form, Robert Benchley. It was a little gambit built around a statement by a doctor that males had quite a few female cells and vice versa. Two decades earlier Stephen Leacock, the Canadian humorist and economist, had produced a definitive "nonsense" short about his youthful confusion in a bank, where he had gone to deposit a few dollars. Benchley's masterfully confused "Treasurer's Report" was in the same vein. Confusion was the humorist's chief stock in trade.

White's piece was different in that, beneath the whimsey, he had tried to insert beauty. Benchley's professional attitude would have been confusion and fear of nature.

White continued to supply small, usable items to the New Yorker, for small sums. The check for one of them would have roughly covered the damage caused by a butterfingered waitress who, by spilling a glass of buttermilk over him, wrought an enormous change in his life. Because of her, White started along the road to an important place in American letters.

On a late fall day of 1925 he entered a Child's restaurant on Fifth Avenue in the middle Fifties. He hung up his overcoat, sat down, and ordered a meal. When a passing waitress spilled a glass of buttermilk on him she did not merely dribble a little of it—she turned it all over the dark suit he was wearing.

Her low emotional voice exploded in his ear. "In the name of God!"

Her distress was acute. Beginning to sob, she ran away.

White was sorry for her, and he hated to be the center of attention. But as he sat dripping he could not help thinking that between his own amusement and the girl's tears there was little distance.

> The waitress came trotting back, full of cool soft tears and hot rough towels. She was a nice little girl, so I let her blot me. In my ear she whispered a million apologies, hopelessly garbled, infinitely forlorn. And I whispered back that the suit was four years old, and that I hated dark clothes anyway. One has, in life, so few chances to lie heroically.

White described the episode effortlessly at his little desk near the rubber plant, with the El clattering by. The New Yorker accepted the piece at once, and White felt a burst of confidence and well-being which he knew he would remember all his life. Out of a simple event he had made a story that had brought him money and, more important, creative satisfaction. At last he had found something that made journalistic sense to him.

In the story as published in the New Yorker the waitress did not, to be sure, exclaim, "In the name of God!" She said, "In the name of John!" Ross did not allow profanity in his magazine at the time.

White was not, of course, the first to realize that strong emotions have a place in humor. Mark Twain declared that humor was incidental with him—that basically he was always preaching. Charlie Chaplin had been putting tragedy into his comedies for years. White did not quite agree with Twain about the preaching, but he saw no conflict between humor and straightforward emotional experience. He knew that Twain was a greater humorist because he was a fine storyteller. Later Chaplin praised White's buttermilk piece as one of the best humor things he had read. As it happened, he bestowed the praise on James Thurber, to whom he was talking, in the mistaken notion that Thurber was the author.

Thurber smiled and nodded, in line with an agreement he had with White not to bother to straighten out people who got their work mixed up.

With a single stroke White had made a dent in the contemporary *Life* and *Judge* pattern of the "funny writer." Benchley was personally one of the kindliest men on earth. He was, as a matter of fact, one of the first to hail White as a coming humorist and pressed Ross to encourage him. While Benchley might have squeezed amusing copy out of an overturned glass of buttermilk, his method would not have permitted him to write warmly and humanly of the girl's emotion. He and his fellows confined themselves to the role of confused funny man.

In the buttermilk piece, titled, somewhat obviously, "Child's Play," White did not, it was true, break completely with the old technique. To some extent he falsified his own personality, depicting himself as vaingloriously paying for the buttermilk, to show off before the other customers. But he had made a start at bringing real people, with their disappointments and sorrows, into current humor. Even Mark Twain's Tom Sawyer and Huckleberry Finn had lacked poignancy.

Katharine Angell sent a note to White, inviting him to drop in at the office. She told him that the magazine valued his work highly—a vast encouragement for a young writer who had had trouble getting a curt personal rejection from most magazines. She had some ideas for pieces.

A little while later White was called in again and Mrs. Angell introduced him to Ross, who offered a part-time job writing kick lines for the "Newsbreaks." The task was then the lowest form of editorial life at the magazine. White accepted gladly. He had done only one batch when chicken pox laid him low. While sick at his parents' home in Mount

Vernon, he got a phone call from Ross praising the work he had done. He was hot to be up and about the job, but for several weeks he was ill.

The job was still open for White when he got well, and after a while he began to work full time as an "orderly," as he called it. Before long his poems and his casuals attracted wide attention, and Ross saw him as the magazine's shining light.

White feared the literary life, once he was in it, and fought entrapment. Alexander Woollcott tried to take him up, with remarkable lack of success. Once White did go to the theater with him, an experience which he later described as like being towed in a dinghy behind a large and very expensive yacht. Another time Woollcott lured him to a woman's salon by swearing that only two or three other persons would be present. The roaring, cocktail-waving throng that met White's gaze nonplused him. The moment Woollcott's back was turned he left.

Ross tried his hand at acclimating White to the social life, with equal success. White said he was interested in meeting only two persons: Helen Hayes, the actress, and Willie Stevens, the shaggy, pipe-smoking, supposedly dim-witted witness who was too sly for the lawyers at the Hall-Mills trial. Ross tried to arrange a joint luncheon. Willie declined. But White did meet Helen Hayes at Ross's house.

White was almost as shy around the office as at literary functions. When James Thurber, a gregarious man, came on the staff in 1927 he suggested to White, whom he had known slightly before and with whom he had been placed in a compartment, that they have lunch together.

"I always eat alone," White said.

A few months later he invited Thurber to lunch and they became fast friends.

Thurber was an elderly man, for the New Yorker, of thirty-one, tall, thin, and nervous, with a fairly impressive string of failures behind him, when he applied for work. Ross promptly made him a "Jesus," failing, though, to make clear the exalted nature of the assignment. Thurber learned of it by accident. Every week a secretary appeared and asked him to sign a batch of slips. Though an agreeable man, Thurber finally tired of it and demanded an explanation.

"It's the pay roll," she replied. "You're managing editor."

In a written description of Thurber as a young man, White relates how a little packet boat slipped into a tropical harbor to discharge copra. Thurber stepped ashore carrying a volume of Henry James and leading a honey bear by a small chain. He was a mystery man, this Thurber. It was told how, substituting for the ship's cook, he had tried to make pancakes out of stump powder. The galley had been blown up and Thurber had lost an eye.

White was not a witness to this scene, since neither he nor Thurber had ever been in the tropics. But circumstances alone prevented Thurber from leading a honey bear off a skiff, and White from seeing him do it. One of Thurber's eyes had been put out, true enough, but it happened in a boyhood bow-and-arrow accident.

Thurber grew up in Columbus, Ohio, where his forebears were solid, well-to-do citizens. One of his grandfathers, a fruit-and-produce wholesaler, owned a gracious old fourteen-room house where James and his brothers and cousins spent much of their time. James's father was sometimes in politics and at other times was a businessman. Thurber's relatives were the kind of Midwesterners who do not repudiate a black sheep simply because he goes East and writes for the magazines. After Thurber was on the New Yorker one of his aunts subscribed and displayed it every week on the parlor table. One day a neighbor inquired whether the magazine was any good.

"I really can't say," the aunt answered. "We take it just to help Jim."

James was the delicate one of the Thurber boys. The grammar school he attended, Sullivant, was tougher than Hell's Kitchen. Sullivant's baseball team would easily have beaten the state university if the collegians hadn't been too scared to play.

Seventeen or eighteen was about the right age for a Sullivant fourth-grader, and twenty-two was not too old for a fifth-grade boy. Little James was fortunate in that the center-fielder, a colored boy named Floyd, set up a protectorship over him. Floyd was impressed with James's learning. Thurber is certain that he would never have made it through grammar school had it not been for Floyd's muscle. Years later he liked to think of Floyd still in the fourth grade, helping others.

At Ohio State University Thurber fitted the vague Midwestern idea of a literary man. His heavy dark hair was long and fell down over his glasses. His clothes were unmatched and unpressed. He ambled about with a melancholy, preoccupied air. In the gymnasium he bumped against inanimate objects and in military drill he bumped into people. He carried a sense of doom. There was the constant fear of something falling on his head, and the sudden end of the world would not have surprised or especially displeased him.

Thurber has said that humorists are a "crazy species" who need the shield of their wit and anything else they can get. He got encouragement when he needed it from Joseph Russell Taylor, a famous English professor. For a time Thurber considered the possibility of becoming an English teacher himself. Still another protector was gained after Professor Taylor read one of Thurber's themes aloud. Classmate Elliott Nugent, a star quarter-miler and campus figure, was impressed. He induced Thurber to get a haircut and even to dress a little better. When the lid of Thurber's melancholy was lifted, a gay, wild humor and a high infectious laugh bubbled out. Though by nature a satirist, he was a student of literature and an idealist. His abilities as a mimic got him roles with the Strollers, a campus theatrical group.

During the first World War Thurber was unfit for military service because of poor eyesight. He worked in Washington as a code clerk. After the armistice he got himself transferred to the American Embassy in Paris where he worked on messages during the Peace Conference. Paris fascinated him, but when the conference was over he had to go back to Columbus. He landed a reporting job on the *Dispatch* and also wrote a Sunday humorous page. But Thurber's newspaper work brought him less attention than a bad habit he had. He drew dogs. As long as he confined himself to filling wastepaper baskets with his dogs, no one except an occasional janitor complained. When he took to filling other people's memorandum pads with dogs the situation became less tolerable. It started as a joke on a friend who doodled while talking on the telephone. Thurber drew a dog on each page of his friend's memo pad. The dog was a curious-looking animal. It had a bloodhound's large head and body and the short legs of a basset. No man's memo pad was safe from the sawed-off dogs. Some people came to fear invasion by them the way Dakota farmers do the approach of grasshopper hordes.

Thurber went back to Paris in 1924, thinking the atmosphere would be more conducive for writing a novel he had in mind. He had married Althea Adams, a beautiful, amiable, firm-minded girl, also of Columbus. She usually could calm her husband's jumpy nerves with a few matter-of-fact words. For diversion on shipboard they decided to pick out an interesting-looking man and woman and get acquainted with them. The man Thurber chose turned out to be a gambler. Althea selected a girl whose brother, a lad named Elwyn White, wanted to be a writer.

To earn a living, Thurber worked on the Paris edition of the Chicago *Tribune*. The staff included Elliot Paul and William L. Shirer. Most celebrated of all the expatriates was F. Scott Fitzgerald, whom Thurber happened to be watching across a terrace café, between peeks at a newspaper, when he first learned of the New Yorker. The newspaper carried a story about the furor created by Ellin Mackay's attack on the stag lines. Thurber had given *Smart Set*, *American Mercury*, and several other magazines a chance to reject his work and they had done it. The new magazine, he thought, ought to have an equal opportunity. The New Yorker's editors responded as had the others.

The novel didn't get finished and the Thurbers went back to Columbus. Thurber cast about for a new literary medium. He had been profoundly influenced, like so many of his generation, by columnists Franklin P. Adams, Don Marquis, and the others. His favorite was Bob Ryder of the Columbus *Journal*. He was impressed especially by the generally satirical nature of the columnists' material. Marquis had used a few of his items in "The Sun Dial," but F.P.A. hadn't yet found any of his contributions suitable.

Thurber decided he would write a book-length satire. Among the recent best sellers were *Microbe Hunters*, by Paul de Kruif, and *Why We Behave Like Human Beings*, by George Amos Dorsey. Thurber went to New York and wrote *Why We Behave Like Microbe Hunters*. It took a dim view of many aspects of current civilization. He peddled it morosely, adding nothing to the gaiety of publishers' reception rooms. Finally a literary agent, who declined participation, suggested that he cut the book into pieces and send them to the New Yorker. He did and they were rejected.

Thurber wrote later: "Humor is a kind of emotional chaos told calmly and quietly in retrospect."

At this time he had only the emotional chaos. The Thurbers moved into a Greenwich Village apartment which was heated in a haphazard fashion by pipes that ran through it. It had a large bathroom in which he wrote. Like White, he had the racket of an elevated railroad to steady him. His was the Ninth Avenue El, which when it got below Fourteenth ran along dark little Greenwich Street near the North River water front. The Thurber place was on West Thirteenth, not far from Greenwich. When not writing in his bathroom he wandered about the streets, usually leading a terrier bitch, his melancholy reinforced by failure.

Thurber was about ready to beat another retreat to Columbus—probably for the last time—when he opened the *World* one day and discovered that F.P.A. had given an entire column to one of his sketches. He was heartened enough to stay on.

Not long afterward he walked down the water front to the New York *Post* and landed a job at forty dollars a week. Reporting was more difficult for him than in Columbus. While on his way to cover a fire in Brooklyn he got lost in the subway. A couple of hours later, while riding across the Brooklyn Bridge in a cab, he read an account of the fire in the *Post*. The editors had picked it up from a news service.

Thurber was switched to rewrite, where he did his fellow slaves a service by pointing up the absurdity of an office demand for short leads. Thurber's contribution: "Dead.

That's what the man was the police found in an alleyway yesterday."

Meanwhile he kept firing manuscripts at the New Yorker. A walk along shabby Horatio Street near the water front was the inspiration for his first acceptance, a poem. For it, he was not James Thurber, but James *Grover* Thurber. The issue of February 26, 1927, carried it amidst a welter of other verses.

VILLANELLE OF HORATIO STREET, MANHATTAN

Rusted bed-springs in the street
And rowdy kids that fight and yell,
All in a clutter at your feet.

No matter what the hour, you meet
Brawling children and, as well,
Rusted bed-springs in the street.

Nothing here is clean and neat,
What you'll find you can't foretell
All in a clutter at your feet—

Tawdry signs of life's defeat;
Irate voice, supper smell,
Rusted bed-springs in the street.

A broken keg, a buggy seat—
Stuff that junkmen buy and sell—
All in a clutter at your feet.

If your eyes lift up to greet
The stars you fall on, sure as hell,
Rusted bed-springs in the street,
All in a clutter at your feet.

The next week's issue had a satirical sketch by Thurber about a little man who whirled around in a revolving door for several hours. People cheered him wildly, as they did the channel swimmers and flagpole sitters, and when he came out he was given one hundred thousand dollars. Modestly he explained that he had done it for the wife and kids.

Shortly afterward the New Yorker bought a casual about the tribulations of strong men who were ashamed to ask at candy dealers' for Love Nests, Tootsie Rolls, and the like. The writer had heard a burly fellow say to a dealer, "I fancy a lady has fainted yonder," and then, when the dealer turned to look, saw him toss down a nickel and snatch a Booful Biskit. But the contributions were run-of-the-mill and did not impress the editors.

Althea Thurber had kept in touch with White's sister and Thurber and White had met at a cocktail party. But Thurber's job with the New Yorker was effected through Russell Lord, White's friend at Cornell. As a teacher at Ohio State, Lord had heard of Thurber and they had mutual acquaintances. While peddling his "Microbe" satire in New York, Thurber had called on Lord, who was working on a farm publication. They had become friends, and Lord and his wife Kate began seeing a good deal of the Thurbers and of White, separately. One rainy night White reported to Lord that Ross was in need of editors. Kate Lord put on her rubbers and carried the news to Thurber's pipe-heated flat, which was not far away.

White made an appointment for Thurber with Ross, and from this the confusion arose. Ross got mixed up and understood that Thurber was a close personal friend of White's. He knew that White would not recommend anyone unless certain of his high talents. Ross hired Thurber at a starting salary of seventy-five dollars a week. Then he sent a note saying that he had decided seventy-five dollars was too little for an old newspaperman, and raised it to ninety. Later he had another change of heart and Thurber's first weekly check was for a hundred dollars.

When Ross discovered his error about Thurber's and White's relationship he loosed a small tirade. It wasn't serious because by that time he regarded Thurber as a great editor. This came about because Thurber, no more aware of what was wanted than any "Jesus" before him, maintained a silence that was interpreted by Ross as profundity. The effect was heightened by occasional noncommittal nods by Thurber. He gravely took extensive notes.

Thurber did most of his administrative work at a speakeasy after hours. Reading over some involved instruction, he would get an executive look on his face and shred the note into an ash tray. "That's taken care of," he would say crisply, and proceed to the next item.

Ross was not aware of this ingenious system, but the result was his increased faith in Thurber as an editor. An executive able to carry out Ross's commands literally might have brought the operation to a standstill. In a way Thurber suffered from this faith in his editorial capacities. He wanted to be a writer, not an editor. The legend grew up that in those early days Thurber tried to get himself fired. Actually he wanted to be fired only from editorial duties. He knew the magazine was the place for him and he desperately wanted to stay on it. In the little free time at his command —the staff was working seven days a week—he ground out pieces, and a few were printed.

Another who slaved in the salt mines of the New Yorker before being allowed above ground was Wolcott Gibbs, who joined the staff in 1927. He is one of the two or three native New Yorkers who played an important role in the creation of the magazine, and one of the few who, when he joined the staff, looked as though he *ought* to have been on it. A slender, blond youth, he was dandified but mildly intellectual-appearing. His background was Gold Coast. Among his cousins were Caroline Duer, arbiter of the Social Register listings, and Alice Duer Miller, noted author and a Round Tabler.

Gibbs's immediate family, however, was not wealthy. Upon leaving school, he went to work in a humble capacity for the Long Island Rail Road. In time he rose to the rank of brakeman. After four years of working for the railroad, he was taken off by his cousin, Alice Miller. She didn't mind that a member of the Duer family slummed a bit, but she was beginning to suspect that young Wolcott lacked initiative. She got him a job on a Long Island country weekly.

Although the job wasn't anything special, Gibbs settled down in it. Eventually Alice Miller managed to get him out of there too. She told Gibbs that a man of her acquaintance, Harold Ross, had started a paper and she would speak to him about a job. Ross obliged.

Gibbs started as a minor copyreader and soon made a reputation as a hard worker and a strong competitor for the title of jumpiest man around the shop. Gibbs always claimed to be merely nervous, not neurotic. A friend of his, St. Clair McKelway, an important writer and editor for the magazine, once said that Gibbs looks on his nerves and the things they do to him "with a kind of amused detachment touched with wonder, but never with concern." When, for example, a martini glass flew out of his hands into the face of a bystander, he merely regarded the incident with astonishment.

People with bad cases of galloping fidgets were not, of

course, handicapped in Ross's view. Ross himself once rested at a sanatorium for a while and afterward always spoke proudly of the incident as "that time I went crazy." When Katharine Angell spoke to Ross about her concern for Gibbs—his stomach was bothering him, he was uncomfortable in elevators, became panic-stricken when he went into the street, and had a notion that someone was following him—Ross merely laughed and remarked that all of it proved Gibbs to be a bona fide staff member.

Gibbs's attachment to the New Yorker was fanatical and more personal than most, as if he feared to wake up and find himself swinging a red lantern in a railroad yard. Though amusing and pleasant among friends, his manner came nearer the superciliousness of some of the magazine's material than that of most of the staff members. "Gibbs carries the New Yorker before him as a kind of shield," an acquaintance once said. Another who analyzed Gibbs as being warily on the defensive remarked with mild sarcasm, "God, he's brilliant. He never likes *anything*." After he became an editor Gibbs was sometimes discouraged from seeing authors because he addressed them too cuttingly. There was danger that creative talent would suffer or that he would be slaughtered. Those who wanted to stir Gibbs up could do it by pronouncing his first name as if it were "Woollcott" and suggesting that he was trying to model himself after that master of the gratuitous insult.

But Gibbs had fine editorial possibilities and he soon became assistant to Mrs. White. Under the force of her strong personality he was restive and he was sometimes resentful of being a woman's helper. But his talents were largely derivative and he needed direction. He once declared his own writing to be a combination of White, Thurber, and Max Beerbohm. No claim was made for a jigger or two of Gibbs.

Because of his capacity for absorption Gibbs became the most accomplished parodist the magazine has had and also the best rewrite man on fiction and casuals. While the New Yorker has altered contributors' copy a great deal less than it has been charged with doing, there have been times when authors gave permission for their work to be "run through the typewriter"—a shop term meaning a fairly complete rewriting. When Gibbs was assigned to do this—and he was the best at it—he conscientiously read and reread the manuscript until he had a feeling of the author's style, intention, and a thorough knowledge of the characters. Then he put himself as best he could in the author's place and rewrote strictly as a technician.

Eventually Gibbs held nearly every kind of job on the magazine except that of "Jesus." He was art editor. He wrote profiles—the most cutting the magazine has published. As substitute "Comment" writer he imitated White's style better than anyone else. He reviewed movies and in time became drama critic.

The Editorial Wars 11

As THE magazine grew sleeker, with richly coated paper, scores of pages of luxury advertisements in many colors, and the art and the text became ever more urbane, the editorial violence increased. Ross had come to believe, many of his associates were firmly convinced, that turmoil was good for the magazine.

At top level, the war between Ross and Fleischmann raged hotter than ever. Fleischmann was not combative by nature, and thought of himself as a partner with Ross. He believed in the separation of editorial functions from the business department. So do many other publishers. But in practice there is a strong tendency for encroachment by the man who writes the pay checks. Ross knew that he would have to fight for editorial independence. The vituperation sometimes employed by him to gain his points doubtless stemmed in part from the very early days when he had had no choice but to accede to many editorial suggestions that Fleischmann and his counsel, Hanrahan, made.

The legend that business office personnel must not enter the editorial zone without permission contains, however, a degree of hyperbole. A joke of Fleischmann's was largely responsible for the currency of the story. One day when he was in the editorial section he ran into Janet Flanner, the

Paris correspondent. She inquired with mock alarm what he was doing there. He replied, in like vein, that he had permission to come. In the retelling the story was garbled into seriousness.

Ross soared to a lofty ethical plane during the conflicts with Fleischmann. He owned a good deal of the magazine's stock himself, and people on whom he could count for support held more. But meetings of the board of directors did not seem to him to be the proper and best field of battle. He quit as president of the company and later resigned from the board of directors.

"I can't really open up on Raoul while I'm a big stockholder," he sometimes declared.

And so during the angrier exchanges he would sell off a batch of his stock.

Other business firms have had conflicts where the personal bitterness was deeper, the poison of the venom deadlier, but it is doubtful that an office war was ever fought in a more curious way. Sometimes Ross won points by threatening to quit. During one period he kept a typed resignation in his desk for the purpose. When he wanted something—money for salary increases or a new interoffice communication system—he would pull the worn resignation from his desk.

Once he sent the current "Jesus" to Fleischmann with a request for some money. When the emmissary came back Ross was surprised to see him looking unruffled.

"You get it?" he asked.

The "Jesus" said he had. He had simply explained the reason the money was needed, and Fleischmann had agreed pleasantly.

Ross looked displeased. "Wrong way entirely," he said. "I wanted you to beat it out of him."

There were times when Fleischmann tried to clip Ross's

wings, and even to replace him, but none of these sallies ever produced results. The magazine was so closely built around Ross, despite his constant designation of someone else as the "Hub," that he could not be quickly replaced. In addition, his ability to bind editorial workers close to him, or to the principles for which he made himself the symbol, was so great that if he left the best of the staff members might go with him.

Inevitably there grew up factions—the Ross faction and the Fleischmann faction. One man whom many staffers believed Fleischmann was backing in an effort to reduce Ross's power was Art Samuels, who with Hanrahan had written the early promotion advertisements. Samuels, a dark, good-looking Round Tabler and a former popular song writer, was greatly admired by Fleischmann, who had been at Princeton with him. Ross accepted Samuels as a top editor. As it turned out, Samuels was far better off from a financial standpoint than others, for he drew a substantial sum above his nominal salary from the business office's budget.

Ross was suspicious of Samuels, and he asked Thurber to see the magazine to bed at the printer's to "keep Samuels from doing anything." On one occasion Samuels got jumpy about the possible bad taste of an item White had written about a little dog eating tulips in the graveyard of St. Mark's on the Bowery. Thurber insisted that any change would ruin it. Samuels demanded that Ross be called for a decision. Thurber left the composing room, pretended to telephone, and came back and reported that Ross had said for God's sake not to make any change as long as they were sure dogs ate tulips. As an old dog man, Thurber said they did.

Ross finally dismissed Samuels by cable while Samuels was on his way back from a vacation in Europe. Later Ross told a friend: "Samuels came in here and gave me hell about that cable. He had a right to. I did a thing no decent man would have done."

After Samuels was gone Thurber told Ross about the dog and the tulips. The incident stuck in Ross's mind. Several years later he said to Thurber when Samuels' name was mentioned, "Dammit, he wanted to take out White's line about the dog eating those lilies."

Out of the turmoil in the lower ranks, Ross thought, might come something new, some little attitude, some pungent bouquet, that would improve the formula. He kept himself busy forcing up the pressure. A man would sit in a cubbyhole, sweating to hold his job, while in another a newcomer sweated to take it away from him. Sometimes they were aware of each other, sometimes not. But the rest of the staff always knew.

Ross had small regard in those days for the personal lives of his helpers, other than to pay them all he could. A seventy-hour week looked about right to him. He hated commuters. Anyone who suggested moving to the country was promptly charged with treason. "You'd spend the whole afternoon catching the five-fifteen." Ralph Ingersoll's announced intention of getting married infuriated him and he treated the project with open scorn. One fear was that he would have to take the afternoon off to attend the wedding. Ross's own marriage was rapidly disintegrating under the pressure of his devotion to the magazine.

There were occasional revolts from below, but Ross easily put them down, either by his gift of gab or by subterfuge. One night several key workers called at his home with a grievance. Before they could state it Ross, running his hand through his hair, his face twisted with mental pain, began, "I live the life of a hunted animal. . . ."

It was an opening line they had all heard scores of times,

and they knew he intended to lead them a wearying chase. After two hours they departed without having stated their case, feeling sorry for him.

On another occasion, when a committee called on him in his office, he jumped up and put on his hat. "I never thought the magazine would last anyhow," he said from the door. His tactics were unbeatable.

Ross had even developed what he considered a sound reason for the terrible hammering and crashing as partitions were nailed up, torn down, and erected elsewhere. The proximity of this person to that would, he claimed, set up a current of some kind that would tone up the magazine. He shifted partitions instead of people. A few combinations endured, but on the whole the way of life was nomadic.

The increased size of the magazine did not change Ross's view of it as basically a newspaper. He liked to stop the presses. Since actually doing this would have been prohibitive for a magazine, he found a way to do it figuratively. After his editors and production men had laid their plans he was likely to rip them to shreds. Something had to go in the magazine, this issue. Or he had decided that something had to come out, usually for more rewriting.

One former employee's clearest and most poignant memory is of a production man standing in a corner, weeping quietly, while Katharine Angell tried to comfort him. At the last minute Ross had torn up the edition.

When Ross thought gentle treatment would bring good results he courageously tried it. This led, among other things, to establishment of the New Yorker's private speakeasy. In theory it was supposed to be a club, but the staff treated it as a speak. Ross was bemused with the *Punch* tea ceremony. Each week, he explained, *Punch* held an editorial tea. A writer or an artist who had gained one acceptance was allowed to stay a certain period of time, one who had gained two acceptances a little longer, and so on. A different system would have to be invented to fit Americans and the bootleg era. Ross dispatched his man Ingersoll to find a suitable location, install a bar, employ a bartender, buy liquor, and otherwise arrange a pally atmosphere in which a stronger bond between contributors and the magazine could be forged.

Ingersoll accomplished the physical end of his mission. But owing to competition from Tony's and other speakeasies, patronage was never heavy. Camaraderie did not come up to expectations, either, though too much of it was responsible, in a way, for a padlock going on the place.

One morning Ingersoll on his endless rounds unlocked the door of the speakeasy upon a shocking sight. Stretched out, dead to the world, were two contributors, a male and a female. There was nothing for it but to tell Ross, since the slumberers had to be got up and out of there. Anyhow the news was bound to reach his ears eventually. Scandalized, Ross ordered an end to the venture in good relations.

Ross felt nevertheless that by constant vigilance he could keep sex out of the office.

"It can be done," he would say grimly.

When hiring Wolcott Gibbs, Ross had laid down a policy: "Don't seduce the contributors." Long afterward Gibbs stated that it was the only consistent editorial policy he had known the magazine to have.

But Ross's faith in keeping sex out was probably never as strong as he said it was, and an unhappy adventure tossed his suspicions sky-high. He rarely interviewed job applicants, but to vary his routine one day he went to the reception room to talk with one—a Vassar girl. It was now considered smart to work on the New Yorker.

A few minutes later, running like a wild horse, screaming with pain, he was back in his office. Frantically he pressed the buzzers for his male editorial assistants. When they arrived he was striding up and down, his face white with rage, his mutterings dark. Finally he halted and pointed an accusing finger.

"At last you've ruined me!" he shouted. "You've finally managed it!"

No signs of ruin being visible, they waited. Gradually the story came out. The girl had stated her qualifications and her burning ambition to work for the New Yorker. And then she had averted her eyes and with a note of journalistic martyrdom in her voice declared, "Of course, Mr. Ross, I understand what would be expected of me."

Ingersoll had developed into a sort of quarreling companion for Ross. Countless cuffs and kicks failed to diminish his admiration. He kept a sixteen-hour daily schedule. On some press nights he spent as much as eight hours at the printer's, shifting and reshifting commas according to Ross's directions from the other end of a telephone.

Regularly the two of them fought what was called the Paper Clip War.

It would begin after Ingersoll, growing nervous in a staff meeting, had begun to chew a paper clip. That bothered Ross, but for a while he would endure it with ostentatious nobility. Then the explosion would come.

"Quit chewing that God damned paper clip!"

Ingersoll would guiltily lay the clip on the table. The conference would resume. After a while Ross, every inch the wise and kindly patriarch, would hold up a hand. It would be seen that Ingersoll was again nervously chewing on the clip.

"Now," Ross would say gently, "we're like a family here.

If one of us does something that irritates the other, we stop it. We try not to get on the nerves of one another."

Back to the table would go the paper clip, Ingersoll's head hung in shame.

In a few moments would come Ross's loudest outcry.

"Quit chewing that God damned paper clip!"

By this time Ingersoll's nerves would be completely frayed. He would revolt. It was his perfect God damned right, he would cry, to chew all the God damned paper clips he had a notion to. There was no one going to dictate to him in the matter of chewing God damned paper clips.

With an air of martyrdom Ross would listen quietly until Ingersoll had subsided, and then proceed with the conference.

Sometimes Ingersoll chewed paper wads and laid them in little rows on the table. That caused as much trouble as the clips.

Ross and Ingersoll quarreled so angrily between themselves that physical violence often seemed imminent.

"You're getting ready to slug me," Ross would say to six-foot-three ex-heavyweight wrestler Ingersoll. "You'll sink to the animals and try to settle this by brute force."

He had real cause for alarm, for Ingersoll's history revealed him as a slugger of editors. While working for the *American* he had discovered that an innocuous story he had written about the Veterans' Administration had been twisted into an attack. He felled the city editor with a single blow to the belly.

In the New Yorker offices staff members were never surprised to find Ingersoll at his desk, sweating, fists clenched, eyes frenetic, muttering, "I'm going in and kill him now. At last I'm going to do it."

Ingersoll felt repaid by watching Ross and listening to

him in his creative periods. The chances against the magazine's success had been at least 100 to 1, Ingersoll figured, and he was inclined to agree that ruthlessness was required to get the job done. He was impressed by Ross's enormous vitality. Ross often said that the New Yorker was merely an episode in his life. He would give it half a dozen years and then pass on to other things. The tabloid idea was discussed interminably. There would be other magazines. His heart was set, for example, on a factual detective magazine, printed on good paper and written by accomplished authors. The title he had in mind was simply *Guilty*.

Ross was never satisfied for long with anyone who couldn't or wouldn't stand up to him, no matter the punishment absorbed. In Katharine Angell he met his match. Her integrity was high, she had strong opinions, and she would not retreat without cause. Ross valued her knowledge and judgment, especially in taste. In the vast majority of big and little things there was no conflict. But when Ross finally accepted a hotly debated point the old cry, "This magazine is being run by women and children!" was likely to rise.

An old employee has said, "Katharine Angell is a fine editor, but she also acted as a mother to the staff."

Anyone whose nerves were on the point of breaking usually went to her. Often she would have to take up some question with Ross before the pressure could be relieved. This often meant high words. Ross carefully eschewed profanity when speaking to women—an enormous concession.

E. B. White had fewer fights with Ross than other staff members. He had little contentiousness in him, and he was not very articulate. Ross treated him gingerly out of great respect for his talent and his value to the magazine. But an individualist of White's caliber could not fail to resent, occasionally, Ross's drive to dominate. Once he refused a raise of salary because he thought Ross was trying to tie him down.

Thurber's chief struggle, at first, was to get away from being an editor. While Ross's enthusiasm for a "Jesus" rode high, nothing would dampen it. When a methodical, literal-minded subeditor brought to Ross a long list of errors committed by Thurber, Ross refused to look at it.

White tried to intercede, explaining that Thurber was no good as an editor but would be valuable as a writer.

Ross disagreed. "Got the most damned common sense of any editor I ever had."

"That," White said, "only proves you've lost your mind. Give me one example of Thurber's common sense."

Ross recalled the time a letter had come in from a business firm protesting treatment of its product in the magazine's columns. Asked his suggestion on what to do about it, Thurber had calmly dropped it to the floor and put a match to it.

"Only direct action we ever had around here," Ross said.

Inevitably Ross's ardor cooled, as on every "Jesus," and Thurber barely escaped dismissal. The closest shave was while he was vacationing in Columbus. Ross got a wire from Thurber that his dog was lost and he would have to overstay his time. A dog's interference with the magazine was the kind of thing bound to drive Ross frantic. He talked of sending off a dismissal telegram. Thurber was meanwhile turning Columbus upside down. The fire department was called out. The newspapers ran stories about the hunt.

After the search was successfully concluded—the dog was found next door—Thurber came back to work. Ross made a snide remark about people who get wrapped up in dogs, Thurber threatened to throw him out the window, they went out drinking that night, and Thurber's place on the magazine was secure.

Knowing the rocky "Jesus" road, Thurber tried to make it easier for those who followed him. One day Ross was talking with Bernard Bergman, a young employee whom he was thinking of promoting to managing editor. As usual Ross was approaching the matter obliquely. All kinds of problems had to be solved, he explained—personal as well as editorial. He had been expounding for some time when an overexcited office boy tore in. Thurber had, the boy was sure, gone into the men's room to commit suicide. Thurber had a reputation for nervousness and profound depressions.

Turning to Bergman, Ross said almost triumphantly, "You see? That's my life! Go try to straighten it out."

Thurber was just emerging, whistling, from the men's room when Bergman dashed out of Ross's office.

Bergman put a finger to his lips. "Cut out the whistling," he said. "Ross thinks you're committing suicide. Do you mind if I tell him that I stopped it?"

"Not if it will help you," Thurber replied.

They talked for a while. Thurber had told Bergman earlier that he thought Ross was going to promote him, and he inquired how things were going. Bergman said he didn't know yet but would telephone him later.

Ross seemed impressed when Bergman told him that Thurber was all right. "By God, I think you'll be able to handle the job," he said.

Bergman telephoned Thurber that night and began to report his conversation with Ross.

"Never mind," Thurber said. "I put a rug down on the floor and listened at the keyhole until I got bored."

Ross's failure to hasten personally to save Thurber was due to his feeling that, while something terrible might be happening, self-destruction was not among the probabilities. The dispatch of Bergman illustrated, though, his growing isolation. His key-jangling corridor pacing had decreased. He discouraged detailed reports of unfortunate occurrences.

Thurber found nervous release in rolling around the big bottles in which water was brought for the water coolers. Once he broke a bottle. "Go out and find what the hell is happening," Ross said to Bergman. "But don't tell me."

The terrific office pressure was withstood fairly well by the staff members because they were young, their spirits were high, they believed in what they were doing, and they had faith in Ross. But sometimes they needed an outlet. One way they got it was by plaguing Ross. An easy method was to insert risqué material into copy handed to him. Or, better yet, to suggest that something was a double-entendre when it was not. Ross set new and presumably unsubverted editors to watch for off-color meanings. But he could never be sure that his subscribers were not giggling lewdly behind his back.

Whenever Ross's preachments on integrity and good taste became wearying, staff members would mention Fleischmann's Yeast. In those days the Fleischmann Yeast Company (owned by relatives of Raoul) was busily flushing the bowels of the American populace, thereby removing pimples from faces and doing other worth-while things. The yeast advertisements, which appeared regularly in the New Yorker, were tastefully illustrated with sketches of the alimentary tract. Ross abhorred them. In editorial copy he would not even permit Lois Long to use the word "armpit." But the revenue was helpful. Editors inquired smugly: What about taste? What about integrity? Ross would explain carefully that little compromises had sometimes to be made for the greater good.

He found a way, though, to compensate for the indignities of the yeast ads. He obtained a list of society women and telephoned them one by one. The conversations went roughly like this:

Ross: "This is a representative of the Fleischmann Yeast Company. If you endorse our product we will send a check for a thousand dollars either to you or a charity you name. Do you agree?"

Society Woman (*after proper hesitation*): "Yes."

Ross: "Thank you. We ask you only to declare that before using our yeast your face was a mass of blotches and unseemly pimples."

Staff workers let off steam by means of escapades of their own. A man digging a hole in the street with a pick and shovel might just as easily be from the New Yorker as the Department of Sanitation. If harassed, he was probably a New Yorker man paying off a bet. The furtive little man slipping down a midtown fire escape would be White, on his way to hide in Schrafft's until the visitor who had inquired for him, but whose name he had not recognized, had departed. For a while any mysterious strangers lurking around the New Yorker office were assumed, at least by Thurber, to be plain-clothes dicks, watching White. A Buick owned by White had been used in a bank robbery, and the cops, faced with White's taciturnity and the scrawls and dentist's dates on his office walls, suspected him of being the brains of the gang. Whenever Thurber heard a police siren he thought they were coming for White.

Ingersoll and White found some relaxation in a scientific voyage with the double purpose of discovering the headwaters of the Bronx River and providing material for a piece spoofing travel books. The expedition was fitted out with a canoe that White owned, a tent, a camera, food, and the department-store dummy, Sterling Finny. This dummy belonged to White and had been used by him in a series of parody promotion ads.

Conditions were not the same as when Joliet and Champlain paddled the rivers through the silent, trackless wilderness. Every time White and Ingersoll stopped to take pictures, large crowds gathered. Traffic was halted on nearby roads. The presence of the dummy caused raised eyebrows and even ridicule. The police objected to the traffic jams. In the end the expedition had to be abandoned, and they returned, dispirited, like many an explorer before them.

No aboriginals had been encountered, but Indians got mixed up in another venture, when several staff members undertook the instruction of a women's club in the history of Sitting Bull. They were pretty sure that the ladies would be enthralled, and they were right. Among the New Yorker's employees was a high-spirited girl named Haydie Eames Yates, who looked something like an Indian. She had landed her job in the first place by means of a sort of prank. Upon her application, Ingersoll had told her, somewhat grumpily, to go out and get a story, any kind of a story, and if it were any good he would hire her. She introduced herself to a cop outside, took him to a speakeasy, and came back with what Ingersoll agreed was a usable tale of her experiences. In time she became an important "Talk" writer.

Haydie went to address the clubwomen disguised as Sitting Bull's last surviving widow. She was supposed to possess clairvoyant powers. Three or four staffers worked on her script. She was to start off straight and gradually broaden into burlesque.

A couple of hours later she came back, considerably shaken, and clanked a hatful of coins down on Ingersoll's desk. She had delivered her lines well—too well. In the parts where her listeners were supposed to laugh they had, to her horror, wept. A few had become overwrought when she communicated spiritually with Sitting Bull. In the end someone had passed the hat for her.

The law was more or less openly flouted several times in the matter of the sign belonging to the office of John S. Sumner, guiding spirit of the Society for the Suppression of Vice. Mr. Sumner was a dangerous adversary, not to be taken lightly. The overt act which started the war was committed by an outsider whose identity was not revealed. One dark night he pried the sign from the front of the society's headquarters, which were in a brownstone house on a quiet street, and scurried home with it. Next day he sent an admission of his sin to the New Yorker. "Talk" reported it in a subsequent issue.

Sumner descended promptly on the office and demanded the culprit's name. It was refused him. Worse, an item was run disclosing that the sign was being used as a cocktail tray by the thief. Sumner threatened to have the law on the magazine unless it divulged the rascal's identity at once.

The task of dealing with the embattled protector of the public morals fell, naturally, to Ingersoll. He enlisted the aid of White. Almost at once they struck on a brilliant stratagem. To their personal knowledge, they told Sumner, alcohol had been spilled on the sign during its use as a cocktail tray. Would not Sumner be satisfied if they had a new sign made for him? The solution appeared reasonable to Sumner.

Ingersoll and White went to Third Avenue and, at a good deal of expense to themselves, hired a skilled cabinetmaker to perform a delicate task. At first glance his handiwork appeared to be simply a sign carrying the name of the Society for the Suppression of Vice. A close inspection was required to reveal that it had a false front. The panel concealed an excellent likeness of Mr. Sumner, losing his hat. It was being kicked off by a girl in scanties.

Ingersoll's and White's plan called for removing the panel, once Sumner had hung the sign. Sumner failed to discover the secret panel, but his goat was not to be had easily. When the plotters arrived for the unveiling they found that, fearing other raiders in search of cocktail trays, he had hung the sign on the second floor of the society's house.

Next night they were back dressed in what they considered proper regalia for the task in hand. White wore a fireman's uniform, complete with helmet, which he had rented from a theatrical outfitter. Ingersoll wore a long-tailed coat and a high hat and had an ax slung over his shoulder. They carried a ladder between them. White held the ladder against the wall. Ingersoll mounted. Just as his ax was poised for the blow to pry off the false front, Sumner thrust his head out of a nearby window.

The tails of Ingersoll's coat billowed as he slid to the sidewalk. As they fled White lost his helmet and Ingersoll his tall hat, but they saved the ladder. Taking counsel between themselves at a speakeasy, they decided that the fireman's and the dude's attire had been too ostentatious.

Next night a tall painter and a short painter, carrying a ladder, buckets, and other tools of their trade, came unobtrusively down the street. They passed the house, for stationed in front was a cop. The city of New York was guarding Sumner's sign.

The task of removing the panel was eventually accomplished, after the cop had been withdrawn, by White and Theodore Pratt, a New Yorker writer. Pratt held the ladder while White removed the panel. Anonymous phone calls to newspaper city rooms resulted, as had been hoped, in stories about the high-kicking chorus girl and Sumner's hat. The false panel was later used by Ingersoll as a cocktail tray. The marauders were never apprehended, and in time the statute of limitations ran out.

There was enough of the old roughhouse left in Ross for him to enjoy accounts of the escapades, and now and again, as with the yeast, he had a little joke himself. One of them he played with the help of Wolcott Gibbs. A man in the financial district had submitted an obscure piece by Stephen Leacock, with his own name signed to it. No one in the office recognized it as Leacock's and it was printed after being edited down from 1200 to 600 words. Nevertheless, several readers recognized it and fired in letters.

Legal action could have been taken against the plagiarist, but Ross and Gibbs thought up a scheme that would punish him and at the same time give them some fun. His note accompanying the manuscript had been on the letterhead of a financial firm. They assigned him to write a weekly financial letter. He strove mightily, but each week his copy was sent back with an editorial notation that it wasn't quite right but that he was getting close.

Finally Ross tired of the game. "Why don't you," he wrote, "send us some more of your intimate recollections of Stephen Leacock?"

Later on Ross was annoyed by some New Yorker legends that popped up in print. An anecdote which might be titled "Thurber in the Telephone Booth" bothered him most. The common version was that Thurber, to protest the installation of a pay booth for personal calls, had torn it off the wall and stretched out in it, arms folded across his chest, as if it were a coffin. A few accounts had his face powdered and yards of crepe wrapped around him.

Ross became so embittered that, when Margaret Case Harriman hinted that unless able to find fresh New Yorker anecdotes for her book about the Algonquin Round Table she would have to put in the telephone-booth tale, Ross quickly supplied several.

To an acquaintance who mentioned the telephone anecdote not long afterward, Ross stated vehemently that he had personally tackled Thurber on the subject and satisfied himself that the whole story was cockeyed.

The acquaintance reported to Thurber, as mildly funny, Ross's vigorous efforts to lay the story. Thurber nodded sympathetically. "Things do get exaggerated," he said. "I was in that booth only a short time. Did it to give Ingersoll a laugh."

The Formula Shines 12

At the end of the second year "Comment" boasted that the New Yorker was carrying more pages of advertising than any magazine in the world except for three. It was not disclosed that the magazine had come near foundering on its success. Advertising contracts had been drawn at a low figure based on a small readership. Circulation had shot up enormously, skyrocketing production costs. To have clamped a lid on circulation would have been disastrous. Fleischmann and others had covered the losses and in the third year the ledgers were kept in black ink.

The generation of the pleasantly turbulent twenties had, it turned out, been as hot for sophistication as for sex and gin. Readers were sure that in the New Yorker they were buying sophistication. Ross worried that his magazine's appeal might be phony—it was a fighting word with him—and was sorry that he had used the term "sophistication" in his prospectus. He discouraged its usage around the office.

By the third anniversary number—in February 1928—the editorial formula had begun to shine. The gingerbread had been tossed out, leaving the pages neat and clean. Writers were surer of themselves. Artists had improved their techniques, and reproduction methods were better. One of the more attractive gleams was manufactured out of humility, of all things. Said "Comment": "Three years ago we had an idea that it would be possible to publish a magazine which would express the city, all neatly, in color, in words, in song." This self-important dream had been shattered. The editors had discovered "to our amaze that the city's electric peaks were higher than our head, its loud follies madder than our heart, its rhythm bolder and finer than our spirit."

Those words were written, to be sure, by E. B. White, who hadn't been on the staff three years before, and who was expressing his own view of the metropolis. Yet he was now writing "Comment," which expressed the editorial tone more directly than anything else in the magazine. White was also leaving his imprint elsewhere.

Whenever a cartoon caption line didn't seem right and others had failed to improve it, the picture was simply brought in and propped on White's desk. After it had been in his way long enough or when he was tired of looking at it he composed a fitting line. In this way there was created one of the New Yorker's most famous captions. The picture was of a young mother and her small daughter sitting at the dinner table. White rolled a piece of paper into his typewriter and tapped out the lines:

> *"It's broccoli, dear."*
> *"I say it's spinach, and I say the hell with it."*

He handed the paper casually to his office mate, Thurber, and asked his opinion. Thurber said unenthusiastically that he thought it would do. When it reached the public it caused a minor sensation, and "spinach" as a term of disapprobation went into the language.

The cartoon illustrates almost perfectly the gradual evolution of the one-line caption from the two-line. It appeared in 1928. A year later the caption almost certainly would have been telescoped into a single line.

White once strayed far enough into the domain of others to paint a picture of a sea horse wearing an oats feeder, which he sold to the magazine for a cover. He did not repeat this victory.

"Newsbreaks" had grown from the filler stage to the dignity of a main feature, and White was chiefly responsible. In a compilation of them into a small book titled *Ho Hum*, White, then at the beginning of a long and busy career of foreword-writing, explained that after the magazine was three weeks old the public had taken over the task of clipping. The staff had soon been hard put to sort them. For his part, White was sorry the magazine had ever begun paying for those used. A typographical error in an advertisement for a window dresser, making it "widow dresser," would net the government up to five dollars in postage. "Immorality" for "immortality," "bride" for "bridge," "martial" for "marital," were errors that strained the backs of the postmen. Printers abetted with such concoctions as "Bloomers, ½ Off." White was pretty sure that the jokes would be clipped out of *Ho Hum* and sent right back to the New Yorker.

The comments under the clippings, bearing White's light touch, often ranked with the cartoons in popularity.

Erratum. We regret to state that we did not have the information about John Ehlich, '28, correct. He is not an instructor, but just a fellow. Dr. Wolf is not head of the botany department. It's not Durham University, but Duke University at Durham, North Carolina.—The Cornell Countryman.

Maybe you're not correcting the right article?

Sex slipped easily into the magazine through the "Newsbreaks."

Thank you for the lovely, sane letter telling the little ones. With a box of seeds planted in the window, a mother cat with two babies under my kitchen stove, and your wonderful letter tucked away in my desk I feel ready for anything.— "Just Among Ourselves" Department in the *Pictorial Review*.

Watch yourself, lady, watch yourself!

Dear Mrs. Lee: Am a woman nearly 40, old enough to know what I am doing. I am very much in love with a married man, whose wife is an invalid. He gives me about $50 a month and says just as soon as he is free we will be married.

It is just killing my mother. He says don't pay any attention to her, it is our business, not hers. I am getting very nervous. Seems like I will go insane. He says if you go back on me you will regret it. What would you do in my case?—Advice Column in the Cleveland News.

Ask for a hundred a month.

Fillmore Hyde's "Comment" had often been caustic. White was easygoing. "There have been rumors," he wrote in the 1928 anniversary number, "that we were about to adopt a policy, but the blessed event seems as far off as ever." He was expert in the use of exaggeration—regarded by some as whimsey.

To date New York has shown nothing but progress. Hopefully we await the first signs of decadence—partial decadence being the only condition under which anybody can exist with any degree of grace and civility. In a wholly progressive city noontime is the most discouraging time of day—the noon's roar and blaze, an orgy of soda water, sandwich counters, heat, traffic, heavy hotel table d'hôtes, blue plate specials, and luncheon club speakers. There are few places you can go where the atmosphere is anything but pompous or hasty. Business goes on right through the top of the day, prosperity mounting over a clank of coffee cups.—*By E. B. White, from "Notes and Comments," August 11, 1928.*

White was equally adept at describing the kind of poignant little events that New Yorker readers felt they were just the kind of people to notice.

One morning last week we took a turn in Bronx Park. There is a little valley, just west of the rose garden, through which the river flows in idyllic ease, guarded by tall hemlocks whose feet are almost in the stream. The sun, pouring through the green tops of the trees, strikes the water and gives it a fine sparkle where it tumbles off a ledge. For a quarter of a mile, sauntering along the footpath, we saw no one, heard nothing save the sound of the water against the hemlock roots, the honk of a duck going overhead, and occasionally—at what seemed an incredible distance—the murmur of a train. It was hard to believe that this lovely deserted glen was in New York City. Sooner or later (we told ourself) we are going to discover a reason for it being here—here where everything, to exist, must have a reason. And we did. Rounding a bend, we came upon a bridge crossing the stream, and on the bridge, leaning against the stone railing, were a young man and a girl. And the girl (because of something her companion had just said) was crying.

In five minutes we were in the subway, feeling intensely vernal.—*By E. B. White, from "Notes and Comments," April 21, 1928.*

Sometimes White took a common experience and raised it to a mildly philosophical plain.

The heavy-footed moving men have come and gone, but their ghosts linger on the stairs. The populace wears a drawn look around the eyes and there is a haggard expression on the faces you see in the street. The Consolidated Gas Company locked up 52,905 meters, unlocked 43,384, their men creeping about the town at midnight, locking, unlocking, locking, unlocking. The Telephone Company changed three hundred and fifty thousand telephones, their men slinking out with an instrument under an arm, slinking back in the next day with another to put in its place. It was an eerie time, a time of grand pianos and mattresses and old boxes of love letters, a gas time, a telephone time, when life itself was smothered under its own cumulus. A gaseous people we are, moving restlessly about from one abode to another, phoning each other constantly.—*By E. B. White, from "Notes and Comments," October 13, 1928.*

In commenting on the city's life White often employed the surprise ending.

A life insurance man told us of a remarkable business migration which took place in Madison Square recently. He said that one division of the Metropolitan Life moved en masse from one building to another, across the connecting bridge. At 2:30 the one hundred clerks ceased work and got up from their desks. At 2:41 the first desk was up-ended by a porter. At 3:35 the whole works had been transferred to the other building and electricians were installing the telephones. At 3:36 the clerks sat down and took up their duties. "And didn't any of the clerks escape?" we asked. But it was the wrong question.—*By E. B. White, from "Notes and Comments," May 26, 1928.*

In one way the jester-philosopher has an easier time of it than his sterner colleague, for when called upon to stand and defend himself he can merely shrug and laugh, bang a bladder on his hip, and express wonder how anyone was foolish enough to take him seriously in the first place. In another way the jester's task is harder. The serious philosopher is permitted to send forth his ideas in murky rhetoric. The jester must be instantly clear. Dullness is never allowed and cuteness for only a short time. White achieved his success as much, or more, by the clarity and grace and sudden sparkle of his prose as by his attitude toward life and the city.

"Comment" usually filled a little more than the first page of the 5-page "Talk" section. Thurber rewrote most of "Talk" from copy turned in by reporters and also did at least one original story a week. Thurber acknowledged his style debt to White. But "Talk" was faster-paced. It dealt with facts, "Comment" with ideas. It was necessary to get along more rapidly with facts.

A fairly typical "Talk" section—in the issue of October 27, 1928—had five long items separated by four short ones. The "we were there" technique was now commonly employed. The first of the long items described stage actors taking Movietone voice auditions at the Fox Film Company studios on Tenth Avenue; the second of the long items described a house in which Al Smith, the Democratic candidate for President, had once lived; the third had to do with a collection of ancient English clocks in a midtown store; the fourth described the hurly-burly of bus terminals; and the fifth reported on the unruliness of the crowd which went to Lakehurst to see the Zeppelin come in from Germany.

In the short items the gag and the celebrity anecdote had given way to the human-interest story, usually with the heroine or hero drawn from the city's anonymous masses. The reader, in short, might conceivably have been in on it.

Separating the voice test and the Al Smith stories was this one.

At rush hour, the other day, a subway guard at the BMT station at Union Square had a time of it with people who were trying to jam into a crowded northbound express, and got the doors closed only after a great struggle. When the train moved off, those left on the platform heard him murmur: "My Gawd, you'd think they was in the Bronx."

It illustrates the magazine's lack of concern with readers who were not familiar enough with the city to know that the passengers were boarding a train in Manhattan that ran to the Bronx, therefore were doubtless Bronx residents, and that the guard was accusing them of behaving as if they were at home. As it happened, the intelligentsia of the provinces rather liked this intimacy, which gave them an illusion of being a part of a sophisticated world metropolis. Quite a few people in Dubuque were buying the magazine. Ross was surprised but he recognized its value in getting general advertising. The New Yorker began putting out two editions—a national and a local one. Local advertising was omitted from the national edition.

The casuals were improving because of Ross's clearer knowledge of what he wanted, more sensitive editing, and the appearance of talented new writers. Casuals took any form. One of the first parodies was by Ernest Hemingway of Frank Harris, the English editor whose autobiography contained many lurid details. Thurber then parodied Hemingway's hard-boiled fiction.

Elmer Rice contributed a series about his New York childhood, setting a tone of nostalgia that was to become a major ingredient of the formula. Herbert Asbury, a *World* reporter, wrote a series, "When New York Was Really Wicked." Russel Crouse, another newspaperman, furnished a set of studies, "They Were New Yorkers," starting off with Steve Brodie.

Wolcott Gibbs appeared under his own name for the first time with a casual dealing with his effort to work a pun,

"Neither beer nor there," into a conversation, and his frustration upon saying, "Neither here nor there," when the opening presented itself.

Every bit as nervous as Gibbs was John O'Hara, a tall, big-eared young man from Pennsylvania, who worked on the staff and wrote casuals. He was usually pretty sure that people were conspiring against him. When out drinking with a group he was apt to interrupt any conversation with a warning to quit talking about him. At first O'Hara was John H. O'Hara, but soon he dropped the middle initial. Among his first contributions was a half-column satire on alumni bulletins. Never having been to college, he was, like Ross, enormously skeptical of them. His pieces were often straight dialogue or monologue.

Arthur Kober specialized in dialect conversation pieces laid in the Bronx. He was a cherubic youth so much in love with the theater that he had gotten a job as a producer's press agent. His wife, Lillian Hellman, was in love with the theater, too, but she had put aside her career to be a housewife. Kober knew the Bronx. As a schoolboy when passing Hogan's Alley, where the big Irish kids hung out, he had always put his cap on sideways and faked a pitiful limp. He hadn't finished school, which was why he began writing in dialect. He reasoned that if he used the speech of uneducated people he wouldn't be asked to write good English. He had contributed doggerel to F.P.A. under the name of A. Narcissus Kober. For the New Yorker he was writing a series of monologues of a dumb girl talking to her boy friend.

White's casuals had his special qualities, one of which, of course, was their truly casual tone. Thurber, on the other hand, often ended with something fairly close to a short story. Ross hadn't contemplated fiction for his formula, but the magazine was beginning to use a few of the slice-of-life stories of the kind pioneered by *The Little Review* and *transition*. There was, for example, Sally Benson's little tale of an elderly couple who adventured to Greenwich Village to eat, blundered into a speakeasy, and went back bewildered to their hotel to dinner. Thyra Samter Winslow, a *Smart Set* veteran, most nearly approached the short story form with a sketch about a woman feeling drunkenly sorry for a poorly dressed working girl in whom she saw her old self.

A stark little piece by Thurber, called "A Box to Hide In," contributed to an attitude which toned up the formula.

I waited till the large woman with the awful hat took up her sack of groceries and went out, peering at the tomatoes and lettuce on her way. The clerk asked me what mine was.

"Have you got a box," I asked, "a large box? I want a box to hide in."

"You want a box?" he asked.

"I want a box to hide in," I said.

"Whatta you mean?" he said. "You mean a big box?"

I said I meant a big box, big enough to hold me.

"I haven't got any boxes," he said. "Only cartons that cans come in."

I tried several other groceries and none of them had a box big enough for me to hide in. There was nothing for it but to face life out. I didn't feel strong, and I'd had this overpowering desire to hide in a box for a long time.

"Whatta you mean you want to hide in this box?" one grocer asked me.

"It's a form of escape," I told him, "hiding in a box. It circumscribes your worries and the range of your anguish. You don't see people, either."

"How in the hell do you eat when you're in this box?" asked the grocer. "How in the hell do you get anything to eat?" I said

I had never been in a box and didn't know, but that that would take care of itself.

"Well," he said, finally, "I haven't got any boxes, only some pasteboard cartons that cans come in."

It was the same every place. I gave up when it got dark and the groceries closed, and hid in my room again. I turned out the light and lay on the bed. You feel better when it gets dark. I could have hid in a closet, I suppose, but people are always opening doors. Somebody would find you in a closet. They would be startled and you'd have to tell them why you were in the closet. Nobody pays any attention to a big box lying on the floor. You could stay in it for days and nobody'd think to look in it, not even the cleaning-woman.

My cleaning-woman came the next morning and woke me up. I was still feeling bad. I asked her if she knew where I could get a large box.

"How big a box you want?" she asked.

"I want a box big enough for me to get inside of," I said. She looked at me with big, dim eyes. There's something wrong with her glands. She's awful but she has a big heart, which makes it worse. She's unbearable, her husband is sick and her children are sick and she is sick too. I got to thinking how pleasant it would be if I were in a box now, and didn't have to see her. I would be in a box right there in the room and she wouldn't know. I wondered if you have a desire to bark or laugh when someone who doesn't know walks by the box you are in. Maybe she would have a spell with her heart, if I did that, and would die right there. The officers and elevatorman and Mr. Gramadge would find us. "Funny doggone thing happened at the building last night," the doorman would say to his wife. "I let in this woman to clean up 10-F and she never come out, see? She's never been there more'n an hour, but she never come out, see? So when it got to be time for me to go off duty, why I says to Crennick, who was on the elevator, I says what the hell you suppose has happened to that woman cleans 10-F? He says he didn't know; he says he never seen her after he took her up. So I spoke to Mr. Gramadge about it. 'I'm sorry to bother you, Mr. Gramadge,' I says, 'but there's something funny about that woman cleans 10-F.' So I told him. So he said we better have a look and we all three goes up and knocks on the door and rings the bell, see, and nobody answer so he said we'd have to walk in so Crennick opened the door and we walked in and here was this woman cleans the apartment dead as a herring on the floor and the gentleman that lives there was in a box." . . .

The cleaning-woman kept looking at me. It was hard to realize she wasn't dead. "It's a form of escape," I murmured. "What say?" she asked, dully.

"You don't know of any large packing boxes, do you?" I asked.

"No, I don't," she said.

I haven't found one yet, but I still have this overpowering urge to hide in a box. Maybe it will go away, maybe I'll be all right. Maybe it will get worse. It's hard to say.

Part of Thurber's purpose was to kid the stream-of-consciousness technique being employed by "modern" writers. But the piece is an exaggerated example of the way the magazine reflected the restlessness of the city, especially the neurotic security-seeking of the wealthy, the rootless intellectuals, and the upper white-collar classes. And yet in the story one can easily read a feeling of safety in the arms of the city itself, a sort of security in anonymity.

Most of the people responsible for creating the New Yorker had fled smaller communities for the metropolis. So had many of its New York readers. Many of those outside the city felt ill at ease in their environment. The average New Yorker writer, editor, and reader wanted to be free of restrictive rules. Even if he did not actually want to break any, he was not happy under his neighbor's gaze. All through the works of Thurber—and he was the chief setter of this atmosphere—there is talk of the possibility of his being run out of town by unfriendly neighbors.

The profiles had been considerably expanded from the vignettes of the early issues. Often they were of literary figures, such as Dorothy Parker's study of Ernest Hemingway (his definition of guts: "Grace under pressure"). But subjects of more massive proportions, for example William Randolph Hearst and Henry Ford, were also being treated. While the average textual matter in each issue was kept between 2000 and 3000 words, the profile might run in several parts. John K. Winkler's study of Hearst ran to five, and later appeared as a book. Niven Busch, Jr., assessed Ford in several installments, finding that "no one could better represent this time in the United States."

Morris Markey was perfecting the "Reporter at Large" technique. For a long time the department belonged to him alone. Then a piece by Karl Schriftgiesser, a Boston literary critic, about his city's Watch and Ward Society, suppressor of books, seemed to fit and it was run as a "Reporter" piece. The heading was thereafter used occasionally for the work of others.

Markey had relinquished entirely his department of press criticism. The new man was Robert Benchley, who wrote over the signature of "Guy Fawkes." After a little the heading, "The Press in Review," was discarded for a more fortunate choice, "The Wayward Press." Though he never claimed to be much of a journalist himself, Benchley was a champion newspaper reader. He had a system. Starting at the top left side of the front page, he read straight down the column, moved to the top of the next, read down it, and continued in this manner right through the paper. He skipped but he never jumped around.

Benchley kept an eye on personalities and controversies.

When the *World* changed its position on the Sacco-Vanzetti case, starting its famous fight with Heywood Broun, he wrote:

> Mr. Broun, who, not having been informed of the editorial shift, thought he was writing for the old *World*, found himself standing alone in the middle of the field with the ball and his interference in a huddle conference 50 yards away. Although the *World* maintained that Mr. Broun was still on the team, when last seen he was in the locker building and in street clothes.

Benchley commented on a newcomer:

> One of the phenomena of modern newspaper writing is the position attained by Walter Winchell in the belles lettres of the day. Within a year Mr. Winchell has become an institution, both as a personal reporter and a compiler of folk sayings. People buy the Graphic who never knew it existed and hide it between the sheets of their *Evening Post*. His words, and the words of people he quotes, are taking their place in the national language.

Ross took some satisfaction from Alexander Woollcott's suggestion that he contribute a weekly page. After all, less than four years had passed since Broadway's glittering rajah had looked with disdain on his old protégé's fumblings and at one point had withdrawn his name from the editorial advisory board. Lately Woollcott had been claiming that the idea for the New Yorker had been his in the first place—that Ross had expropriated it during the *Stars and Stripes* days.

This sort of thing didn't bother Ross. But his opinion of Woollcott's value had undergone a change. At the beginning he had paid Woollcott a higher rate than anyone else and had been afraid to change so much as a comma in his copy. Now he doubted that Woollcott ought to be in the magazine, at least regularly. Woollcott's stuff never rang very true, Ross claimed. Besides Woollcott's aversion to accepting editorial suggestions, there was his love of inserting double-entendres. The search for them might well keep half the staff busy.

Another thing Ross didn't like about Woollcott's practices was his acceptance of gratuities for inserting commercial plugs in his copy. Once when Woollcott received a hundred neckties from a manufacturer for whom he had done a favor, Ross managed to steal half of them. On a day that Woollcott was expected in the office Ross issued them to elevator men, office boys, editors, writers, and to Sterling Finny, the dummy in his private office. Woollcott's usually imperial entrance was marred by recognition of his neckties. The staff was impressed by the way he stormed into Ross's office and by the sounds of conflict which emerged.

In the end Ross bowed to his editors, who felt that Woollcott might add something to the magazine.

As a title for his page, Woollcott chose "Shouts and Murmurs," which had served him for a book about the theater. Though feeling that his name ought to stand at the head of the page, he agreed to let it abide at the end, and promised to behave. Not many weeks had passed before Katharine Angell, who was assigned to edit him, was using all the force and tact at her command to hold him in line. Even so, he managed to devote a whole page to an ancient risqué story about a celebrated Parisian lady of pleasure who, deeply moved that the students of a French military school had conducted a lottery to enable a lucky student to enjoy her favors, had unselfishly returned to the winner the price of his own ticket.

But Woollcott had more to offer than ladies of the evening. He had ghosts and grisly murders and famous friends. His page was very popular.

The departments had become the sturdy base fluid into which the bright colors were mixed. Charles Brackett, a young novelist, was now drama critic. The cinema column was being written by John Chapin Mosher. He was also first reader of fiction and casuals. As such he was considered one of the most valuable members of the staff because of his tireless interest in the hunt for new talent and his sharp eye for recognizing it. "The Art Galleries" was the domain of Murdock Pemberton. Robert Simon conducted "Musical Events." Dorothy Parker seldom reviewed books any more and the job was divided between various persons who used pen names. Lois Long's "On and Off the Avenue"—the area had expanded from "Fifth Avenue"—had grown in comprehensiveness, and as "Lipstick" she could fill a new cabaret with a favorable mention in "Tables for Two."

Ralph Ingersoll would wrap himself in a coonskin coat and go to the Yale football games, a venture which was either courageous or masochistic, for when Yale lost, his horror was doubled by the necessity of writing a report of the game. Win or lose, he hung sadly over the shoulder of Wolcott Gibbs, the kind of copy editor who would cruelly change "pigskin," "spheroid," or other Ingersoll synonyms to plain "football." Among the other departments were "Indoor Polo," "Tee and Green," "The Oarsmen," "Motors," "On the Air," "Horse Shows and Hunts," "The Race Track," "The Tennis Courts," and "New Apartments."

Brightest flashes, as they had always been, were the cartoons. The two-line caption appeared infrequently. Artists with individualistic styles and subject matter had refined the drawings. Soglow's were neater and had a sure touch.

He got an early grip on the sandwich-sign carriers. His men fitted their signs. One in a fur coat advertised a storage company, another wearing glasses represented an optician. Best of all was the naked man huckstering for a Turkish bath.

Peter Arno had dropped the "Whoops" girls and was bringing into focus two characters who were to serve him well. One was a lecherous, commanding, explosive, and aristocratic old gentleman with a white mustache. Most of the time the old boy pursued fair and presumably innocent maidens. But he could get excited about other things. Once when reading a tabloid he shouted: "Good Lord. They've misspelled grandma's name!" Arno's second best figure was a little man with a long, wispy mustache whom the young ladies pursued. As a rule he was seen lying in bed with a beautiful lass in a bursting nightgown. He never seemed exactly bored. But then he was never much interested either. "I was discussing the Mexican situation with Bottomly today," he said on one occasion to his voluptuous companion. "It seems fraught with interest."

A legend that sex jokes got in only when Ross didn't comprehend them has been widely accepted. Several writers have cited an Arno cartoon that showed a young couple appearing at a police station dragging an automobile seat, one saying, "We want to report a stolen car." The inference is that Ross didn't understand that the couple had taken the seat out of the car to make love on. Marc Connelly had passed the idea to Ross from a girl who had originated it, and the usual small payment was sent to her. Ross in turn passed the idea along to Arno. Once Arno had drawn the cartoon he owned the idea, since the New Yorker allows its artists to benefit exclusively from subsidiary sales. Connelly is still smoldering because the girl received no share of two hundred dollars a movie company later paid Arno for use of the idea.

The legend of Ross's blindness to sex-situation humor grew, of course, out of fear that he *might* miss a point. Sex humor was a fairly important part of the formula, and some of it was in questionable taste. The magazine several times repeated an Arno drawing of a guest necking his host's wife in a porch swing. In one gag line he thanked her for a pleasant week end. Others were in a similar vein.

Helen Hokinson had taken so firm a grip on fat women that for any other artist to try them was almost presumptuous. A series of cover paintings had a very plump, uppish lady busy about town, always with the aid of her butler or chauffeur. One or the other baited her hook when she fished, brought her picnic hamper when she lunched under a tree, handed her water-color brushes to her. Hoky did children, too, and did them well. Said a boy to a department store Santa: "You know damn well what I want for Christmas! I told you last Saturday at Loeser's."

Most of the New Yorker cartoons reflected the times, the city, and the mildly editorial attitude toward what people were up to. A man went for his gun and shot down another who had succumbed to the "Ask Me Another" craze. A woman shopper inquired of a clerk: "Who endorsed this cream?" An intellectual type said to a friend: "I'd love to visit with you but I'm on my way to discuss *Strange Interlude*." A man pleaded with his analyst: "Don't you think, Doctor, in view of my marked improvement I might resume my affection for my mother?"

Probably the most famous of all New Yorker artists was required, though a staff member, to break into print elsewhere. Ross thought he was being kidded when White and others suggested that Thurber's scratch-pad animals and people ought to be used in the magazine. True enough, Thurber's draftsmanship was, technically speaking, no better on the hundred millionth sawed-off dog than it had been on the first millionth. (Some years later he claimed to have achieved a certain tightening of his lack of technique.)

Finally White officially submitted a Thurber drawing to the art conference. It was drawn with a pencil on a sheet of yellow paper and showed a seal on a rock watching the approach of some explorers. The seal's simple comment: "Hm. Explorers!" In an indulgent note Rea Irvin pointed out that the seal's whiskers went the wrong way and drew a picture showing nature's way with them. White resubmitted the drawing with the comment: "This is the way a Thurber seal's whiskers go." This time it was rejected without a message.

Thurber's drawings were first accepted as illustrations for a book, *Is Sex Necessary?* by White and himself, which was published by Harper in the fall of 1929. The two authors carried their manuscript and a sheaf of Thurber's drawings to the publisher's reception room, where, White reported later, they had a desultory and seemingly unsatisfactory interview with Eugene Saxton, the editor. The lowest note was struck when White spread the drawings out on the floor.

"These, I take it," said Saxton, "are the rough sketches for the drawings themselves."

"No," White replied cheerfully, "these are the drawings themselves."

Thurber was not prepared to argue for the drawings. But White was determined. He had bought a bottle of waterproof ink and inked in some of the drawings. Thurber, who drew with light pencil strokes, had required only a few minutes to dash off the illustrations. It took White hours to ink them. "The difference," he explained, "between genius and pluck." After some thought the Harper editors decided to use them.

As the 1920s drew to a close a vast stream of books on sex and marriage flowed to the public, not always in plain wrappers. To Thurber and White it seemed that, the way things were going, sex as nature intended it was on the way out. After a while people would just sit around and read sex books. Boldly they undertook to save the human race from extinction. They also hoped to make some money.

Is Sex Necessary? was a pretty good example of the White-Thurber attitude toward life and humor which readers spoke of as "New Yorkerish."

The dedication read: "To Daisy and Jeanie." It was not explained that these were Scotty dogs. Jeanie, Thurber's dog, was the mother of Daisy, White's dog. Thurber bred dogs and sometimes entered them in shows. White went along to one and was impressed with Thurber's training methods. When a dog wouldn't get up on a bench Thurber jumped on the bench himself, on his hands and knees, and shouted, "Damn it, like this!"

In Thurber's opening chapter, "The Nature of the American Male: A study in Pedestalism," he expressed concern about man's worship of woman. But in a moment the sound of trumpets was heard and Thurber was caught up in the war between the sexes. He plainly believed that the legions of women were the mightier, and the better generaled.

The chapters were unsigned, although the pronoun "I" was employed. The casual reader may not have been aware of any difference in the chapters' authorship, but they revealed the chief differences between White and Thurber as humorists. Thurber concerned himself mainly with individuals. He recorded, for example, the shattering experiences of a young husband whose bride had been taught by her mother to believe that children are conceived by the presence of bluebirds. The war between wife and husband was always brought down to the specific. Dealing with the boxed-in feeling that husbands get, he wrote: "He will strive to get out of the home, and his wife should allow him to go." Thurber's basic approach was fictional. He created scenes and individuals.

White wrote as an essayist, dealing with general problems. His chapter, "The Sexual Revolution," while very funny, might have been turned into a serious essay by a relatively small amount of stripping and adjusting. The sexual revolution, he explained, had begun with man's discovery that he was not attractive to woman, as such. "The lion had his mane, the peacock his gorgeous plumage, but Man found himself in a three-button sack suit." Man therefore had to find a substitute, and inadvertently became intelligent.

Man put some thought to selecting a mate, with consequent worries. He feared that she might grow fat, that if only he waited twenty-four hours longer some better mate would turn up—the girl, maybe, of his fantasies. Woman then made a grave error. She chose to imitate man. (There was, of course, a discrepancy between the views of Drs. Thurber and White. Thurber never did get woman off her pedestal. White hauled her down right away.)

White credited New York with being the capital of the sexual revolution, partly because of its magnificent harbor, partly because of its queer-shaped apartments, especially those in Greenwich Village. Young ladies flocked to the big city, bent on erotic experiences, though they always told their mothers it was concerts they were after. Unfortunately the erotic impulses were usually sublimated by making parchment lampshades and being literary. "She had a way of leading young men on into exhilarating topics, and sitting with him in provocative attitudes, and then putting on her hat and going quietly home to bed." Later on she stepped placidly into an old-fashioned marriage.

The question in the book's title wasn't answered, but 40,000 copies were sold, making quite a little extra pocket money for the authors. White took his share and stepped into marriage, with Katharine Angell, who had been divorced some years earlier. The parents of Thurber and White read the book, blushed, and were sorry they had ever let their boys go to the city.

Harper had felt impelled to ask White to explain Thurber's art to the readers. White spoke of the "uncanny faithfulness with which he has caught—caught and thrown to the floor—the daily, indeed the almost momentary, severity of life's mystery, as well as the charming doubtfulness of its purpose." To White, Thurber's men were perplexed, frustrated, or frightened, while the women seemed better adjusted. When someone suggested to Thurber that his women lacked sex appeal he replied, "They have for my men."

Ross used only a little of *Is Sex Necessary?* in the New Yorker, but in a series about a Mr. Monroe, Thurber was developing his theory of the war between men and women. Mr. Monroe was a small and timid man with a large imagination. One time when his wife, who was not afraid of anything, went to town to visit her mother she left him to hold the fort. There were strange noises and, though he had a gun, he ended by driving to the station to wait for her.

Sinclair Lewis told Thurber, "I read you into Mr. Monroe and I admire you. Everybody's afraid to stay alone in a house at night, but you said so."

Mr. Monroe could buck himself up by identifying himself with the hero of something he was reading. Few more imperturbable men were at the ship the day Mrs. Monroe came back from Europe. He was so cooly poised, as a matter of fact, that she knew he had been reading something. Everything would have been all right had she not confided that twelve bottles of benedictine were concealed in her luggage. While she was clearing customs he began to get shaky. He imagined himself in the witness chair, listening to a devilish prosecutor read a letter purported to be in his own handwriting. Mr. Monroe began to protest audibly, and Mrs. Monroe had to shush him.

Ross, the cold realist where his magazine was concerned, troubled himself, now that he could afford to, with getting the advertising matter into a companionable relationship with the text. It should be typographically pleasing to the eye, he felt, and the sensibilities of aesthetic readers should be taken into consideration. Fleischmann and the others of the business department were wholly in accord with the concept. Deodorants, laxatives (including yeast), and bathroom accessories were declared out of bounds. A rule was laid down that when the advertising department was dubious about a piece of copy Katharine Angell would read it for taste.

The New Yorker made an uncalculated contribution to the advertising profession. Merchandisers and agency men, desiring to brighten their copy, noticed the eye-catching qualities of the cartoons. The art department received inquiries about the purchase of drawings. The struggling artists were happy enough to oblige, but Ross was leary of overcommercializing the talent he was creating. As it turned out, the work of the artists appearing in advertisements drew attention to the magazine. Writers were also hired to turn out copy. And so the New Yorker was at least partly responsible for bringing a lighter touch to advertising.

Ross was rapidly outdistancing his competitors in the humor and sophistication field. *Vanity Fair*, sticking to its formula of bright essays, shiny caricatures, beautiful photographs, and reproductions of modern, usually European, art, was coming nearer than the others to keeping the pace. Crowninshield liked big names and the owners of the big names liked to appear in *Vanity Fair's* glossy pages. Otherwise they wouldn't have been there, for the magazine's pay was low. Fairly regular contributors were Walter Lippmann, Percy Hammond, Aldous Huxley, Heywood Broun, Sherwood Anderson, André Gide, Deems Taylor, Arthur Schnitzler, Edmund Wilson, Dorothy Parker, W. O. McGeehan, Alexander Woollcott, William Bolitho, and Harold Nicholson. The only concession Crowninshield made was to run more parodies. Most of them were by Corey Ford, who signed some with his own name and some "John Riddell," who was described as a Welshman of great reticence. Each issue of *Vanity Fair* carried about as much advertising as a contemporary number of the New Yorker. The latter was issued, of course, slightly more than four times as often.

Life appeared totally unaware of the New Yorker's phenomenal rise and the revolution being worked in humor. Charles Dana Gibson was still boss. Robert E. Sherwood was editor and movie reviewer and Robert Benchley was theater critic. John Kieran wrote sports, Elmer Davis editorials, and Walter Winchell conducted a department called "Along the Main Stem." None was given much space, for the average issue was only 32 pages. Even the Christmas numbers seldom rose above 48. All the advertisements *Life* ran in a year could have been fitted handily into four or five of the bigger issues of the New Yorker.

An exclusive reader of *Life* had no way of knowing that

the two-line caption was out of date, that real situations could be amusing. Gag lines were designed, apparently, to spell out wheezes for twelve-year-olds. One picture showed a boy running to pick up the train of a lady's dress. The caption: "Feudal Lord: 'Hey, boy!' Page: 'Can't stop now—I'm hurrying to catch a train!' " A picture showed a Negro servant standing before an author at his desk. Caption: "Why, Columbia, you are not leaving?" "I is, boss; dey tell me you is one of dem ghos' writers."

Even the Christmas issues of *Judge* seldom ran more than 32 pages. Norman Anthony, with whom Ross in 1924 had hotly debated the best way to run a humor magazine, was now *Judge's* sole editor. George Jean Nathan covered theater and Pare Lorentz the movies. But *Judge* relied chiefly on a hodgepodge of cartoons and he-she jokes. One cartoon showed a half-finished painting of a woman on a signboard that covered the side of a tall building. A painter was talking with his partner, who was down on the street. "Sign Painter: 'How's she look from there, Bill?' 'O.K.—but move the ear up about three stories.' "

Coasting Uphill 13

The depression years were the greatest of the New Yorker's first quarter century. The humorists matured, yet were still in the bloom and power of their youth. (For some reason not a single major American writing humorist started his career after the stock market crash of the autumn of 1929.) Ross's magic formula, invented for an era of prosperity and gaiety, turned out to be even better for the years of darkness. Advertising declined, but not by so much as that of most other publications. Circulation rose from 77,500 in 1929 to 121,000 in 1931. In 1934 it was 125,000.

Ross, who became thirty-seven years old a month after Wall Street began to totter, had become an important, though oddly obscure, figure in the publishing world. Suppression of his editorial identity left him a stranger to his readers and a man of mystery in the trade. He seldom mingled with fellow editors, and those who did know him got little hint of his theories and practices, since he rarely talked shop. The general view held by his associates and fostered by Ross was that he simply lacked interest in what anyone thought about him. Some believed that another factor or two might be involved. One was his desperate fear of ridicule—though a satirical view of others remained a fairly important part of the formula. Therefore he wanted to keep out of the public's gaze. Another suggestion was a possible fear that, since he didn't look the part of the editor of the New Yorker, his beloved creation might suffer from his public association with it. This was in line with the opinion, held firmly by some members of the Algonquin set, that the magazine had become so intertwined with Ross's personality that separation of the two was neither possible nor, for him, desirable. He had always said that he would give at most ten years to the New Yorker, before moving to new fields. Though only five years had gone by, he could easily have expended a large share of his energy in another direction without harm to his first-born. He did continue to talk about launching a true crime magazine, and even got John T. Winterich to work up plans. One of Ross's close friends was Ray Schindler, owner of a private detective agency. But Ross decided that businessmen wouldn't put enough advertising into a crime magazine to make it pay.

From Hearst-owned *Harper's Bazaar* there began to issue rumors that a rival to the New Yorker was in preparation. Ross's fierce pride in his creation redoubled and, surrounded by his staff, he grimly awaited the onslaught. It didn't come, probably because of the depression. If it had, the going for it would have been difficult. (Heavily backed imitations of the New Yorker have been started at one time or another in Philadelphia, Chicago, Boston, and other cities. All have failed.)

Nerves were jangled again when a rumor swept the office that Henry R. Luce had bought New Yorker stock with the intention of getting control. The story had it that he expected to give the magazine to Clare Boothe, whom he was planning to marry, as a wedding gift. She was managing editor of *Vanity Fair* at the time. Ross's galloping contempt for the Luce publications was well known, and as the rumor assumed galelike proportions the staff began to feel as sorry for him as for themselves.

It was finally ascertained that Luce *had* purchased a substantial block of stock—about a hundred thousand dollars' worth. Terror yielded to fury. What traitor, what rat, was guilty of selling?

He was soon exposed. Name: Harold W. Ross.

Fears of the staff turned out, however, to be unfounded. Ross wanted to invest in something else and had been ready to put the stock on the market. Ralph Ingersoll, who had moved into a top job on *Fortune*, had negotiated the deal as a straight financial investment for the Luce enterprises. The stock was resold later in other operations.

No one familiar with the wild, topsy-turvy New Yorker operation would have been surprised to learn that at one time Ross unknowingly was in competition with himself. John Hanrahan, Fleischmann's consultant, had become publisher of *Stage*, a monthly aiming at largely the same readers—and consequently the same advertisers—as the New Yorker. To finance it, Hanrahan had enlisted the backing of Fleischmann, who, with the board's approval, was using New Yorker funds for the purpose. Ross's contemptuous hands-off attitude toward business affairs prevented him from knowing anything about it.

Only the loyalty of the majority of the editorial staff kept Ross from being unseated during a palace revolt. It was generally believed around the office that Fleischmann backed it as another effort to at least clip Ross's wings. The form taken was an argument that Ross was tired and deserved a rest. If necessary, this good thing would be forced upon him.

The revolution collapsed before Ross knew about it. At any rate he didn't let on that he did. Later he steadfastly refused to admit that the rebels had meant any harm. "There is no real duplicity in them," he told a loyal staffer.

Ross had gained the deep—often emotional—loyalty of most staff members chiefly because of their attachment to his editorial ideals. Those who stayed acquired a good deal of his own fanaticism. Whenever one did depart, say for Hollywood, Ross sincerely wished him success, though convinced that, if not a downright traitor, he was a weak character who had deserted for a handful of silver.

One time when Ross was visiting Hollywood a publicity man asked him to comment on former New Yorker writers whose contributions had forwarded the moving picture industry. Calling for a typewriter, Ross sat down and tapped out a statement to the effect that not a single writer worth his salt had ever left the New Yorker for Hollywood.

Ross in turn became loyal to the brilliant helpers who remained with him—became, as a matter of fact, ever the fiercer father, the patriarch fending off hostile destroying forces. He had learned also that in the bosom of his family the father should not be unduly harsh, that understanding and tenderness are at least as important to a creative person's productive ability as a galloping neurosis. The suicide of Ralph Barton, the artist, shook him badly. Barton had told him several times of the contemplated act, but Ross had believed that anyone who talked of suicide wouldn't do it. Afterward he couldn't escape a feeling that he might somehow have stopped it. He began to take a deeper interest in personal troubles, and he could show rare tenderness coupled with hard-boiled practicality.

More important, Ross had learned the value of showing appreciation. He realized that writers and artists need more than anything else a sense of importance in their work. He found a way to express his pleasure for an outstanding accomplishment if only by a compliment expressed personally or by a note. Those who wanted to try something new got his encouragement. Thurber has stated that Ross's major quality as an editor in the early days was willingness to give writers a free rein. True, Ross had discouraged Thurber. But in the end perseverance had won, and perseverance is one of the more valuable qualities editors find in writers.

With more money at his disposal, Ross was working out a plan to give his creative workers a measure of security. It had to be a complicated plan, for he was sure that if *too* secure they would lie all day under apples trees, doing nothing. The wolf had at least to be in sight, he believed.

One of the first to benefit in a fairly typical way from Ross's system was Frank Sullivan, who, though a staff writer for the *World*, had contributed regularly. Ross considered Sullivan one of his best humorists. When the *World* folded in 1931, Sullivan found himself out in the cold, scared. There weren't many newspaper jobs and anyhow he was pretty sure he had been ruined by the by-line. Sullivan occupies a niche in journalism as the only newspaperman who was ever sorry (he still is) that the privilege of signing his work was offered.

When he went to work on the *Herald* in 1919, Sullivan, a small, round, retiring youth from Saratoga Springs, felt good merely to have landed a job in the big city. After a while he moved to the *Sun* and was put on rewrite. He had a quiet, pixy sense of humor that he translated easily into his copy. Leg men who had got hold of something funny called in and demanded, "Gimme Sullivan." He sat pleasantly, tapping out the copy. He liked to sit. When off duty he moved from one bar to another under some protest.

The *World*, to which he moved in 1922, thrust the by-line upon him. With Heywood Broun, Franklin P. Adams, and other stars he shared the famed opposite-editorial feature page. Most of the shining writers had offices. Sullivan chose to occupy a desk in the city room. He was the kind who, if a cub sat down at his typewriter by mistake, waited unobtrusively until it was free. His columns were in the nonsense school and often dealt with his imaginary secretary, Martha Hepplethwaite, who wore garters with bells on them. A couple of introductory paragraphs to a book of his collected pieces is fairly typical of his work.

> The book was shaping itself nicely along those [monumental] lines when one day not long ago, as the manuscript lay on a table near an open window, a storm came up and a wind whisked the sheets from under my very nose and scattered them to the four winds. Oh, there were *more* than four winds that day. I counted seven. There must have been nine or ten in all.
>
> It was impossible to retrieve all the sheets. Many of them had been buried in remote, inaccessible sections of the subway excavation in the street outside. Others were filched by the spies who had been stationed outside the house by rival authors immediately after the rumor spread that the book would be monumental. . . .

It was after the arrival of fame that the by-line—Sullivan has called it the Iron Maiden—began to torture. Sullivan didn't care much whether people said his stuff was good. He did hate it when they said, "You weren't quite up to standard today." He longed to be back on rewrite, turning out an occasional funny piece if asked to, not caring greatly whether it turned out flat. On the other hand, it would be bothersome to answer people who demanded, "What's happened to you, Sullivan—dried up, get fired, or what?" He let the by-line ride.

Even before the *World* folded the mellow nonsense essays and quips of the great humorists were on their way out of daily journalism. Sullivan was faced with trying to make a living as a free lance in a tightening market, and he was without a sufficient financial backlog for it. Ross inquired how much money he had been making on the *World*. When Sullivan told him, Ross said he would deposit a check for a like sum to Sullivan's account every week. He would do it for a year. Payment for whatever the New Yorker bought would be applied against the debt.

At the end of the year Sullivan owed around fifteen hundred dollars. But he had sold fairly widely to other magazines and felt confident. Ross did not ask for the cash, nor did he levy totally on subsequent contributions. Ten per cent was subtracted until the debt was almost liquidated, after which the deductions were simply stopped.

The "drawing account" system, as finally worked out, was more complicated. Writers and artists drew fixed weekly stipends or lump sums, as they chose, which were liquidated when contributions were accepted. This provided a degree of security, and, for the larger producers at least, went a long way toward solving the free lance's problem. Some were not happy. They likened themselves to sharecroppers who go to the landlords for loans to pay grocery bills and repay them out of their crop—if they get a crop.

Artists or writers whose crops didn't come in were left in debt. The magazine thus did not *guarantee* anything. If, for example, a writer were assigned to a profile and the material proved inadequate, he took the loss. A newspaper reporter would have drawn his salary no matter what happened. The strain of sitting at a typewriter, palms sweating, trying to work out of debt by being amusing, was too much for some and they cracked.

On the whole the system was advantageous for creative people because Ross was never overly harsh about the debts.

Money could not be paid out forever, naturally, without something usable for the magazine coming back. But a man who worked for a year without getting more than an acceptance or two could usually be depended on to leave under his own power. He was rarely pursued, but if he got an acceptance later he was expected to pay something—perhaps ten per cent—on account.

The greater concern for individuals did not mean that peace and quiet reigned. Ross still drove people crazy by tearing up the magazine at the last minute. His punctuation, grammar, and fact manias grew bigger than ever. In the old days he had been limited to expressing vigorous doubt about a writer's facts. Now he was building a checking department like nothing ever seen in magazine publishing—except at *Time*. Anyone who gave a fact, however small, to a reporter was in grievous error if he thought he was finished with the matter. The checkers were apt to ask all over again and perhaps cross-examine him.

Ross was doing more editing himself, carrying home a crammed brief case at night and for week ends. He had become a fine technical editor as well as an intuitive one. When he wanted to and had the time he could sit down with a writer and explain how weak spots could be shored up. But usually he confined himself to written comments. His later famed "What mean?", "Who he?", and the like began to appear on manuscripts and proofs. He preferred to work on proofs. Sometimes he drew a line through a stretch of type and ordered simply, "Fix." "Fix" was a favorite word. A bad piece of writing took a lot out of him. When badly upset he made a kind of frantic double curlicue which editors and writers understood to mean that he had passed beyond the state of coherency. The mark looked something like "ge" or "ga," and it became known as "the terrible gay." Other editors adopted the practice of making scathing queries and comments. These, along with Ross's, were often toned down before being shown to writers.

With a weighty editorial budget and a strong flow of copy, Ross could be choosy. His judgments were still largely intuitive, even hunchy, and he didn't always take time to explain them. A writer's morale suffered when a piece on which he had worked for months was discarded for a reason obscure or downright unintelligible to him. Artists were asked to try and try again without being given specific suggestions, until often they threw the drawing away in disgust.

Ross was wandering less about the offices, and his key-jangling had almost stopped. But now and then he dropped into somebody's cubbyhole with the question, "Are we important?" The answer usually was, in line with the customary outward cynicism: "We're only a fifteen-cent magazine."

Out of the office Ross was beginning to conduct himself more like the top-hatted gentleman of the anniversary cover, in a roughhouse sort of way. His marriage with Jane Grant had ended in 1929. As one of the town's more eligible bachelors, he was turning into something of a gay dog. Among his residences during the early years of his new bachelorhood were, fittingly, the Ritz and a Park Avenue apartment. He allowed his hair to grow longer and it more or less lay on his head. Yet despite his cosmopolite background, which he liked to enlarge on, there remained something rustic about him. His clothes were of good material but the fitters weren't able to make a clotheshorse of him. He had to be careful about drinking. There was his bad stomach, and cold drinks made his front teeth ache. Sometimes he filtered cold drinks into his mouth through a napkin. At best there was a good deal of spilling and the method did not sweep the fashionable set.

For a while big Ed McNamara, known on the stage as the singing cop, shared his apartment. This was while Ross was between wives. McNamara's gaiety and vast charm made him a welcome guest, sometimes for years, in the homes of Heywood Broun and other celebrities. But the prevailing opinion was that when living with Ross he earned the roof over his head by keeping his host out of the clutches of unscrupulous females. His task was made no easier by Ross's fear that some lady would commit suicide in his presence. One of his brokenhearted lady friends had a habit, after numerous drinks, of showing up at his door late at night and shouting through it that she intended to do away with herself then and there. It was McNamara's job to sally forth and quiet her.

Ross's mother, who had come on from Salt Lake City, was distressed by the night life he was leading and constantly admonished him to get in by eleven o'clock. He was unusually solicitous of his mother, and making excuses to her kept his imagination busy. When he got in at 3 or 4 A.M. she was often waiting up for him, and his explanations grew more elaborate. Once he told her that at eleven, just as he was starting home, his host had suddenly locked all the doors and said, "No one will leave this house until three o'clock in the morning." Mrs. Ross said she had never heard of such a thing in her life.

Another time, desperate, Ross told her that he had been attending a men's embroidery class and had got so interested in his embroidery that he hadn't noticed the hour. She was pleased and he was pleased with his excuse. And then she asked to see some examples of his work. He began telephoning women, asking, "Do you know where I can get hold of a doily or two that looks as though it had been embroidered by a man?"

Some of Ross's friends were not above taking advantage of the situation. One day Mrs. Ross saw Harold with dark circles under his eyes and looking rather haggard. She consulted Ed McNamara about Ross's health. Was he working too hard, or what? No, McNamara said, it wasn't that. It was that terrible gym Harold went to every day. Harold was *such* a fiend for exercise. Mrs. Ross thought it was nice that Harold exercised. McNamara said yes, it was, but he didn't know whether Harold ought to chin himself a hundred times and fly about on the trapezes the way he did. When Ross came in his mother gave him a lecture about overdoing the trapeze. He promised to cut down.

Mrs. Ross was proud that her son had made good in the city and had many people working for him, even though his offices were dreadfully untidy. She expressed the belief that he had reached a point where he could sell out and get a job with the *Saturday Evening Post,* a magazine both she and her friends read.

Ross's love of horseplay and his passion for gambling continued undiminished. He played cards regularly with what remained of the Thanatopsis Literary and Inside Straight Club. While other men at parties made *bon mots* for the entertainment of the ladies, Ross was dragging people upstairs for gaming. His bumptious self-confidence had increased, if anything, since the days when it had irritated F.P.A. to the point of public outcry. But his ability to win wasn't much greater than it had ever been.

A gambling bout at the home of George S. Kaufman, the playwright, illustrated Ross's blind confidence and the kind of broad humor he liked. Kaufman was giving a party for two publishers, Bennett Cerf of Random House and Harold

Guinzburg of Viking Press, who were leaving the following morning for a tour of Russia. Ross challenged them sharply to go upstairs and get their ears beat off at backgammon. They agreed to play three games. At the finish Ross was in the hole. He remarked that if they weren't scared they would give him a chance to break even and go ahead, as their respective playing abilities warranted.

Cerf had some jokes he wanted to tell around and was anxious to be off. But Guinzburg offered to play for both. A couple of hours later when the players came downstairs, Cerf could tell from their expressions that he had made some money.

The two publishers departed next morning before there was a chance to collect their winnings—a matter of about fifteen hundred dollars apiece. In Russia they bought some rubles and discovered that owing to the favorable rate of exchange a long cable could be sent to the United States for about thirty-five cents. Every day they dispatched a cable to Ross in which they spoke cuttingly of people who allow friends to set off for far lands without paying monies owed to them. Ross enjoyed the insults, but, totting up the cable costs in dollars, he concluded they had gone mad.

Fairly typical of Ross's practical jokes was his use of a fluid which, when spread on a chair, made whoever sat down feel that his kidneys were about to let go. His detective friend, Ray Schindler, and Ed McNamara were his main cohorts on this one, and Heywood Broun was probably their best subject. Broun's face was very expressive. Guests who had been let in on the joke were able to watch the play of expressions across his face for a full five minutes before he excused himself politely and scampered for the bathroom. It was the only time anyone ever saw Broun scamper.

A natural stamping ground for Ross was the fabulous

booby-trapped house of Joe Cook, the stage comedian. Ross was a close friend of Dave Chasen, Cook's straight man. Cook's guests might be bundled into automobiles and told they were on their way to a hidden rural speakeasy. They would be driven over back roads for hours. Finally they would halt at the rear of a house. A door panel would swing open and a bald pink-faced man would stick his head out suspiciously. The head would belong to Marc Connelly. Inside the travelers would find Ross behind the bar wearing a long and spotless apron. They were back at Cook's.

Ross decided in 1934 to give up his bachelor-around-town role, and married Frances Elie, a beautiful girl of French descent about a dozen years his junior. They moved to Fairfield County, Connecticut, not far from Stamford, in the heart of literary suburbia. Among his neighbors were Broun, Westbrook Pegler, George Bye, Deems Taylor, John Erskine, and Ursula Parrott. Commuting time to New York was about forty-five minutes. Not many years had gone by since he had hurled the charge of treason at those who spent all afternoon catching the five-fifteen.

The New Yorker was slow to get into the subject of depression. The stock market break in the fall of 1929 was hardly noticed at first, and then was treated lightly. The magazine's most effective attitude—the combination of sense and nonsense—was present in a "Comment" item a little more than a month after the initial crash.

Fear, running through the jungle like flame, strong as ever. Doom still makes a crackling sound, like summer thunder. Thousands of minor clerks and small tradespeople, hearing faint noises of railroads they had never seen, mines they had never worked, steel they had never tempered, fled before the terror of dark. Then came the voices. Two hundred and five for twenty-five thousand steel, said a Morgan, gritting his teeth. The fundamental business of the country is on a sound and prosperous basis, said President Hoover. No buildings were burned down, no industries have died, no mines, no railroads have vanished, crooned Arthur Brisbane. The great comforters. There, there, my children. Try and catch a little sleep. Mother is near.

The collapse of the market, over and above the pain, couldn't help but be amusing. It is amusing to see a fat land quivering in paunchy fright. The quake, furthermore, verified our suspicion that our wise and talky friends hadn't known for months what they were talking about when they were discussing stocks. Forcing us to breakfast on copper and oil, dine on sugar and food products, and sleep with rails and motors, they had succeeded in boring us to the breaking point. Uninformed dreamers, running a fever. Then came the debacle. They still talked, in husky voices; but we at least had the satisfaction of knowing that it was costing them anywhere from a hundred to two hundred and fifty dollars a word every time they opened their mouths. Many of them have gone quietly back to work. They may not be the most useful citizens in the world, but from now on when they talk they'll talk about their business or their love affairs and know a little something of what they're talking about.

What finally stemmed the tide and averted an actual panic in Wall Street was not the intervention of the bankers but the arrival in town of the Rodeo. Things had come to such a pass that nobody had faith in anything. What restored the public's confidence in the national speculative life was the sight of the men from the West, who would take their chances with a bucking horse for a prize of fifty dollars. Wall Street took one look at the horses, heard their hooves banging the sides of the chutes, and decided that the gambling spirit had not quite died out.

The psychology of boom was still reflected in the magazine's pages. A cartoon showed two men at the side of a construction project, one saying: "It's going to be the biggest, or the tallest, or the somethingest building in the city." A workman on a skyscraper asked: "I've lost track, Jim. How many stories we got to go yet?" Diners in a roof restaurant looked far down on the spire of the Chrysler Building, the largest in the world, pending completion of the Empire State Building. The Rockefellers had made plans for a vast project to be called Radio City. Lewis Mumford had denounced the project in "The Sky Line" department and the editors shared his dread of "the organized chaos of the Rockefellian dream." Later on a cartoon character said of an acquaintance: "He's quite sophisticated—he's against Radio City."

At first the New Yorker cartoons depicted only upper-income crash sufferers who were not to be greatly pitied. Observing an elderly gentleman, a coupon-clipping type, sitting disconsolately alone on a park bench, a passer-by remarked: "They were an ideal pair until he sold her United Shipping at forty-two and a half." A businessman pointing to a downward sales curve said to his wife: ". . . and you ask for sables." A dignified old boy minding his apple stand bade a swanky friend good-by: "Well, so long. I'll see you at lunch at the Bankers Club." A lady told her milliner: "Let me see some plain, simple little hats—something I can wear in my unemployment work."

Most readers, sick of what they saw in the newspaper, were happy for a brief escape into the New Yorker's calm pages. But occasionally, as distress mounted, a really somber note was struck. White was the man to do it, and "Comment" the place.

We walked over to Union Square the other morning to dry out our soul in the sun, and sat a while with the dismal on the benches—the men who were thinking, and waiting. (We ourself were only waiting.) Before leaving the Square, we read the motto on the monument, a quotation from Thomas Jefferson:

"How little do my countrymen know what precious blessings they are in possession of. . . ." Uneasily we glanced around at our countrymen. The only precious blessing most of them were in possession of was the cup of coffee they had recently got from the relief shanty nearby. In such graven words, it seemed to us, the disconsolate must taste the ultimate bile.—*By E. B. White, from "Notes and Comments," March 5, 1932.*

A book had appeared which tried to eke humor out of suggesting silly jobs people might try. White mixed acid with his ink.

Such suggestions are funny till you realize that many an intelligent man now starts his day wondering whether there isn't a wheelbarrow somewhere he could paint, or an escaped canary bird he could capture for the reward. Being out of a job perforates the walls of the mind, and thoughts seep off into strange channels. To say that the country is as rich as it ever was is a joke: something is gone that used to be here—the spirit of millions of men is gone, and a man's spirit is just as real a national resource as gold or wheat or lumber. A few weeks ago a motley bunch of ex-soldiers descended on Washington to ask for a handout. They were tagged bonus-grabbers, and got short shrift, which is what their cause deserved. Yet that army was something more than just a lobby: it was the expression of men's desire to huddle together when their courage is gone. Going to Washington meant a change of scene, a temporary escape from the aimlessness of idleness, and they jumped at the chance. This is something our statesmen and economists might well consider: the establishing of a real Army, to give men a change of scene and a change of heart; an army in which men could enlist for a short term, not to destroy the enemy, but to recapture their own souls.—*By E. B. White, from "Notes and Comments," July 2, 1932.*

(Not long after Roosevelt took office he set up a Civilian Conservation Corps, whose youthful members, gathered in

CCC camps, were employed in preserving forests and other natural resources. "Comment" remarked the prompt attention given its suggestion.)

Once the baselessness of President Hoover's optimistic promises had been established, the cartoonists began to have real fun—much of it devastating. In one of a series titled, "The Turning of the Tide," J. P. Morgan helped things along by purchasing a doll from a pushcart dealer. In another a Canadian trapper was commissioned to bag two beavers. A third was captioned: "The Hoover anti-hoarding commission induces Master Peter Delancy Witherspoon to deposit the contents of his penny bank." The commissioners wore high hats. An apple seller displayed a sign, "Business going on as usual during alterations," while he hammered a nail into his packing box. Following a brief flurry in Wall Street, "Talk" added a factual note: "The forlorn gentleman who sells apples at the corner of Forty-fifth and Madison Avenue put up a little sign on his stand last Friday: 'The rise in the stock market does not affect my prices.' "

With less anger but equal accuracy the cartoonists reflected other social phenomena. A minister declared from his pulpit: "And, may I add, there are still a few desirable apartments available over the church, with free gas, electric refrigeration, and maid service." A dowager declared apprehensively: "We can't simply dismiss the talk of revolution, my dear. This morning Burke neglected to touch his cap." Increasing radicalism, especially of youth, was noticed. "I'd like to hire a hall suitable for a small political convention," a long-haired young man told a renting agent. Even the children of the rich were affected. On the porch of a sumptuous house a girl introduced one youth to another: "Mr. Elliott, too, is an ardent Socialist." The bitterness of intellectual youth was caught in a picture of a mother pleading with a heavily thatched, spectacled lad sitting at a typewriter: "Aw, be a good boy and leave your pa out of your novel."

After Roosevelt's inaugural the editors, like nearly everybody else, went along on the honeymoon. Benchley noted in "The Wayward Press" that the newspaper headline writers were experimenting with the President's initials, some liking "FR," others "FD." Benchley liked "FR." One of the more famous of the New Yorker cartoons, and one of the few dealing with real-life individuals, had a coal miner looking up from his work and exclaiming: "For gosh sakes, here comes Mrs. Roosevelt." It was by Robert Day. There were other comments on the economic and political scene. During the early mad days of NRA, Arno's wispy little man lay beside his voluptuous young lady, remarking, "Codification, codification, codification! Where will it end?" A shovel-wielder declared: "Oil, gold, maybe basements—the CWA just said dig."

But for the New Yorker audience there was a more fascinating upheaval in the body politic. Prohibition was on the way out, and the speakeasy generation watched with mingled titillation and trepidation. A cartoon showed a man nailing up a bock beer sign while a speakeasy proprietor watched from underneath the steps of a nearby brownstone house. Before many gallons of legal, three-point-two beer had gone down the gullets of the populace Benchley, unable to find that Home, American Womanhood, or Part Singing had benefited, demanded the return of needle beer. When strong drink was finally legalized, "Comment" suggested to the Waldorf that it fix up a fake speakeasy for memory's sake, and worried whether Schrafft's restaurants, if they put in martinis, would be able to resist the little dab of whipped cream on top.

The whole thing was summed up by a young ex-Harvard man named Ogden Nash, who had taken to writing verses which gleamed brightly in the formula.

I think it will probably be quite a spell
Before I and a great many others can get used to having a drink in a hotel.
Not that I especially plume myself on holding any brief for the speakeasy, for I think that in consideration of services rendered everybody of common decency ought to hold a brief, or at least a brief two minutes' silence, for the speakeasy,
For I do not know where we would have been without Jack and Charlie and Mac in the fourteen years preceding the happy day when the Crusaders and Mrs. Sabin were able to cry "Veni, vide, vicisi!"
But after all those years of intimate and secluded sipping I find that to order and drink a drink in a hotel
Gives me the naked fceling of a scallop torn from its shell,
And sitting in a dining-room full of 500 assorted debutantes and dowagers all engaged in trifling with alcoholic nectar and ambrosia
Makes we wonder why it was necessary in legalizing cocktails also to legalize such indecent exposia.
When I drink a drink in a hotel
I feel as unhappily open to the public as one of those unfortunates who live in tenements on Ninth Avenue where every time they dress or undress or brush their teeth or make love their actions are observed through the windows by interested passengers riding by on the El.
And in spite of the consoling fact that in a hotel you do not a bill as big as in a speakeasy run up,
The unconsoling fact remains that while quaffing the items that go to make up the bill you have the embarrassing sensations

of a mole above ground or a politician in church or a ghost caught out after sunup.
It seems sort of sacrilegious that the secret and mysterious rites of drinking
Should be carelessly revealed to the unthinking,
And a great pity to find liquor reduced to the state where it is something to be taken with meals normally
And is now merely a means to an end instead of being an end in itself as it was formerly.
Everything is so respectable and orderly that the process of imbibing has lost both drama
And glama,
And its humdrumness is even such
That nobody feels any more like taking just a little bit too much.
Having a drink in a hotel is an operation from which I am afraid I will for some time shrink.
Let's all go over to the hotel and have a drink.

Nash got the idea for his curious kind of verse from the labored country newspaper poetry which F.P.A. sometimes reprinted in "The Conning Tower"—a custom borrowed by the New Yorker. While working as a bond salesman and advertising man he had begun to contribute to F.P.A.'s column.

He had served time as a "Jesus." Ross met him for the first time in a speakeasy and, taking him for a man about town, and momentarily convinced that he was badly in need of a man about town, hired him on the spot. Much of Nash's time during the six weeks he lasted was taken up with searching the copy of Dorothy Parker and Benchley for double-entendres. (His successor was James M. Cain, who after *his* time had run out wrote the sensational novel *The Postman Always Rings Twice.* A list of celebrities who served their brief and inconspicuous hour at the New Yorker would be a long one.)

The magic formula fitted the depression, but there were other reasons why the first half of the thirties was the golden era of the New Yorker's first quarter century. It was probably as fine an all-around magazine—for entertainment, for literary quality, for journalism, for influence on the nation's culture—as any ever published in the United States. Most of the editors and contributors were fortunately the product of years without tension (the first World War did not seriously frazzle the nerves of many). The movies and radio were not yet absorbing talented young men and women before they had a chance to think of themselves as individuals. The magic formula was fluid, with no signs of the hardening which Ross so desperately feared.

Ross was now able to get the best work of the Round Tablers and others he had admired. Benchley had become theater critic besides writing "The Wayward Press." Ross was able to give him far more space than *Life*, along with an opportunity to wield the meat cleaver if desired. "The only new offering last week," he once wrote, "was a play called 'Perfectly Scandalous.' It was one of those plays in which all the characters, unfortunately, as it turned out, enunciated clearly."

Dorothy Parker substituted on theater and book reviews and contributed an occasional prose piece or bit of poetry. Alexander Woollcott was in fine fettle with his "Shouts and Murmurs." Franklin P. Adams occasionally provided a little poem or skit. Marc Connelly was available when pressed. Heywood Broun, angered by the widespread economic suffering, was generally pitched too high emotionally for the New Yorker, but he wrote with such ease that Ross knew he could always be pushed down to a typewriter in a pinch.

Frank Sullivan was developing a couple of specialties. He

put a "weather wit," a Mr. Tattersall, on the witness stand and allowed the district attorney to question him closely on weather repartee. It was the forerunner of Sullivan's celebrated reports on clichés. Mr. Tattersall's knowledge, as it turned out, was confined chiefly to weather, but Sullivan managed to locate a Mr. Arbuthnot, who worked in all fields. At Christmas time in 1933, Sullivan, feeling merrier than he had for some years, greeted his friends through the New Yorker's pages, starting off:

Hail, Yuletide, merry and jolly,
Season of mistletoe, Santa, and holly!

His annual greetings became a winter holiday feature.

Ross was happy, both for his magazine and for himself, to be able to employ, and pay well, Ring Lardner in the last years of his life. Ross kept another magazine's rejection of Lardner's masterpiece, "Golden Honeymoon," framed on a wall of his office. Not long after the New Yorker began, Ross had talked with Lardner about contributing regularly. The idea appealed to Lardner. But he had a large family which required a fairly heavy income. If Ross would pay him $500 a week he would write only what he really wanted to and turn it over to the magazine. Ross was excited but at the same time depressed. He didn't have the money.

Lardner had furnished small pieces from time to time over the years, but it was not until he lay mortally ill—he was in his late forties—that he began to contribute regularly. In the hospitals he had little to do except listen to the radio, and, since he hated most of what he heard, the criticism he wrote for the New Yorker was a release for him, as well as entertainment for readers. Usually his reports were datelined, "No Visitors, N.Y.," but occasionally he wrote from "Do Not Disturb, N.Y." and from "Nowheres, Calif."

"Eight months of constant listening," he once noted, "have whetted the undersigned's intellect to a keenness that renders it incapable of composing a questionnaire, let alone replying to one." He was pretty bitter about Donald Novis' renditions of "Trees" and Tony Wons's syrupy poetry and Morton Downey's singing. But what riled him most were double-entendre lyrics of the current popular songs. He campaigned to clean them up, but without visible success. And he had little time. He had been contributing regularly only a few months when, in the autumn of 1933, he died.

The New Yorker printed his last piece, a satire on O. O. McIntyre, the interpreter of the Big City for the sticks. Lardner had started off with a little poem.

Each morn when the neighbors are through with the papers
And stealthily slide them beneath our front door,
I grab the *American*, knowing that there I can
Find O. O. McIntyre's column of lore,
You ask what it's like? I've no copy right here,
But p'rhaps I can give you some sort of idear.

He imitated some of McIntyre's favorite devices: "Thingmabobs: If they did not wear identical hats, Jack Dempsey and Connie Bennett could pass for sisters. . . . There is something about the name Babe Ruth that suggests rare old Dresden filigree work. . . . Tallulah Bankhead and Jimmy Durante have profiles exactly alike." Thoughts while strolling ". . . Damon Runyon's feet . . . Damon Runyon's feet . . . There is a strong resemblance between Damon Runyon's feet and Ethel Merman."

"Comment" added a bit to the Lardner lore, and, in evaluating him, indicated Ross's ambition for his magazine.

This issue of the New Yorker contains a piece by Ring Lardner—the last piece of his we will have the privilege or the fun of publishing. We recall how he fussed with it, to get it exactly the way he wanted it. He seldom thought his stuff was quite right. Even after he had made a name for himself in the calendered-stock trade, he continued to regard himself essentially as a sporting writer who might sometime knock out a short story for the magazines if he could get a break. (What he most wanted to do was to write lyrics.) Any magazine that thought Lardner was working for it was crazy. He was always working for the newspapers.

It was a curious thing about Lardner that he was one of the easiest writers to imitate—if anybody wanted to try that. A lot of beginners have thought they were forging ahead in belles-lettres by using his little phrases: "further and more," "no one hundredths," "and etc." But Lardner had an ear for the dim sad music of America that nobody else could touch. The funnier his stuff was, the more deadly the aim. "Odd's Bodkins," which appears in this issue, happens to be a good example of Lardner; but if it were below par it would still be better than most anybody else's masterpiece, and it would certainly be the best obituary notice we could give him.

Finally Ross got into his pages an older humorist, Clarence Day, who obviously should have been there all along. As far back as 1920, Day had begun writing about his stern but tempestuous father, and life in New York in the days when a spanking team of horses was a young blade's heart's desire. A book, *God and My Father*, had already appeared before Day began contributing to the New Yorker. But it was *Life with Father*, selected from pieces that had appeared in the New Yorker and his earlier writing, that brought Day into his own as a humorist. He died before it was fashioned into one of the most popular of all American stage plays by Russel Crouse and Howard Lindsay.

Thurber was struck with Day's childhood pieces and decided that the world ought to know more about the things he had had to endure. The most fitting over-all title he could think of was simply *My Life and Hard Times.* He dwelt only a little on his suffering, properly giving over most of the series to dogs of strong and unique personalities, his slightly-at-seas-while-at-home father, his competent but fun-loving mother, two brothers, a grandfather who occasionally thought he was living in Civil War days, and such spear carriers and mob-scene extras as were required. It was an autobiography of childhood to end them all, even if it didn't.

Thurber was a careful writer who had exchanged years of sweat for his craftsmanship. The tremendous popularity of his drawings, once they were allowed in the magazine, pleased him. Yet he drew them so effortlessly that the writer in him was jealous of the artist. There was the way he improved the seal idea when, after *Is Sex Necessary?* had been a success, the art conference asked to see the cartoon again. Thurber placed the new seal on the wooden headboard of a bed. In the bed were a crushed-down husband and his crushing mate. Said the woman, "All right, have it your way—you heard a seal bark!" Psychologists were beginning to study New Yorker cartoons and even to use them therapeutically. That one they let alone.

Thurber's feeling that the female usually has the upper hand over the male was apparent in almost all of his drawings of people. A man said through a speakeasy peephole, "Don't you remember? I was here three nights ago with a lady who beat me up?" In a night club a weeping man mourned to his companion, "My wife had me arrested one night last week." Sincerity was plainly lacking in the woman who said, "I yielded, yes, but I never led your husband on, Mrs. Fisher." Thurber's great series, "The War Between Men and Women," began at a party with the overt act of a man throwing a drink in a woman's face. The battle raged over hill and dale, afoot and on horseback. The worst kind of military chicanery was practiced, but the women did it the more effectively.

On the wall of a corridor in the New Yorker offices Thurber drew a small, dejected man about to turn a corner. Waiting around it was a big woman with a poised club.

At first Thurber didn't force his dogs on the magazine. He put an occasional one in for balance. But they got ever bigger and after a while gained attention and even domination. A woman spoke irritably to a great, sad hound: "For heaven's sake, why don't you go out and trace something?" A man lugged his dog, feet upright, to a veterinarian, saying, "Here's a study for you, Doctor—he faints."

Ross seemed nonplused by the immense popularity of the drawings.

"An intellectual fad," he told Thurber.

Thurber inquired, "How long does an intellectual fad last?"

"Not long, Thurber, not long," Ross replied.

Thurber was a hazard first to speakeasies and later to saloons. He drew pictures on the walls. Most of the proprietors had the bad judgment to wipe them off. One of those who didn't was Tim Costello, a large, morose Irishman whose Third Avenue dispensary was turned by Thurber and other New Yorker writers into a literary oasis. When Costello moved many years later he went to enormous expense to take along the wall sections containing the drawings.

White was in full production during the early thirties. In addition to casuals, poetry, and sharp and sad comments on the times, he spun gossamer paragraphs which preserved the New Yorker's reputation for humor combined with chichi. "Comment" quoted from an advertising man's memo to his boss: "The suggestion for the New Yorker will put us into an influential magazine published with an exclusive circulation reaching people who, relatively speaking, lead fast lives and who are in that sense good prospects for mineral salt baths." White added: "It brings us no little happiness to close our eyes and conjure up visions of our thousands of readers, all of them leading fast lives and constantly taking baths of mineral salts."

Minor victories continued to be noted. After a poem by Arthur Guiterman protested about the colored lights on the Empire State Building's mast, Al Smith had them changed to white. But victory was sometimes tasteless on the tongue. "We succeeded," lamented "Comment," "in getting the information booth at the Pennsylvania terminal moved out into the middle of the floor—and then discovered there was no information we needed."

The New Yorker's self-appointed role of policing the railroad stations was nevertheless continued. In 1935 its delicate sensitivity to noise in terminals (which a decade and a half later was to bring Ross out of his self-imposed obscurity to plunge headlong into public battle) was demonstrated. Pennsylvania Station was again at fault.

We walked into the main hall the other afternoon to buy a ticket; the place was a nasty smear of sound, a hemorrhage of tonality, an old song "Marcheta" defiling the authentic peace of the terminus. We felt immediately defenseless, uneasy, and cheap. No sound in music should be universal. It made us mad as hops to realize that "Marcheta" could be, and was being, heard in the place for which we were buying a ticket, the effect being to nullify the romance of the intervening miles and make our journey seem pointless and banal.

S. J. Perelman showed up in the New Yorker's pages for the first time during the depression years. Though only twenty-six at the time, he had already gained a reputation as a humorist. He had come off the farm, but not off the kind of farm people usually think of when bucolic life is mentioned. He came off a chicken farm. The Perelman family lived in Brooklyn when the future humorist was born, but not long afterward it moved to Rhode Island. Perelman fell in love with chickens. It was not until he reached voting age that he could be really happy without knowing a few chickens to call on for company.

At Brown University, Perelman was editor of the *Brown Jug*. It was the great day of collegiate wit, when *College Humor*, which clipped most of its material, had a big national circulation. Perelman and his fellow editors battled to get the magazine to pay for the clips, without any success. At Brown he was a member of a writers' group which included Quentin Reynolds and Nathaniel West. It was led by Percy Marks, author of *The Plastic Age*.

After leaving college, Perelman became one of *Judge's* most prolific writers and artists. This didn't amount to much financially, since pay was low and harder to collect. He spent a good deal of his time, along with Gardner Rea, Frank Hanley, Donald McKee, and other humorists, waiting in *Judge's* reception room in the hope of catching the treasurer and forcing him to yield sums due them. The treasurer had to enter through a corridor, visible from the reception room, whose walls were painted a battleship gray. For camouflage he took to wearing a suit of the same color. Perelman and friends, stomachs grinding hot dogs, felt themselves lucky that he had a red face which could sometimes be spotted. While Ross was *Judge's* co-editor Perelman had been acquainted with him, but only slightly.

Perelman's drawings, which resembled woodcuts or engravings, made fun of stereotyped book and stage characters. A typical drawing, carrying in large block letters the words, "I will never assist your wicked designs defied the honest stable-boy firmly," showed sleek mustachioed villains menacing the stable-boy. This sort of thing, present also in his writing, had a wild, preposterous quality that made Perelman a natural script writer for the Marx brothers. He was at work on a screen play for them when he began contributing to the New Yorker.

Perelman's first piece was in his authentic style. A girl had written to the *Mirror* that the strangest sight she ever saw was a man, whom she took to be sozzled, kissing the statue of a horse. Perelman was hurt and outraged. The gentleman described, he explained, had been himself. Far from drunk, and entirely without amorous regard for the steed, he had simply been trying to catch a white horse which he thought had run away.

Ross had never been completely satisfied with the New Yorker's book section, and until 1933 it had always been signed with a pen name. Then he read in the *Nation* an analysis of Ring Lardner by a young critic and editor named Clifton Fadiman. Lardner, said Fadiman, had a low, almost savage opinion of mankind, including himself, which was the motivating force in his work. Ross was impressed and made further inquiries about Fadiman. He was a native New Yorker, had attended Columbia University, and afterward had taught in a private school. Now he was editor in chief of Simon and Schuster.

Ross took Fadiman to lunch at the Ritz and suggested that, if interested in writing book reviews for the New Yorker, he might work up a few samples. The Lardner study had been one of a series that Fadiman was writing for the *Nation* and he offered to stand or fall on them. Ross waived samples and it was agreed that Fadiman should write weekly reviews, sign his name, and send his copy over by messenger.

It was a time when proletarian literature was attracting wide attention. H. L. Mencken, though a political conservative, had been among the first to give space to radical young authors picking at America's ugly spots. Fadiman gave generous coverage to Josephine Herbst's *Pity Is Not Enough*, Jack Conroy's *The Disinherited*, Robert Cantwell's *Land of Plenty*, Granville Hicks's *The Great Tradition*, John Chamberlain's *Farewell to Reform*, and many other sour views of American life and letters.

It was a review of Matthew Josephson's *The Robber Barons*, a story of the railroad magnates, forest strippers, and other buccaneers, that brought to Fadiman his only editorial rebuke of the decade he spent as reviewer. Ross regularly sent back all kinds of queries about references and facts and with his copy editor, Rogers Whitaker, fussed endlessly with syntax. Fadiman considered it an excellent writing school. But there was never any effort to dictate opinion. Fadiman's rebuke came after his review had been printed. The robber barons, he had said, were not fit to sit at table with.

Ross mulled that over for a while. "By God," he said to Fadiman the next time he saw him, "*I'd* have eaten with them."

The abundance of talent at Ross's command was apparent on the New Yorker's every page. In addition to poets Ogden Nash and Arthur Guiterman, he had Margaret Fishback, Phyllis McGinley, and many more. Edmund Pearson's studies in murder were immensely popular. James Reid Parker, Richard Lockridge, Morris Bishop, Frances Crane, and Emily Hahn were supplementing the casuals furnished by the regular stable.

Arthur Kober was perfecting his stories of the Bronx. For a play he had created Bella Gross, a stenographer in search of a husband. Pa and Ma Gross did all they could to help. The play didn't come off and Kober broke it up into sketches for the New Yorker. Most of the scenes were laid in the Gross's Bronx apartment, as one in which Bella was about to set off on a picnic with Max Fine, her current boy friend. Pa had been nibbling the cold cuts. Ma Gross comments:

"Eat like a huss. Stoff yesself op. Get sick. Get even gullstones. So who cares?" She placed an enormous piece of lettuce on a slice of rye bread.

"Look, look!" exclaimed Pa, pointing to the lettuce. "Why alluva sudden such fency-shmency senwiches?"

"Because Bella says Mexie likes to eat a piece lettiss with his senwich. What'sa metta?" she asked, "by you a piece lettiss is poison?"

"Lettiss!" Mr. Gross held up a piece and eyed it dubiously. "A cow eats lettiss! A huss eats lettiss! It's just like a piece gress!" He shrugged his shoulders. "Where does Mexie come to lettiss?"

Just then the bathroom door opened and Bella appeared. Her face, freshly hued, looked like an artist's palette. She glanced at her wrist watch and her features clouded. "Gee, I better hurry. How's the food coming, Ma?"

Mrs. Gross paused as she poured the coffee into the thermos bottle. "Is coming in a train the food," she replied. "Is coming in an uttomobill. So how should the food come?" Bella was now rummaging through the top drawer of the bureau in the dining room. "Miss Hurry-Shmurry," Mrs. Gross shouted at her. "What you looking fur in such a rush?"

"My khaki pants. Whereja put them?"

"Miss Blind Girl," her mother chided as she opened the bottom drawer and extracted the trousers. "You ain't got eyes in head, God fabbid, you can't see?"

Bella headed for the bedroom. "Now don't forget the tishya paper for the senwiches, Ma," she said.

"What'sa metter tishya paper alluva sudden?" Pa wanted to know. "Plain senwiches Mexie can't eat? He's maybe gung eat op the tishya paper, too?"

The Gross family provided the best of the New Yorker's strictly city humor. Kober worked up a couple of glossaries of spellings, one for the Old World people, another for the new generation. After a while, largely because Marc Connelly had a lucky run at roulette, he got another chance to write a play. Connelly was listening to Kober tell about his experiences as social director at a summer camp, and promptly shelled out part of his winnings as an advance. Kober got to talking with Moss Hart, another old social director, and decided that Hart's experiences had been more interesting than his own. He packed up, went to Hart's old camp, Kopake, kept his eyes and ears open, and wrote *Having Wonderful Time*, which Connelly produced successfully.

The form which was eventually to be labeled "the New Yorker short story" was beginning to emerge. The blood lines were visible in Kay Boyle's "Kroy Wen," which appeared in the summer of 1931. It was the kind of story-without-an-ending which the author and others had been writing for the obscure little magazines. A movie producer-cameraman on the brink of a nervous breakdown takes a ship at the beginning of a six months' rest. In the steerage he finds two young Italian acrobats, husband and wife—the wife pregnant—who he thinks would be good photographic subjects. The husband, after being given some money, tries to arrange the posing so that his wife will not be upset. She is frightened and refuses to co-operate properly. The climax is simply that they all become upset.

These plotless stories usually had other compensating qualities—sensitivity, often introspection—which New Yorker editors felt were important in good fiction. They felt that there had been, perhaps, too much emphasis on rigid plot development.

Other pioneers of the New Yorker short story were Sally Benson, Donald Moffat, Thyra Samter Winslow, John Collier, Robert Coates, John Mosher, Nancy Hale, and John O'Hara. The editors made three major contributions. The first was insistence on greater clarity of writing—for which Katharine White and Wolcott Gibbs, in line with Ross's policy, were chiefly responsible. The second was payment of cash, which established a market for experimental writing. The third was a wider audience than was available in the little magazines.

A group of brilliant cartoonists turned up in the New Yorker's pages during the depression years. There was William Steig with his Small Fry and undershirted proletarians. Sydney Hoff drew the kind of people Arthur Kober wrote about. George Price began with a long sequence about a man who floated halfway between a bed and the ceiling. His wife finally shot him down. Others beginning long careers were Daniel Alain, Richard Decker, Whitney Darrow, Jr., Robert Day, Richard Taylor, Chon Day, Charles Addams, and Mischa Richter.

14 The Journalistic Frying Pan

THE NEW YORKER'S PROFILES, like the "Reporter at Large" pieces, have had an enormous influence on American journalism. A quarter of a century ago the personality articles in the magazines were either inspirational or the kind in which the authors praised famous men. Typical *Hearst's International* subjects, for example, were Dr. Charles W. Eliot of five-foot-bookshelf fame and Clarence Darrow. O. O. McIntyre gushed about "My Dad." Irvin S. Cobb furnished moralistic pieces such as "The Convict Who Refused to Be Beaten by Fate." In *Harper's*, Gamaliel Bradford studied the wives of some of history's famous and infamous, while the *Atlantic Monthly* reader found himself "Face to Face with Lincoln." The *Ladies' Home Journal* featured Brigham Young and "How the Rockefellers Give Millions." The *American* let it be known that "Madge Kennedy Is Lucky—but She Doesn't Trust to Luck." *Collier's* celebrated the public's great friend and "hired man," utility magnate Sam Insull (this was quite a while before Sam took to his heels, closely pursued by representatives of the public). Nearest to the human-interest pieces of a later day were Alexander Woollcott's pally studies, in the *Saturday Evening Post*, of Irving Berlin and the Marx brothers.

During its early years the New Yorker had made no startling innovations. Woollcott had simply written about Harpo Marx, his favorite, rather than all the brothers. Even the many-part profiles, as of Hearst and Ford, had been in the old tradition. The trouble was that Ross's formula severely limited the old-style subjects. The inspirational note would have been jarring in a magazine that ran fairly heavily to satire. And its topicality obviated most men in the twilight of their careers.

The writer who did more than anybody else to develop the profiles technique was Alva Johnston, a tall, slender Swede who, like Ross, had come out of the Far West. He was one of the two persons older than Ross and already established in his field—the other was of course Rea Irvin—who had a large hand in developing the magic formula. A star reporter for the New York *Times* and a careful, hard worker, Johnston had won a Pulitzer prize for his clear reporting of the abstruse proceedings of a science convention. He wrote also on frothier subjects, notably prohibition.

Many years later, after Johnston's death, the New Yorker in one of its rare editorial comments on a contributor said: "When the New Yorker in its earliest days was trying to establish the Profile as a new journalistic form, it was Alva Johnston more than anyone else who set the pace, clarified the idea, and produced the pieces. He gathered and assembled facts in such a way as to give a fresh, candid, gay, and occasionally satirical picture of an individual. . . . His contribution to this magazine was, as its faithful readers are well aware, very important."

The statement was not strictly accurate, for Johnston was not around in the earliest days. He did not, as a matter of fact, appear in the pages until 1928, when the magazine was already a success. And most of his energy during the next four years went into his regular job on the *Herald Tribune*, to which he had moved from the *Times*. It was not until the early and middle thirties that Johnston's influence was felt strongly in the profiles.

Ross and Johnston had in common a friendly feeling for raffish characters. Ross had known and liked them. In point of fact he had been something of a raffish fellow in his youth. Johnston, on the other hand, was a proper, almost sedate type. He liked the raffish characters because they did the kind of things he wouldn't do.

Ross had a difficult time persuading Johnston to join the regular staff, but he finally managed it by offering three hundred dollars a week—more than almost anyone else on the magazine was getting.

Johnston found the almost perfect subject in a man known in various world capitals as Prince Dmitri Michl Obolenski-Romanoff. His real name was Harry F. Gerguson and he hailed from Illinois. He had behind him a successful career as an impersonator of royalty. Ross took a personal liking to Prince Mike and later sent him to Hollywood to free-load off his friend, restaurant owner Dave Chasen. The prince learned the trade so well, and ingratiated himself with so many of Chasen's customers, that he was soon able to open his own restaurant.

Johnston found other subjects in fields ranging from a left-wing politician (William Z. Foster) to a somewhat stuffy clergyman (Bishop Manning). On his profile list were such lusty characters as W. C. Fields, Sam Leibowitz, Grover Whalen, Christy Walsh, John S. Sumner, Nicholas Murray Butler, Jake Ruppert, and Jack Curley, the wrestling promoter. A patient digger of facts, Johnston was also a fine, sharp writer and a humorist. Authors of magazine personality pieces had seldom employed wit. Foibles were usually ignored or played down. The standard practice was to interview the subject and his friends. Johnston was careful to look up his enemies also. He did not consider a subject necessarily a good source about himself, and consequently did not always bother to interview him. He did not meet Prince Mike, as a matter of fact, until after the profile had been printed.

Ross was expanding, meanwhile, the "Reporter" department. In the early days Morris Markey had often gathered his material one night and written his piece the next morning. Now he was often busy on other projects, and anyhow Ross wanted longer and more involved pieces. A writer might now work several weeks on one of them. They remained casual in tone only.

Many capable "fact" men were trying out for the magazine, and those who made good were put on drawing accounts. Among those who stayed or produced fairly regularly while on other jobs were Milton Mackaye, Geoffrey T. Hellman, A. J. Liebling, Joseph Mitchell, Meyer Berger, Sanderson Vanderbilt, Philip Hamburger, Russell Maloney, E. J. Kahn, Jr., Brendan Gill, and St. Clair McKelway. In 1935 the editorial handling of "fact" or non-fiction was separated from fiction and McKelway was made editor of it.

Use of the profile form for humor and especially satire entailed considerable danger. It was not always possible to put a man in the journalistic frying pan without ill consequences. He kicked and flailed. Burning grease popped and burned the faces and arms of the cooks. And once the victim got out he often heated up a frying pan of his own and tried to reverse the roles.

The first big job Ross undertook was to fry his old neighbor, Henry R. Luce. That was in 1936. In the decade since the little staffs had labored forlornly not far from each other, Luce, a few years younger than Ross, had risen to greater heights—materially at least. *Time* was a huge success. Rich, heavy, ornate *Fortune* was the capitalist's bible. Luce had just extinguished the guttering flame of *Life* and was about to use the title for a picture magazine. (Tottering *Judge* took over what *Life* circulation remained—29,000 compared with 200,000 when the New Yorker was launched.)

When a New Yorker editor asked Luce if he would co-operate on the profile by furnishing information about himself and his enterprises, Ralph Ingersoll's advice was asked. Ingersoll was now Luce's general manager.

"They hate you over there," Ingersoll told him. "They'll take long knives and cut you into little pieces and put you over a fire."

Luce decided nevertheless that it was his moral duty as a journalist to co-operate. After all, his men went all over the world asking questions. His writers and researchers, especially *Fortune's*, took up a fantastic amount of busy people's time.

Wolcott Gibbs, the most cutting satirist available and a fine parodist, was selected to do the job. Gibbs did not see Luce himself—the research was done by John Bainbridge and others—but it was his parody that made the piece probably the New Yorker's most celebrated profile.

Gibbs described Luce: "Ambitious, gimlet-eyed . . . co-founder of *Time*, promulgator of *Fortune*, potent in associated radio & cinema ventures." The rest, in a like vein, left no doubt that Luce was able, hard-working, and important—but a man who took himself with a rather overwhelming seriousness without the ameliorating grace of humor. Since *Time* was known for its unhappy adjectives ("horsy," "pig-eyed") and the intimate details it sometimes gave of people, the article went into Luce's expensive way of living and other private matters.

Another reason for the intimate nature of the portrait was that a couple of years earlier Ingersoll had written a long piece about the New Yorker for *Fortune*, revealing, among other things, the salaries paid various people. This was regarded at the New Yorker as an undue invasion of privacy. Ingersoll had written that Gibbs took an "adolescent pride" in being cynical. It was also noted in the piece that Katharine White was "hard, suave, ambitious" and that in office warfare she had occasional "recourse to tears." Gibbs described Ingersoll, whom he called the No. 2 heir apparent to Luce's headman job, this way: "Burly, able, tumbledown Yaleman Ralph McAllister Ingersoll, former *Fortune* editor, now general manager of all *Time* enterprises, descendant of 400-famed Ward McAllister. Littered his desk with pills, unguents, Kleenex, Socialite Ingersoll is *Time's* No. 1 hypochondriac, introduced ant palaces for study & emulation of employes, writes copious memoranda about filing systems, other trivia, seldom misses a Yale football game."

"Backward," Gibbs wrote, "ran sentences until reeled the mind." One of *Time's* favorite phrases was "Upshot of this . . ." Gibbs switched it to "Shotup of this . . ." The piece ended: "Certainly to be taken with seriousness is Luce at thirty-eight, his fellowman already informed up to his ears, his future plans impossible to imagine, staggering to contemplate. Where it all will end, knows God!"

When the profile was finished and in galley proofs it was shown to Luce. He was not pleased. He went over it several times and so did Ingersoll. For a while there were negotiations between McKelway, acting for Ross, and Ingersoll, acting for Luce. They got nowhere. Nothing was left but for the principals to face each other.

"Bulls like to fight," a New Yorker staffer, fearing the carnage, said resignedly.

The meeting was held one night at Ingersoll's house. Ingersoll seconded Luce. Ross was handled by McKelway. Gibbs waited outside in a bar. In the last analysis all decisions were to be left, as was the New Yorker policy, to the writer. Ross wanted no final agreements made in the heat of the battle.

The great adversaries sparred cautiously at first, but things soon warmed up. Luce didn't feel that *Time* was ever crass, scandalmongering, or insulting. Ross disagreed.

"I say frankly, but really in not an unfriendly spirit," he declared, "that you are in a hell of a position to ask anything."

Luce doubted the accuracy of several items. Gibbs had calculated the "weekly recompense for informing fellowmen" at $45.67802 per worker. Luce inquired whether the Chicago staff had been figured in. He didn't know that Gibbs had merely hit what typewriter keys had come under his fingers, believing that the reader would gather from the five decimal points that the figure was part of the parody. Ross maintained that a few errors would heighten the general effect.

Gibbs had quoted drama critic Richard Watts's review of a play by Mrs. Clare Boothe Luce: "One almost forgave 'Abide With Me' its faults when its lovely playwright, who must have been crouched in the wings for a sprinter's start as the final curtain mercifully descended, heard a cry of 'author,' which was not audible in my vicinity, and arrived onstage to accept the audience's applause just as the actors, who had a head-start on her, were properly lined up and smoothed out to receive their customary adulation." Luce considered use of the quotation unkind. Ross retorted that it was the sort of thing *Time* would run, and smoothed things over by offering to run it as a footnote—where it attracted twice as much attention as it would have in the text. Luce didn't think the apartment he lived in had fifteen rooms and five baths. Ross said he would try to check.

At one point Luce sighed and remarked, "There's not a single kind thing about me in the whole profile."

Ross snarled, "That's what you get for being a baby tycoon."

Luce was particularly bothered by these sentences: "He drinks not at all at midday, sparingly at all times, takes sometimes champagne at dinner, an occasional cocktail at parties. Embarrassed perhaps by reputation for unusual abstemiousness, he confesses proudly that he smokes too much." During the evening Luce hovered near a liquor decanter in what seemed to the others an ostentatious manner, now and again taking a small nip. After Ross got home Ingersoll telephoned.

"What do you mean, Harry doesn't drink?" Ingersoll said. "I'm thinking of putting him under a cold shower right now."

The whole thing was taking a good deal out of Ross. He wrapped up a before-final-press copy of the issue containing the profile and sent it, along with a 2000-word letter, to Luce. The letter was later pirated out of the files of either Ross or Luce (probably out of both) and mimeographed. It has since passed surreptitiously from hand to hand in editorial circles.

Ross went over the reasons certain items had been allowed to stand. As for the fifteen-room, five-bathroom apartment, an earnest checker suspected that Luce did not know about five servants' rooms. Luce was offering to rent the place, and the checker, posing as a prospect, had counted the rooms. The Clare Boothe quotation and the wage figures were gone over again.

And then, taking a clear sight down his nose, Ross delivered a lecture on journalism. While not doubting Luce's passion for accuracy, he expressed a doubt that he attained it all the time. He possessed evidence, he claimed, of "slithering insults" inserted in copy by Luce's writers. *Time* started fantastic rumors by denying them, he charged; it invaded people's privacy, threw facts out of focus, and its style hurt the ear. After the recent meeting he had polled quite a few people and concluded that *Time* was generally thought of as "mean as hell." The whole matter had reached a childish state, he concluded, and now he prayed that it was all over.

It was not quite. The New Yorker continued from time to time to make fun of the Luce publications. But they, being printed on Olympus, treated Ross and the New Yorker graciously.

Other profiles took a good deal out of Ross. McKelway and A. J. Liebling wrote a long study of George Baker, better known as Father Divine, in which he appeared something less than God. Meyer Berger wrote a piece about one Marty Franklin, described as a Broadway chiseler. There was a close line to be toed on Alva Johnston's piece about John Sumner and another on the Society for the Suppression of Vice itself. Mr. Sumner's threat to call the law about the stolen sign had not been forgotten.

Big trouble did not come, however, until Ross tripped up Alexander Woollcott, landed him in the frying pan, and sizzled him pink. Gibbs performed the rites for that one too.

"Ross," an awed New Yorker staffer declared, "is attacking his former god."

Woollcott and Ross were not seeing much of each other any more. Woollcott was by now planning his social life weeks, even months, in advance. Ross was lax in keeping engagements and when verbal chastisements were unavailing there was nothing but for Woollcott to treat him as dead. Ross was sure that the real cause of Woollcott's anger was disruption of the patron-protégé relationship. He nevertheless remained in considerable awe of his old mentor. Once he telephoned Heywood Broun, his Connecticut neighbor, and begged him to come to dinner, explaining that Woollcott had agreed to come only if he were there. Broun was in bed with a cold. Woollcott came to Ross's anyhow, but directly after dinner he insisted on visiting Broun.

Woollcott's page had been dropped because Ross thought it had deteriorated below the magazine's standard. Fleischmann carried out the terrible task of informing Woollcott he was through. From the first there had been, of course, a lot of trouble. Gibbs, who had alternated with Katharine White in editing Woollcott's copy, said risqué stories were the cause of most of it.

> About once a month a specimen would turn up which would usually not only be unprintable in any magazine not intended exclusively for the United States Marines but would also be drearily familiar to all worldly editors. Its removal from the copy was always the signal for a fierce battle, with Mr. Woollcott passing from blank astonishment that anyone could be virginal enough to object to such a pretty story, then to a vehement lecture on the subject of taste, and finally to the cold tendering of his resignation. On several occasions, when some editor had as usual proved adamant, he actually did resign and had to be won back with humble telephone calls and ardent letters. These lovers' quarrels turned up periodically and while they brought two or three editors close to nervous collapse, Mr. Woollcott enjoyed them thoroughly.

Gibbs's profile was titled "Big Nemo" and ran in three parts. Woollcott's public thought of him as a gay man about town. Gibbs cast some doubt on his masculinity. Edna

Ferber, who often fought with Woollcott (and Ross too), was quoted as remarking that he sometimes mistook his pinafore for a toga. Howard Dietz was said to have called him "Louisa M. Woollcott." (In his biography of Woollcott published in 1945, after Woollcott's death, Samuel Hopkins Adams stated that in his youth Woollcott was subjected to feminizing influences but was never homosexual.)

Woollcott's careful way of planning his engagement schedule and his fury when anybody disrupted it was related. Ross himself, disguised under the name Smith, appeared in a watered-down version of Marc Connelly's story about the broken theatrical appointment and telegram. Included also were Woollcott's more pleasant qualities, with emphasis on his generosity with money.

When the piece was finished Woollcott read the proofs and told Gibbs he felt as Bruno Hauptmann would have felt if a piece had been written about him with all reference to the Lindbergh kidnaping omitted. Among his friends Woollcott did not mind being considered vicious. But people began to tell him that he had been hurt in the public's mind—and therefore in his pocketbook. He never spoke directly to Ross again.

Many editors asked him to write a profile of Ross. Assuming a hurt and bewildered air, he always refused, at the same time carefully stating that he regarded no man more highly. Once, when feeling that he was about to die, he wrote Ross suggesting a reconciliation for old times' sake. Ross agreed. Woollcott began to feel better and withdrew his offer.

Walter Winchell was the wiriest subject, with the toughest meat, that Ross ever put into his frying pan. Winchell was easier to put there than Luce because proofs were not shown to him. But once out, he took a bellows, pumped a forge to white heat, and dangled Ross over it every chance he got.

The idea for the profile originated with McKelway, who proposed himself as the author. At first Ross was not enthusiastic. Inevitably there would be an air of moral indignation about it, he thought, and that was one thing he wanted kept at a minimum. Finally he told McKelway to go ahead, that Winchell ought to be tackled and it might as well be them.

McKelway set to work with the aid of John Bainbridge, who had helped Gibbs with Luce, and all other researchers and checkers who could be spared.

"Now, Walter," McKelway would tell Winchell as they sat at the table just inside the Stork Club which was Winchell's second office, "you may not like what I write."

Winchell always brushed off the remark. He either felt that McKelway couldn't help but make him look good, or else he didn't care what was written.

The profile was in six parts—the largest number the magazine had ever run. One night in a restaurant many years later, Ross ran into McKelway, who was just back from a writing stint in Hollywood. "That God damned Winchell thing was too long," he said, and walked on.

McKelway had a man at the Stork Club gauging Winchell's reactions to the installments as they appeared. Winchell registered pleasure at the first, which described his powerful influence and his rise from a small-time hoofer. Thereafter his gloom, the spy reported, deepened until by the fifth installment he was plainly unhappy and angry. It was in the fifth part that the backbreaking toil of the researchers was apparent.

They had taken Winchell's Monday morning columns for a month—five Mondays—and by telephone and letter had checked each item for accuracy. There were 239 items. Of these 108 were "blind"—that is, had no names and therefore could not be checked. Of the rest, McKelway decided from the evidence supplied him that 54 were completely inaccurate, that 24 were partly inaccurate, and that 53 were accurate. Winchell had been right slightly less than half the time, according to the analysis.

Since Winchell often spoke of his ability to be in the know, usually ahead of other columnists, this was the sort of thing that stung. It damaged him little with his vast newspaper and radio audience. But with Stork Club customers it hurt. They looked at him with less awe as he sat at his table making left-handed notes.

Ross was a fairly regular Stork Club patron, though not much impressed by its proprietor, Sherman Billingsley, an ex-speakeasy operator. For his part, Billingsley regarded the New Yorker as a caviar and champagne magazine and therefore occasionally sent a gift of champagne to one or another of the contributors. This displeased Ross. At another club he ordered a case of champagne to be sent to Billingsley.

"Make it cheap champagne," he stipulated.

One night Ross entered the Stork Club with a group of friends. It was an engagement party that Lela Rogers, mother of Ginger Rogers, was giving for Bennett Cerf and Phyllis Fraser, Ginger's cousin. Ross—divorced again—was at the time escorting Ginger about town. Winchell was sitting at his regular table. Ross thought he saw him blanch as he passed by.

As the party was leaving, a note from Billingsley was delivered to Ross, explaining that thereafter he would be *persona non grata* in the place. No restaurant in New York can legally exclude any well-behaved person able to pay his check. The Stork Club and others nevertheless habitually "bar" people. Rather than resort to law, the victim usually leaves quietly on request and does not come back unless sure of courteous treatment.

"Never liked the place anyhow," Ross said.

Some members of the party have stated that Billingsley claimed later that Winchell had threatened to leave the club for good unless Ross were barred. McKelway had written in his profile that Winchell was largely responsible for the Stork Club's success. The inference was that Billingsley sent the message after Winchell's ultimatum.

Ross went to his office after leaving the club, typed out a notice, and pinned it to the bulletin board. In it he told of his experience and suggested that other New Yorker people might be subject to embarrassment at the Stork Club, and therefore ought to proceed accordingly.

McKelway took it for granted that he was barred and, for the hell of it, appeared a few nights later at the club. Billingsley didn't recognize him. Some time later McKelway and Richard Watts, Jr., were sitting at a table with Billingsley and others.

"Sherman," Watts said, pointing to McKelway, "this is St. Clair McKelway."

"Oh, Dick, you and your jokes!" Billingsley said, hastily getting up and departing.

In the end McKelway's past caught up with him. One night as Billingsley passed by, McKelway asked in a strong voice, "Who is that man?" It is the sort of remark that in the Stork Club is taken for an insult. Billingsley learned McKelway's identity and sent him his notice.

"I Am Sorely Pressed. . . ." 15

Ross was as patriotic as the next man during World War II. His habitual look of injury stemmed simply from a belief that he had been personally affronted by Hitler, Mussolini, and Tojo. They were bent on driving him to his wit's end by pinning down a large part of his staff in out-of-the-way parts of the world.

"I am sorely pressed," he would cry suddenly to a companion, and then hurry on to relate the deterioration of his staff and his stomach. By now he had ulcers—duodenal—and they were in terrible shape. He gobbled pills like a famished chicken pecking up corn.

There were reasons for worry aside from the diversion of his people to the armed forces. As far back as 1938 he had suffered the partial loss of the talents of three of his most important people—Thurber, White, and Katharine White.

Thurber had been driving in the country one day when the wheels of his car began to go off the pavement. He wasn't sleepy and he hadn't had anything to drink. He noticed that the fields were beginning to blur. He got home all right, but from that point on his sight failed until he was nearly blind. For many years he spent much of his time in hospitals undergoing delicate operations on the eye that had survived his boyhood arrow accident. The doctors were amazed, as a matter of fact, that he had been able to see at all after the age of six. Thurber got a feeling that they regarded his refusal to go blind at that age, or at least short of forty, as sheer bullheadedness.

He was definitely stubborn about refusing to let the misfortune throw him. He had been divorced and was remarried to the former Helen Wismer, a tall, attractive Nebraskan who was an experienced editorial worker. With her assistance he tried to carry on as if nothing had happened. After the trouble began, but while he was still able to get around fairly well by himself, they went on a shopping trip to a town near their Connecticut home. Mrs. Thurber ordered her husband, rather sharply, he thought, to buy a pair of rubbers. This little incident, together with his ancient Man-beaten-down-by-Woman theory, resulted in "The Secret Life of Walter Mitty," probably his most celebrated work. (Mitty was played by Robert Benchley for broadcasts to the troops during the war and by Danny Kaye on the screen. Thurber objected violently to some changes made in the movie version.)

"Mitty" was a short piece—a little less than two pages in the magazine. Thurber hadn't viewed it as much better or worse than the scores of casuals he had written. It turned out that a vast number of people, like Mitty, were accomplished daydreamers. Mitty's wife had ordered him, as had Thurber's, to buy some rubbers, and also a box of dog biscuit. While driving to the parking lot, trying to park the car, and carrying out his errands, Mitty had several lapses of judgment and memory. For every one of them he compensated brilliantly in his daydreams. He was a daring air commander, a great surgeon, and the hero at a trial. Finally he was shot against a wall, inscrutable to the end.

As Thurber's sight grew worse he simply got bigger pieces

of paper on which to draw and, writing by hand, put fewer words on each sheet of paper. After a while the drawing paper was four feet wide by five feet high. The going was slow, but it was a challenge, and he worked long hours, drawing his men and women and dogs. Writing was even harder, for he was a slow hard worker who got his effects by assiduous polishing.

"Never read a first draft of my stuff," he had told his wife. "It will be terrible and you'll be discouraged with me."

Fortunately Thurber's memory was excellent ("He has total recall and then some," an admirer of his imaginative power has said) and he learned to compose in his mind. By 1941, when he was able to make out only a constant light, he could revise about three hundred words in a lump without resort to paper.

His output was nevertheless cut, and Ross was hard put to fill the gap even with material of lesser quality.

White left the offices, though not ceasing altogether to contribute, because he felt restless and confined. After working at his New York apartment for a while he and his wife moved up to a farm in Maine. For Katharine White, leaving her desk was a blow. She was involved in the big things of the magazine, as well as the little ones down to the personal problems of small jobholders. But her husband believed he could write better and be happier in Maine, and that was enough for her. A bundle of manuscripts was sent to her each weekday.

After Mrs. White's departure Gustave Lobrano became head of the fiction department. A Cornellian, he had been one of those sharing a Thirteenth Street apartment with White when White first began to contribute to the New Yorker. Lobrano had worked unhappily for a travel agency, until White, thinking he would make a good editor, helped him get a job on *Town and Country*. Later White recommended him to Ross. A tall, graying, polite man, he was less jumpy than many of the magazine's key workers. He quickly won the confidence of Ross and the contributors.

White purchased a flock of sheep and went bucolic in a fairly large way. This caused Thurber to comment that, whereas most humorists tried merely to support their families, White had taken on the additional burden of feeding the mouths of sheep. But White was more than a literary farmer and he took his work and his place in the community seriously. He began writing a regular monthly department for *Harper's* titled "One Man's Meat." To make room, *Harper's* dismantled an ancient department, "The Lion's Mouth," one of the last refuges for humorists who had short pieces to sell. White was unaware of his part in narrowing the humor market. When it was called to his attention long afterward he felt guilty.

The Whites returned to New York and the New Yorker office after America's entrance into the war. Ross could thank the Axis Powers for that. But he lost John Mosher through death. Mosher was movie critic besides acting as first reader and doing other important editorial chores. And the armed forces were drawing off staff members at a faster pace. Besides, Ross did a foolish thing in the spring of 1942 that laid him open to public ridicule and even worse. The false elephant's hide that he always wore was quickly stripped away and his own tender skin was revealed.

A few years earlier he had built a new, fairly sumptuous house on his Wire Mill Road property near Stamford. He lived there with his third wife, the former Ariane Allen, a pretty young Texas girl who had studied dramatics and had expected to go on the New York stage. They entertained fairly extensively, sometimes members of the surrounding literary set but more often theatrical and café society people from the city.

The trouble started when Ross learned that the state of Connecticut planned to build a park not far from his property. He rolled a sheet of paper into his typewriter and bore down on the governor: "I address you in a state of considerable panic and alarm. . . . Stamford is on the verge of becoming the playground of the Borough of the Bronx and the dark, mysterious, malodorous stretches of Harlem. . . . I do not mean to be undemocratic, but you couldn't choose a more alarming bunch of people in the world. . . . I write in sheer terror."

The Bronx is widely thought of as having a predominantly Jewish population. Harlem is of course almost totally a Negro community.

The diatribe was first brought to public gaze, ironically, by the tabloid *PM*, which Ralph Ingersoll had started in part to realize Ross's old newspaper dream. Ingersoll was busy being drafted into the Army at the time and was unaware of the letter until after it had been printed. He felt sure that Ross was neither anti-Semitic nor anti-Negro. But he did not want to interfere with his editors, and the letter was, after all, a bad one. It was not easy to explain that for nearly two decades Ross had been writing wild memos which were often open to misinterpretation. The man who wrote the *PM* story was surprised that Ross's style was "utterly different from the urbane, polished prose of the magazine." Ingersoll was not.

Time, unimpressed by Ross's lecture to Luce, found the letter newsworthy and printed it. So did the New York *Times*, whose reporter, sent to interview Ross, found him "taken aback" by the furor. The president of the Borough of the Bronx, James J. Lyons, wrote to Ross: "It is most unfortunate that a grandee such as you should bc editor of a facetious periodical bearing the glorious name the New Yorker. . . . There are thousands of those who love and practice the democratic ideals that are now suffering in internment camps, while your ilk sit in Ivory Towers with a superiority complex. . . . It is creatures like you that create strife and cause wars."

Walter Winchell noted: "Because Harold ('I Don't Mean to be Undemocratic') Ross, the editor of the New Yorker mag, complained to Governor Hurley of Connecticut about 'the alarming people' from the Bronx and Harlem invading his privacy, groups of uptowners are planning armies of pickets—many of the signs to be photos of their kin fighting for him abroad."

Ross called *PM's* editors a "rabble rousing lot"—which *PM* gleefully reported—but admitted that "maybe I stuck my neck out and should learn to keep my mouth shut." To the *Times* man he declared of picnickers who had been in his neighborhood: "I don't care whether they're from the Bronx or from Indianapolis, Indiana. They are extremely numerous." Old hobo newspapermen, reading the charge of "grandee" thrown at Ross, shook their heads sadly. The whole thing quieted down, but Ross was seen pecking medicine harder than ever.

While not especially dollar conscious, Ross could hardly help being shaken when he discovered that his secretary had stolen more than fifty thousand dollars of his personal funds. None of it could be recovered. Young Harold Winney had been with Ross for a long time and he was an efficient and resourceful secretary. He kept Ross's accounts and had power of attorney for use when Ross was away. Winney was particularly helpful to Ross and his friends in their practical joking. If Bennett Cerf, say, wanted to send a nanny goat to somebody—as he once did—Winney knew where to put his hands on a goat in a hurry.

Ik Shuman, who was "Jesus" for longer than anyone—nearly a decade—was responsible in an indirect way for discovering the theft. Shuman had been a crack *Times* reporter and rewrite man. Ross had a great deal of respect for him and he got on especially well as a liaison man with the business department. One day Fleischmann inquired in a friendly way whether Ross was hard up—maybe could use a loan. Shuman reported the conversation and Ross, while sure he was in a secure financial position, called his secretary in to check. Winney gave a long and involved explanation about bonds, checkbooks, and the like, which satisfied Ross for the moment.

Shuman talked with Fleischmann some more and learned that Ross's salary was drawn several months ahead. Ross was surprised and once more called on his secretary for an explanation. This time he was puzzled and told Shuman after Winney had departed that he guessed he would stop by his bank and check up.

When Shuman went out he found the door ajar. Winney had apparently been listening. At any rate he went home and killed himself with gas. He had sold Ross's bond, using the power of attorney, and had falsified his checkbooks for years.

Not long before the discovery, Winney had thrown a champagne party for some of the staff members at the Astor. Ross hadn't attended but during the evening he had walked by the hotel.

"I was hit on the head," he said grimly, "by my own champagne corks."

There was always the bigger worry: how to adjust the formula to fit wartime. One of the regular bulletins to artists and idea men stated: "The New Yorker's problems in these times are perhaps more difficult than those of any other publication." Ross was willing to add new ingredients, if need be. Another bulletin said: "We want our artists and idea men to give some thought to the development of a political type of cartoon that will make pointed comment on the war. . . . We are ready to use serious drawings from time to time." The idea was dropped, though, after a few sinister-looking Japs had appeared.

There were times when the evidence seemed clear that clipper-paster Ross had dug an old copy of *Yank Talk* out of his World War I duffel bag and was dropping it piece by piece into the magazine. Sergeant gags were endless. Said the tough top kick to petitioning recruits: "I don't care *how* many signatures you have. Reveille is still at five-thirty." A girl ruffling a sergeant's hair on a davenport said: "Where do people ever get the idea you sergeants are tough?" Sergeants played cards on a ping-pong table while a couple of recruits fingered their paddles. A top kick at the wheel of an Army vehicle and a traffic cop shouted "Yeah!" at each other. A sergeant told recruits still in civilian clothes: "You men will hear all sorts of wild stories about me—one, that I was suckled by a werewolf."

There were the MP jokes. One said to a cop who was instructing him in traffic directions: "I told him to pull over, and I asked him if he was going to a fire. Now what do I do?" A comical-looking MP stood in the snow watching through a window as other soldiers had fun inside a beer joint.

And the girls. A soldier lad said to his date as they sat on a davenport: "I know we just met, but all I got is a twenty-four-hour pass." Girl visiting boy friend at camp: "Can't you do KP *tomorrow?*" Bride to husband as they left a justice of the peace's office: "Now where do we go for the allotment?" Wac private to male sergeant, on davenport: "Don't pull your rank on me, Herbert!" A girl in negligee to her roommate: "How old is a major?"

Things didn't get much better after the recruiting period was over and the troops were scattered over the world. In Alaska a line of Eskimo girls entered a barracks as a soldier remarked that at least the USO was trying. Soldiers lined up for action after debarking from a plane were warned by an officer: ". . . and one thing more, men. I don't want to hear of anyone eating his emergency chocolate until he has finished his K ration." There were the "locale" pictures: fuzzy-wuzzies in New Guinea watching a bulldozer, a soldier in India showing a rope-trick fakir how to put a loop on the end of his rope, Russian soldiers trying to understand spam, visitors in Paris remarking that the "imported" wine they were drinking was better than the California stuff, in China a soldier carrying to his quarters a huge statue which a host had given him in accordance with custom because he had praised it, a couple of pairs of GI shoes among slippers outside a door in Japan.

"Talk" was full of war jokes, most of them clammy from the sweat of the professional gag man's palm.

A social worker has told us of a touching case she investigated recently—that of a delinquent girl whose delinquency was contributed to (as they say) exclusively by sailors. Sometimes it was a signalman, sometimes it was a gunner's mate, sometimes it was an oiler, and once it was a petty officer; but always sailors. Out of sheer, unprofessional curiosity, the social worker finally asked the girl why this was. "Well, I don't know," the little delinquent said reflectively. "I guess maybe it's on account of sailors ain't all the time talking about how they're afraid of losing their jobs."

One item had obviously been captured while in the wrap leggings and dishpan helmet of the first World War.

The general policy of the Army, we gather, is to encourage the soldiers to sing whenever possible, and of course "Hinky, Dinky, Parley-Voo" is still the favorite, with the men if not with the officers. One outfit we have been told about featured, during a long march, a verse that went:

The second lieutenant carries a pack,
We hope to hell it breaks his back,
Hinky, dinky, parley-voo.

As the men tired of the second lieutenant, they substituted other and more exalted officers. They were getting to work on the major when a courier from the head of the column passed the word along to lay off the song. The men marched a mile or so in hurt silence, and then another message came from Higher Up. They could sing the song, after all, but only about the second lieutenant.

All these things presumably tickled readers of the New Yorker who remained at home. They were less funny to the young men who had made the dreary, painful crossing from civilian to military existence. The problem of reporting real —much more caustic—soldier humor in cartoons and jokes was, of course, enormous. Lack of special military knowledge by civilian audiences made communication difficult, for one thing. But the internal evidence indicates that Ross and his staff did not try very hard. The jolly "GI Joe" picture of the man in service which most newspapers gave was avoided, but not by far. The New Yorker's adless, small-sized service edition was nevertheless welcome to old readers.

The reporting was on a high plane. It was credited by Ross and other editors with pulling the magazine through the difficult war years. In charge of "fact" writing by this time was tiny William Shawn, so youthful-appearing and extra-polite that strangers often took him for a copy boy rather than an editor on whom Ross leaned heavily. A Chicagoan, Shawn had worked on newspapers and traveled abroad before joining the New Yorker in the early thirties as a part-time writer.

A large share of the job of reporting the military life went to E. J. Kahn, Jr., who entered the Army in the summer of 1941. Kahn and his experiences demonstrated the handicaps faced by the serviceman writing for the New Yorker and other civilian publications. Though not of very rugged physique, he was assigned to the infantry, a good point of vantage. His accounts of "The Army Life"—the heading under which his pieces appeared—suffered from the New Yorker's traditional underwriting, so that he seemed to be having a better time than he was. His work was accurate enough, however, to gain the praise of the straight-backed *Infantry Journal.* (The reports for the New Yorker by Walter Bernstein, who wrote less, were somewhat grimmer.) Kahn, who had an obliging disposition and was a hard worker, besides being intelligent and handy with a pencil, was better suited to headquarters work than to the line, and that's where he soon was. In time he became secretary to the general who commanded his division. This gave him time and a place to write, but to some degree it cut him off from the rank and file.

Kahn went overseas early and was soon dispatched, with his division, the famous Thirty-second, into the New Guinea jungles. There his reporting handicap was even greater. The Battle of Buna, one of the most terrible ordeals of American arms, was being fought. Though not a front-line soldier, Kahn was often under fire, and he sent back dispatches to the New Yorker about his journeys forward. They did not seem especially grievous. A major factor in this particular case was censorship. It was the tightest that General MacArthur ever placed on a campaign. The public knew almost nothing of the fearful suffering of the troops, though casualties were heavier than in the well-reported Guadalcanal struggle. Later, back in the United States, Kahn told more of the grim story in the *Saturday Evening Post*.

In Europe the New Yorker had Janet Flanner and Mollie Panter-Downes, its regular Paris and London letter writers, and drew on British author Rebecca West and others. One of its star reporters, A. J. Liebling, was a sort of roving correspondent. He knew French, and before the war he had spent a good deal of time in France, including study at the Sorbonne. A heavy-bodied, high-domed man, he was slow-gaited, nearsighted, and extremely reserved in manner. But he ranged widely. When the Nazi troops burst across France he walked across the French-Spanish border not far ahead of them.

Nearly four years later, after writing many combat pieces from Africa and England, Liebling debarked in France from a large landing craft that had brought assault troops to the Normandy beachhead. His long "Cross-Channel Trip" was ranked by the New Yorker editors as among the best they printed. Excerpt:

A sailor came by and Shorty, one of the men in the gun crew, said to him, "Who was it?" The sailor said, "Rocky and Bill. They're all tore up. A shell got the winch and ramps and all." I went forward to the well deck, which was sticky with a mixture of blood and condensed milk. Soldiers had left cases of rations lying all about the ship, and a fragment of the shell that hit the boys had torn into a carton of cans of milk. Rocky and Bill had been moved below-decks into one of the large forward compartments. Rocky was dead beyond possible doubt, somebody told me, but the pharmacist's mate had given Bill blood plasma and thought he might still be alive. I remembered Bill, a big, baby-faced kid from the District of Columbia, built like a wrestler. He was about 20, and the other boys used to kid him about a girl he was always writing letters to. A third wounded man, a soldier dressed in khaki, lay on a stretcher on the deck breathing hard through his mouth. His long, triangular face looked like a dirty drumhead; his skin was white and drawn tight over his high cheekbones. He wasn't making much noise. There was a shooting-gallery smell over everything and when we passed close under the Arkansas and she let off a salvo, a couple of our men who had their backs to her quivered and had to be reassured. . . .

The "I" reporting style of the New Yorker had the advantage of intimacy, but it was less suitable for the panoramic sweep than many situations demanded. Insertion of the customary little kickeroos often blunted rather than toned up the story. Liebling's craft had performed various chores off the landing beach for several days when, partially crippled, it was ordered back to England. The crew was trying to make it before pub-closing. Another craft, worse hurt, asked them, apologetically, to stand by while it proceeded more slowly. The commander replied good-humoredly: "Never mind. We would have been too late for pub-closing anyway." Liebling thought the message "may someday be in schoolbooks along with Nelson's 'England expects every man to do his duty.' " Readers thinking about the men engaging the Nazis on the beaches, as the report led them to do, found the ending a bit light.

Some of the best New Yorker war reporting was by John Lardner, best known as a light commentator on sports for other publications, who was primarily representing a newspaper syndicate. His story from the Anzio beachhead was acclaimed by many, including some New Yorker editors, as the best reporting of that action. Later his brother David, representing the New Yorker, was killed at Aachen in Belgium. Another of Ring Lardner's sons had died in the Spanish civil war. But John went to the Pacific, where he landed with the troops at Iwo Jima and Okinawa. At Iwo Jima, using broader strokes than was customary with New Yorker reporters, he got a bigger and clearer picture. It contained an over-all dignity of fighting men that was often missing.

I got into a small boat with Colonel Thomas Wornham, regimental commander, and some of his staff, his messengers, and his radio operators. We chopped and splashed through the ocean swells to Wornham's control ship, which was anchored nearer the shore, at the line at which the first assault troops formed up in their amtracks and began their long slow, bobbing run for the beach. They went in in ragged waves, which left the departure line at intervals of a few minutes, coached hoarsely by a loudspeaker from the bridge of the control ship. The men in the amtracks were a fierce and stirring sight as they passed us to disappear in the valleys of water between us and the beach. I stood watching them as well as I could from the rail of the control ship beside a regimental messenger, a Navajo Indian named Galeagon, and we spoke of how most of the shock troops we could see, their hands and faces greased dead white for protection against possible flame barriers, sat up very straight and looked intently ahead. The first wave struck the beach approximately at the appointed hour of nine, and simultaneously the Navy shellfire, which had been raking the shoreline, jumped its range to the ridges and pillboxes farther inland. The central range was in our sector of the island. We could see the wreckage of Japanese planes piled at one edge of the plateau. We knew that an airfield lay just beyond this junk—one of the two airfields for which the Marines were beginning the dogged battle of Iwo Jima.

The short-story writers had a better chance than reporters to get some of the poignancy of the civilian-at-war into their copy. Robert McLaughlin wrote effective pieces, mostly of the early recruit days. Edward Newhouse was limited by his job as an aide to a high Air Force general, but he got some of the flavor of the armed forces into his work. Irwin Shaw, looking more to the rank and file, achieved probably the best effects of all.

The most serious tone in the New Yorker was set, as might have been expected, by E. B. White. His license as a practicing humorist was in danger of being lifted. He would start a piece, decide that the time to be funny was either in the past or the future, and tear it up. His thoughts turned more and more to the problems of the nations, and he became an advocate of "one world." This did not mean that Ross had gone in for "cosmic thinking." White once explained the New Yorker's editorial position this way: "Most publications, I think, make rather hard demands on their editorial writers, asking them to be consistent and sensible. The New Yorker has never suggested anything of that kind, and thus has greatly eased a writer's burden—for it is easier to say what you think if you don't feel obliged to follow a green arrow. The New Yorker is both aloof and friendly toward its opinionated contributors, and I am grateful for this. I am reasonably sure that if some trusty around the place were to submit an editorial demanding that the George Washington Bridge be moved sixty feet further upstream and thatched with straw, the editors would publish it, no questions asked."

In the spring of 1943 White penned a typical item for "Comment."

Dr. Gallup, the asker, has asked people whether they favor an international police force, and three out of four have said they do. That is very nice. It is also quite misleading. Asking a man whether he wants an international police force is like asking him whether he wants the Rockettes. Of course he does, but the question is not whether he thinks the Rockettes are a good idea but whether he knows what is in back of them, making them effective; in short, whether he is in earnest about the girls and willing to give up time and money to build a stage big enough to hold them, hire an orchestra loud enough to accompany them, buy costumes rich enough to adorn them, and in general sustain an organization orderly enough to give them meaning and make them click. Dr. Gallup should ask his question again, this time adding, "And you people realize, of course, that a police force is no good if simply used as a threat to strengthen agreements between independent powers, that to have meaning it must be the certified agent of the law, that to have law we must first have a constitutional world society, and that to achieve that each nation must say good-bye to its own freedom of action and to its long-established custom of doing as it damn well pleases. *Now* how many of you want an international police force?"

Here's one hand up, Dr. Gallup.—*By E. B. White, from "Notes and Comments," May 15, 1943.*

With the world in arms, it was only fitting that the New Yorker should have a civil war. By this time the atmosphere was supercharged because Ross had learned, a few years earlier, of the three quarters of a million dollars of the New Yorker's money that Fleischmann had lost in backing John Hanrahan's *Stage* magazine. Ross was ready to quit and Fleischmann was ready to accept his resignation before better counsel prevailed. Where the earlier differences between the two men had been regarded as bitter office squabbles, now there was a deep cleavage. They rarely spoke to each other.

The cause of the new outbreak was the passing of a quarterly dividend in 1943. Advertising was down. The war had ruined the travel business and trade with France and other

European nations. Some of the stockholders felt that, nevertheless, the business department could bring in more revenue than it was doing under Fleischmann's direction. Ross agreed with them.

The fight—led by Jane Grant—was a brisk one and for a while there was a strong possibility that Fleischmann would be removed. But in the end a compromise was reached, with Hawley Truax, long a director, coming into the business department as treasurer and keeper of the peace. Dividend payments were resumed before the year was out.

Plush-lined Rut? 16

Now and again these days Ross will cry out to a member of his inner circle, "Our trouble is we're in a plush-lined rut!" The term "formula" comes less readily to his lips than in the old days. Occasionally, though, he shakes the editorial bottle as violently as in the period of frantic search. In his mind there seems to lurk a suspicion that his ancient fear of the formula hardening was well founded.

Undeniably the New Yorker's circulation and advertising are at their highest pinnacles. Subscribers and newsstand buyers average around 350,000—twice as many as a decade ago. Two thirds of them live outside of New York City. No strenuous effort is made to increase circulation. People subscribe or resubscribe on their own initiative, with cost per renewal therefore much lower than for the average magazine. More advertising was carried in 1950 than ever before. Bored with the conflicting claims of big popular magazines to volume leadership, the New Yorker took full-page newspaper ads to announce that it stood in fourth place itself. At the end of 1950 a plump melon was cut by the stockholders which brought the take for the year to slightly less than eleven per cent on the current stock value. Ross now holds hardly more than the one per cent of stock necessary to get him a listing in the official published statement of ownership.

The magazine's three large floors of offices at 25 West Forty-third Street, two blocks south of the original offices, are still far from plushy. Artists and writers under contract are usually allowed at least desk space in one of the countless cubbyholes that open off the labyrinthine corridors. Technical progress has not, however, been altogether ignored. Anyone who wants air conditioning may have it.

A buffer of secretaries and editors protects Ross so thoroughly that to many staff members he is an almost mythical figure. Many have never spoken with him. He has been known to meet an author of fairly long tenure in a corridor and, not recognizing him exactly, congratulate him for a piece written by someone else. It is considered bad form to straighten him out. All this has resulted in an office legend, nurtured by those without knowledge of Roughhouse Ross, that he is a sensitive genius in need of protection from the thorny outer world.

Ross's seclusion has not, of course, been owing to his view of himself as a "grandee." In the very early days he had, after all, delegated personal relations, especially the firing of employees, so far as possible, to others. There isn't a "Jesus" any more. Ross has a titular assistant, but elsewhere he would be called an executive secretary. Since Ik Shuman left a few years ago the role has been divided among several persons.

Ross's passion for detail, along with his retirement from wide personal contacts, has reduced the rate of personnel turnover. Some believe he is unconsciously atoning for the sudden dismissals of the early days. As the operation is constantly and ever more mysteriously subdivided, the tendency is merely to add new workers. "If an office boy should chronically louse up paper-clip distribution," an old employee has said, "he would not be dismissed, but another boy hired to watch him." Greater security does not mean that tension has disappeared. Ross is capable of stirring things up by remote control, and often does.

The magazine's wealth in dollars has not brought editorial satisfaction to Ross. The mystery of the dearth of rising young humorists has taxed the minds of many persons, including, naturally, Ross's. Shaking his head dejectedly, he has declared that funny writers have come up, but no humorists. A theory held by some is that the movies and radio, paying heavily for inferior material, have stopped humorists short of full development. Others believe that depression and then war knocked all the humor out of the younger generation.

The New Yorker has had experience, it is true, with promising young humorists who turned to grim matters. Ruth McKenney's "My Sister Eileen" series, which appeared in the late thirties, attracted wide attention. Then suddenly she was writing books about strikes and was deeply involved in left-wing politics. Leonard Q. Ross's tales of the adventures in a night English class of an adult immigrant who liked to write his name H*Y*M*A*N K*A*P*L*A*N were immensely popular. Leonard Q. Ross was really Dr. Leo C. Rosten, a research expert in the social sciences. He chose to follow his professional career, working in occasional slick novels.

One school of opinion lays responsibility for the shortage of humorists, ironically, at the door of the New Yorker itself. According to this theory, Ross has simply been too successful. The humorous *Life* ended in 1936. *Vanity Fair* went to its grave in the same year, though ostensibly combined with *Vogue*. For a few more years *Judge* staggered along and then gave up the ghost. Don Marquis is dead and even F.P.A.'s column has disappeared from the papers. Almost no place is left for a humorist to appear outside the New Yorker. Because space is needed for its longer journalistic pieces, departments, and fiction, the New Yorker does not experiment with humor as in the days when Thurber and White and Arthur Kober and the rest were developing. There is another penalty of success. The editors, hunting for something fresh, find that young writers are imitating the New Yorker.

Ross is prepared to set out a red couch, caviar, and champagne for any writer able to produce the kind of humor he would find suitable for his pages. Many are trying, which proves, at least, that the new generation *wants* to write humor despite catastrophes. Thurber gets a big mail from young hopefuls and answers it religiously. Perelman and Corey Ford have worked with youngsters. Peter De Vries comes nearest to filling the bill for the New Yorker. He had been struggling in Chicago as the small-salaried editor of *Poetry* when Thurber read some of his manuscripts and carried them to Ross. De Vries has written poetry, short stories, and casuals for the magazine, besides sitting in on the selection of art.

Of the elders—White, Thurber, Sullivan, Perelman, Gibbs, Kober—Perelman is the most active in magazine humor, and his popularity is on a brisk upgrade. A man signing his name as Namlerep once gave the following description of Perelman.

> Under a forehead roughly comparable to that of the Javanese or the Piltdown Man are visible a pair of tiny pig eyes, lit up alternately by greed and concupiscence. His nose, broken in childhood by a self-inflicted blow with a hockey stick, has a prehensile tip, ever quick to smell out an insult. At the least sus-

picion of an affront, Perelman, who has the pride of a Spanish grandee, has been known to whip out his sword-cane and hide in the nearest closet. He has a good figure, if not a spectacular one; above the hips a barrel chest and a barrel belly form a single plastic unit which bobbles uncertainly on a pair of skinny shanks. In motion the man's body may best be likened to a New Bedford whaler in the teeth of an equinoctial gale; in repose it is strongly reminiscent of a giant sloth. In point of fact, from what small exterior evidence we possess, it would appear that he has modeled himself closely on that luckless animal. A monstrous indolence, cheek by jowl with the kind of irascibility displayed by a Vermont postmaster while sorting the morning mail, is perhaps his chief characteristic.

It is just possible that Perelman sees himself in the above light. At any rate it is his professional view, and anyone tampering with it runs the chance of being run through with a sword cane. It may not be dangerous to say that many of his acquaintances look on the portrait as an exaggerated, even a boastful one. They point out that, not being a large man, he is at best keg-chested. In cool weather he wears big, loose coats that miss the ground by only a little. These undeniably give him, when he is in motion, a look of being caught in an air movement. But the term "gale" is too strong. It is more as though a gentle but capricious breeze propelled him. Comparison with the Piltdown Man is generally thought to be his sly way of trying to picture himself as a brutal, irresistible type.

Perelman's identification of himself with the sloth is a peccadillo common with writers. Those blessed with true slothfulness always try to give an impression, even to themselves, of being hard workers. The industrious work hard to give an impression of slothfulness. Perelman composes slowly and painfully on the schedule of a businessman who arrives ahead of his employees and leaves after they have gone home. While in New York he rents an office and keeps business hours. When Al Hirschfeld, the artist, and Perelman were touring Siam and other far-off places for *Holiday* magazine, Hirschfeld always accompanied his partner to the post office when a manuscript was finished. Perelman's arm usually had to be twisted before he would mail it. His natural instinct was to peek into the envelope, find a word that seemed wrong, and go back to his hotel and change it. If he changed it he retyped the whole page.

When dealing with Perelman the most dangerous land mine on which to tread is his professional reputation for irascibility. In print he is nearly always angry. Even when not threatening to cane somebody he is likely to be so obstreperous that he has to be chased and caught, or disposed of in some other manner. In real life—the words have to be measured carefully—he is quiet, good-humored, and obliging. That is, unless a manuscript is changed without his consent.

Lacking a stable of young writing humorists, Ross has concentrated on the cartoons. Here again he misses Thurber. After some years of nearly total blindness, during which he did no drawing, Thurber, seeing a little better, is back at work on his cartoons. He uses a white pencil on solid black paper. But his output is small.

A terrific blow was the death, in the fall of 1949, of Helen Hokinson. Her ample-bosomed characters, serious-minded but often befuddled, had become so famous that the term "Hokinson woman" was part of the American language. Hoky had herself become a celebrated personage, but fame sat lightly on her, and she continued to be a careful, hard-working reporter. At women's conventions and the flower and dog shows she filled her sketchbook, just big enough to fit into her small hand, with likenesses of exhibitors and visitors. A large, broad-beamed woman once remarked to those near her, "Watch out, I understand that Helen Hokinson often comes here for material." Hoky, busily drawing the woman, laughed politely, but did not miss a stroke.

Most of the buxom women who saw Hoky's work were her fans. One wrote, typically, "My husband thinks you must have seen me trying on hats." Another reported, "Oh, you were drawing me two months ago, all right, even if you never actually laid eyes on me. But not now! I've taken off 20 pounds." Many sent in accounts of their own small misadventures.

Hoky saw many of her "women's" characteristics in herself. Not physical ones, of course, for even the added weight of middle years brought her to no more than 110 pounds.

"I refuse," she once said, looking into a mirror and speaking like a true Hokinson woman, "to have gray hairs in my bangs!" But she grayed early.

From her efficient Connecticut summer studio she could go out to her garden and be as capricious as any of her women. "I can't seem to get through her head," a man helping with the garden told a friend of hers, "that this is the wrong season and especially the wrong time of day to plant tomatoes." Hoky, on hands and knees, went gaily along at high noon, the tomato plants wilting behind her.

She was devoted to pets and dealt with them as far as possible on a human level. A tiger tomcat named Swenson Mousilini was the smartest she ever had. Some people thought he rose above the human level, if the creature comforts he secured were any indication. Swenson was a big gray cat with black stripes and white vest and feet. He hated men and horses. Whenever a party including men arrived for lunch or tea, Swenson took off for the top of the house or a tree, where he pretended to be fearful of toppling down. When Hoky sent one of the men aloft to the rescue Swenson gave him a fight. Horses were responsible for Swenson's death. During the war the maker of his favorite food—he always ate dog food—changed the formula, substituting horse meat for beef. Swenson refused to touch it. Malnutrition and old age laid him in his grave.

Quick enthusiasms were as common with Hoky as with her women. She "took up" cooking—she had never married—after hating kitchen duties all her life. Out of her experiences around a stove came ideas for drawings, such as one of a harassed woman muddling a "Happy Birthday" on a cake while her cook looked on with unconcealed contempt. She had first a bridge and then a canasta phase.

The popularity of the "Hokinson women" resulted in an indirect way in their creator's death. Hoky was bothered by a feeling that people were laughing *at* instead of *with* her women. She repressed her natural reticence and launched a crusade by radio and platform appearances to explain and defend them. Finally she set to work on a play about them in collaboration with Nancy Hamilton, a successful stage writer. For dramatic conflict Miss Hamilton wanted to create a catty woman or two.

"But my women are honest, they're good, they're well-meaning," Hoky would cry.

Once while Miss Hamilton was away Hoky, to be helpful, rewrote the play, leaving out the plot.

Hoky took a plane on the first day of November 1949 to Washington, where she was to speak at the opening of a Community Chest drive. It was her second plane trip, and because the other had worried her mother, who shared her apartment in New York, she said nothing of her journey, but left a supply of cash in a handbag on the kitchen table in case of emergency. As the airliner came in for a landing it was rammed by a small plane and crashed.

There was drama in the New Yorker offices, for the news, flashed to Ross by the wire services, struck him like a thunderbolt. His patriarchal instincts were roused to their fullest. He dispatched two men to Washington and stood vigil at his telephone until it was certain that all passengers had died. Ross, together with Hawley Truax, was immensely helpful in making funeral arrangements and aiding the distressed family in other ways.

Nowadays Ross is busier than ever in the hunt for suitable cartoons. He sits as always in the weekly art meetings. After a quarter century in which he radically changed cartoon art, he is less humble.

The conferences, held each Tuesday, are similar to those of the early days. Rea Irvin remains as art consultant, but, as before, he comes to the office only for the meeting. At seventy, wavy haired and young-looking, he spends most of his free time during visits to New York—he lives in rural Connecticut—at The Players, likely as not playing pool with Franklin P. Adams.

The full-time art editor is James Geraghty, in charge of sorting out the two or three thousand contributions which are sent in every week. Affable, aggressive, prematurely gray, his first connection with the New Yorker was as a supplier of cartoon ideas. (Professional gag men are kept under contract.) Geraghty brings to the conference two baskets of "roughs," which are unfinished drawings with suggested caption lines. One of the baskets contains work of artists either under contract or whose work is accepted fairly regularly. In the other is the best by "unknowns."

At one side of a long table sit Ross, Irvin, Geraghty, Lobrano, and whomever else Ross wants there. Above the table is a rack on which the roughs are placed. Ross demands accuracy, as always, and his own opinions are stronger than they used to be. One time he objected to a mustache on a cartoon figure.

"People don't wear mustaches any more," he said.

After a moment Geraghty, Irvin, and Lobrano began to stroke their small mustaches.

"I don't think of those as mustaches," Ross said.

The cartoon mustache was removed.

Ross demands perfection in the final drawing. Every detail must be authentic. Artists are asked, for example, to produce evidence that a truck is of a known manufacture. Researchers check the smallest details. Once they discovered that the screw threads on a fire hydrant ran the wrong way. The artist managed, however, to convince the editors that the matter was not vital.

Ross spends a lot of time worrying about the art. He takes drawings to his office and mulls over them. Sometimes he thinks of a change that will make a piece of work acceptable. Or he merely says, "I think there is something here," and has it passed back to the artist to tinker with. Specific changes are often suggested and the captions are likely to be reworded. Lobrano is considered especially good at rewording. Occasionally a regular, disgusted with the numerous changes demanded, refuses to submit drawings for a while. But the New Yorker pays more than others and the prestige is important and profitable. Advertisers usually prefer to hire New Yorker artists, and the magazine's advertising columns appear sometimes to contain nearly as many drawings by regulars as do the editorial. Peter Arno went a step further not long ago, reaching the sublime, when a photograph of him endorsing a beer was published in the New Yorker.

For a reason which may or may not have something to do with the times, the macabre drawings of Charles Addams are now the most popular with New Yorker readers. Addams is a big, good-natured man of thirty-eight. He likes powerful foreign-made automobiles which he sometimes enters, with himself as driver, in cross-country and hill-climbing races. Any good joke will make Addams chuckle, but he has admitted that macabre humor has always fascinated him. He first appeared in the New Yorker in 1933, and even then his cartoon people were usually in some kind of trouble. In one of the earliest a man was drawing heads of horses on a wall. He had started with a big head and was down to a tiny one. A friend declared: "Why, hello, Otto. They *told* me you were getting an inferiority complex."

Addams invented the huge, eerie old "Addams House" in 1937 when he was working out a cartoon about a vacuum-cleaner salesman calling at a haunted house. He liked the house and began to populate it with his sadistic, horror-savoring characters. The master of the house, Addams admits, looks a little like a bloated Tom Dewey, but he doesn't think he had Dewey in mind for it. The huge manservant, who is too stupid or too morose ever to say anything, may have been unconsciously modeled, Addams thinks, after Boris Karloff's Frankenstein monster. The grandmother could be any witch. When people comment on the little boy and girl, who are as perverse as their elders, Addams inquires innocently, "Aren't *all* children like them?"

People who meet Barbara Addams, his wife, for the first time often do a double-take and a moment later whisper to someone that she resembles the slim, jet-haired, withdrawn mistress of the "Addams House." The natural conclusion is that his wife serves Addams as a model. That is not quite correct. He created his cartoon character *before* he met his wife. Addams doesn't see anything unusual about drawing a type of woman that attracted him and then marrying her after he had found her in the flesh. But he admits that the lady of the cartoon is more attractive now than she was before he married.

Addams' face, particularly his nose, which is fairly prominent, was partly responsible for the appearance in the New Yorker's pages of Sam Cobean, whose male characters are usually in some kind of trouble in saloons when they are not stripping women naked with their eyes. Addams and Cobean were in the Army together. To while away spare hours Cobean, who had worked for Walt Disney, drew pictures of Addams—sometimes of the nose alone. After the war Addams took these to the New Yorker and convinced the art selectors that Cobean had possibilities.

Like Addams, Cobean was a fancier of powerful and exotic automobiles. Early in the summer of 1951, while driving his Jaguar, he crashed into another car and was killed.

Another bright star of the magazine's newer cartoonists is Saul Steinberg. He had seen the New Yorker in his native Rumania and in Italy, where he studied architecture, and had thought of it as one of the world's few civilized magazines even before he was able to read English. On faces of the people he drew for an Italian magazine between 1936 and 1939 he was not allowed to show either bitter or puzzled expressions. Therefore he covered the faces with mustaches and beards.

Steinberg came to the United States in 1941. He was already well known in Europe and the New Yorker accepted his work at once. Except for taking off beards and mustaches to reveal puzzlement and a good deal of sadness on the faces of his people, he altered his style little in changing from Europe to America.

The so-called "New Yorker short story" probably causes more debate, and results in more distemper, than anything else about the magazine. To many, the stories are merely stretches of type separating the cartoons, as the sea lies around islands. A fairly large number of people read them out of active dislike, apparently as a way of getting blood pressure up. Not only are there complaints about the stories seeming to get nowhere, and ending as if the authors had gone out for a drink and forgot to come back, but it is charged that neuroticism comprises too large a portion of their basic content. The last criticism, at least, appears to be unfair, since the magazine endeavors to report the times. Stories from the New Yorker are more widely reprinted than those from other magazines.

For their part, the editors deny vigorously that there is any such thing as a "New Yorker" type of story. They are particularly irritated by any suggestion that they rewrite stories or are a "closed" magazine with a few favored authors. There is a rather large staff of fiction editors—seven of them—who are conscientious, sensitive, considerate, and always extremely hopeful of discovering new talent.

Katharine White is still active, both in manuscript reading and in working with authors. But Lobrano, who is listed officially with the Post Office Department as one of the two managing editors—William Shawn is the other—is a sort of general supervisor or clearing point for the fiction department. He wouldn't like to call himself *the* fiction editor, partly because of the vagueness of office titles and partly because he is as retiring as he can be. All seven fiction editors prefer to be anonymous except when communicating with authors.

When an unsolicited fiction manuscript comes into the office it is read by both of the two first readers. If the writer seems to have talent or if somehow the story is out of the general ruck they pass it on. At least two more editors read it, on the average, during the next stage. Unless it is then rejected the rest of the editors read it. They may point out weak spots, inconsistencies, and the like to the author, and, if asked, perhaps suggest possibilities for solving problems. They do not, however, rewrite, make assignments, or suggest topics. The manuscript of a regular contributor is treated not much differently. One editor may correspond with him and be the first reader of his work. Otherwise his manuscript passes through the same machinery.

Ross is the final editor and the final authority on acceptance. He doesn't get so deeply involved in fiction as in "fact" copy, but he is on hand with his queries. He notes muddy passages, keeps the characters in focus, and calls for references. He is credited with being brilliantly penetrating sometimes.

To add to Ross's general troubles, John O'Hara, probably the best known of the story writers, has been throwing rocks at him. Hostilities began, according to New Yorker editors, when O'Hara insisted on full payment for submitted manuscripts whether they were used or not. Many story writers are, like artists and non-fiction contributors, under contract and are rewarded for allowing a first look at their manuscripts. O'Hara had always kept a respectable eye on his own cash register and often accompanied his contributions with suggestions that an increase in his rate would cause him no unhappiness. In better times Ross had answered one of O'Hara's particularly eloquent beefs by presenting him with an engraved gold watchcase which Ik Shuman had bought for three dollars in a Second Avenue shop. O'Hara's most recent request was turned down flatly.

There were other factors as well. The New Yorker ran an unfavorable review of O'Hara's novel, *A Rage to Live.* He was displeased by the magazine's rather battered profile of Ernest Hemingway, whom he ranks alongside Shakespeare. The Hemingway profile brought a blast from O'Hara in the *Times*'s Sunday book section: "The most recent, and most disgusting, example of the intrusions into Hemingway's private life was made by a publication that reports on Hemingway's drinking habits, somewhat in the manner of a gleeful parole officer. . . . For Eustace Tilley to raise an eyeglass over anybody's drinking is one for the go-climb-a-lamppost department. . . . With the long piece on Hemingway the magazine achieved a new low in something."

The Hemingway profile drew wider adverse comment than anything the New Yorker has published in recent years. Its author, Lillian Ross, a young former *PM* reporter (no relation to Harold Ross), did not paint an appealing portrait of Hemingway. He seemed to be going to pieces before her eyes while emitting loud, ungraceful boasts, somewhat like a punch-drunk prize fighter in his cups. Though it ran under the profile heading, the technique was nearer that of "Reporter" pieces. Miss Ross described, using considerable dialogue, several visits with Hemingway, his wife, son, and friends, including Marlene Dietrich.

Around the New Yorker offices it was said that Miss Ross greatly admired Hemingway and believed her picture of him to be a favorable one—and that Hemingway after reading it thought so too. There was a long debate over whether to publish it or not. To letters of protest the editors replied that Hemingway had read it and raised no objection.

Ross showed a flash of his old will to experiment when

he startled the commercial magazine world by devoting an entire issue to John Hersey's account of the havoc wrought by the atomic bomb at Hiroshima. The original idea had been simply for a number of pieces. Then it was discovered that the story did not break up well for serialization. It was Shawn who came up with the suggestion of running it as a whole. The magazine could have withstood a bad gamble, but as things turned out, it was a very good one. Newsstands were snatched bare of the issue soon after its appearance, and Ross's acumen as an editor was celebrated. It is true that persons who insist on thinking of the New Yorker as strictly a humor magazine were a bit nonplused. Helen Hokinson, who was then alive, enjoyed repeating a remark a woman made to her about it. "I've read that long Hiroshima article from beginning to end," she said, "and I just wish you'd tell me what was funny about it!"

A few general changes have been made in the "fact" formula. The profile heading has been stretched to cover pieces of a more general nature—as, for example, a "profile" of the sea, and the silt at the bottom of a river. One well-known profile character was actually a work of fiction. This was the ancient and salty "Mr. Flood," a veteran of the fish market. Joseph Mitchell, the author, explains in the foreword to a book in which the pieces were reprinted that "Mr. Flood" was a composite, but the New Yorker allowed the impression that he was real to stand.

Ross decided after the war to give slightly greater coverage of national affairs. For one thing, he concluded that Washington was no longer strictly an American city. It was now international. The regular newspaper correspondents tried out, but Ross always found their stuff too "insidey," too much like the standard columnists. A young ex-editor of the *Nation*, Richard H. Rovere, satisfied Ross by writing much as if reporting on a foreign place, just as Janet Flanner and Mollie Panter-Downes give chatty accounts of Paris and London. But writers who try to get general assignments in America outside New York City have little success. The chance of getting a European subject across is better.

The Korean war caused Ross a good deal of editorial concern. His offhand opinion was that it wouldn't last long. Consequently he sent no correspondent, though Liebling, Kahn, and others pressed to go. Negotiations for peace were almost at hand before Ross dispatched Kahn.

A "fact" writer can be sure that at least half a dozen persons, all holding sharp pencils, will deal with his copy. There will be at least two editors—Ross himself and Shawn or one of his assistants. There will be a copy editor or two. All will read for "taste" and syntax as well as for clarity and accuracy. And there will be the dedicated band of checkers.

Feverish checking has made the New Yorker as detail-accurate a magazine as any published. But sometimes the checkers are remindful of the blind men who examined an elephant, one touching the trunk only, another the tail, and so on, with none of them getting much of an idea what a whole elephant is like. The checkers had no way, for example, of evaluating Lillian Ross's impression of Hemingway.

One detail-accurate "Reporter" piece was so far out of focus that it disrupted a department of a large New York firm. After receiving carte blanche from the firm's president, the writer set to work with the complete co-operation of employees. As a matter of technique he built his story around a man chosen fairly arbitrarily for the purpose. The employee was severely embarrassed when the piece appeared because, although the basic facts in the article were correct, he appeared more important than he was. A rash of jealousy broke out among other employees. Many felt the president had done wrong by forcing them to give up time. By a coincidence the article's hero was fired not long afterward. The president felt obliged to write a general memorandum explaining that the action did *not* stem from the article.

For its silver anniversary in February of 1950 the New Yorker could boast a victory in a crusade. The slain dragon was, once again, a railroad. The magazine's editorials softened it up. Ross—the old Roughhouse Ross—personally forced it to lie down and roll over.

This time the railroad was the New York Central, though the contest was more specifically with the management of Grand Central Terminal. The vast hall, in which E. B. White had whiled away his hours of unemployment, and through which Ross commuted to Stamford, was being filled with amplified commercials.

"Comment" of the New Yorker issue of October 15, 1949, remarked:

> We wonder how a traveler would make out if he were to carry an amplifying device into Grand Central and shout back at the commercials. "Aw, shut up!" would be a proper response to make in the great hall these days. Undoubtedly the traveler would be seized and ejected from the terminal, as a disturber of the peace. But the New York Central apparently is in a safe corner and can disturb the peace 25 times an hour by plugging beer and flashlight batteries in a loud voice when people are trying to get some sleep in the waiting room. Now that the precedent has been set to louse up a public place with audible advertisements, the idea should spread rapidly. Eventually it will spread into hospitals, whose rooms, we trust, will be entirely occupied by railroad executives, each on a bed of pain.

By December 10 the crusade was in high gear.

The radio people have a word for the kind of audience assembled in Grand Central Terminal. . . . The radio people call it the "captive" audience. They are generally agreed that the captive audience proves very attractive to the advertiser—in the same way that a fly entangled in the web is attracted to the spider, or a frog immobilized by fear is attractive to the snake. An audience in captivity is a new stunt in this republic.

A little while later "Comment" mentioned that twenty-five letters to the State Public Service Commission would force a hearing on the commercials. The letters were promptly sent. In the meantime a terminal spokesman had blamed the hullabaloo on an "adult comic book."

When the hearings opened quite a few people were on hand to protest the commercials, including a man who had lost his mother-in-law in the terminal because the noise upset his wife. But Ross, stepping back more than three decades to his days on the San Francisco water front, easily stole the show.

His occupation, he explained, was "editor of an adult comic book." When the counsel charged that the New Yorker had started the fuss, and read from "Comment" to prove it, Ross declared sarcastically, "Sorry, I guess I must have read that in Grand Central Terminal." The counsel revealed a poll which professed to show that most people thought the commercials were fine. Ross claimed that his own polling outfit, the "Datum Diggers," had found just the opposite, by exactly the same percentage points.

As a result of the hearing the commercials were stopped. To show that there were no hard feelings Ross had the terminal manager as his personal guest at a big anniversary party the New Yorker gave.

While he has not again played before an audience, Ross has appeared vicariously on the stage in Wolcott Gibbs's Broadway hit, *Season in the Sun,* which opened in the fall of 1950. Gibbs's own histrionics provided mild amusement to admirers of his Luce profile. For *Life* he posed a sequence purporting to show how a playwright sweats out opening night. The fans of his New Yorker drama criticism whiled away some pleasurable hours imagining what he would have written about his own play. In an apparently frantic effort to escape failure he had inserted cathouse and homosexual gags and other hoary devices of the burlesque stage.

The character whom Gibbs patterned on Ross was the strongest of the play and was probably responsible for its success. The creator of the role, Anthony Ross—no relation—is taller than Ross, younger, and his voice is less raucous, but his portrayal was pronounced basically accurate by those in a position to know. Ross himself was spotted at the play twice, but withheld comment. In the play Ross goes to Fire Island to rescue one of his staff members, presumably Gibbs, who has decided to quit and write a serious book. The most characteristic parts are Ross's hails of words and his way of completely ignoring any reply as he goes ahead with his share of the conversation, the only one that interests him. Gibbs did not have to be absolutely literal, and to help his plot he had Ross looking forward happily to an approaching storm. Not many of the audience knew, after all, that Ross trembles when it thunders.

Today Ross has the satisfaction of seeing his magazine a great success. It is the bible of that part of the younger generation which thinks of itself as sophisticated, and it is still the favorite magazine of most of its older readers who pray for fresher material. Anyone hesitates to experiment with a successful formula. But those who feel that Ross was happiest while the New Yorker was being created are convinced that his instinct is to scramble it and start over again.

Meanwhile Ross works hard, and gloomily goes about accepting gold medals and other honors which are showered on himself and his magazine. Not long ago he was sitting at lunch with an acquaintance, relating the debt he owed those who helped develop the New Yorker. He praised his present staff to the skies. A little later his mood shifted.

"Nobody up there will do a damned thing," he said, pointing in the general direction of his offices. "Have to do every God damned thing myself. When someone wants to give us a gold medal or something, do you think any of them will go after it? Always sick or nervous. I have to go."

He always stipulates that no speech will be required of him, but once he broke his own rule. It was at a dinner of the Laughing Lion Society, composed of former editors and managers of the *Jester*, the Columbia humor magazine. Thurber and Fred Allen were also being honored. Ross, who was sitting by Frank Sullivan, listened to them make witty speeches. When his turn came he arose, got his trophy, and glanced nervously about him.

"Jesus Christ!" he exploded, and sat down.

Sullivan looked at him sourly. "Too long, Ross," he said. "I was bored before you had passed the first syllable."

Index

Adams, Althea, 157–59, 161
Adams, Bristow, 143
Adams, Franklin P., 3, 24, 28, 40, 43–44, 48, 60, 63, 67, 73, 144, 147–48, 158–59, 193, 215, 221, 230–31, 280, 285
Adams, Kenneth, 10–12, 32
Adams, Samuel Hopkins, 39n, 255
Addams, Barbara, 287–88
Addams, Charles, 243, 287–88
Alain, Daniel, 243
Alajalov, 137
Algonquin Hotel, 39, 51
Algonquin Round Table, 39, 43, 115, 163, 169, 212, 231
Allen, Ariane, 262
Allen, Fred, 297
Altman, B., & Co., 95
American, New York, 76, 174, 233
American Legion, 36, 38, 48–49, 53–54, 144
American Mercury, 120, 158
Angell, Katharine, 139–40, 153, 164, 171, 175, 199, 206 (*see also* White, Katharine)
Anthony, Norman, 54, 209
Arno, Peter, 81–82, 131–32, 201–2, 228, 286–87
Asbury, Herbert, 192
Aspen, Colorado, 5
Associated Press, 143
Atlantic Monthly, 139, 245

Bainbridge, John, 249, 256
Baldridge, C. LeRoy, 23, 25–26, 29, 33, 36
Bankhead, Tallulah, 233
Barlow, Perry, 136
Barton, Ralph, 63, 68, 137, 214
Baruch, Bernard M., 91
Baskerville, Charles, 59, 87
Baukhage, Hilmar, 34
Beerbohm, Max, 164
Benchley, Robert C., 40, 42–44, 46–47, 63, 91, 107, 147, 151, 197–98, 208, 228, 230–31, 260
Benét, Stephen Vincent, 147
Bennett, Richard, 91
Benson, Sally, 194, 243
Berger, Meyer, 248, 253
Bergh, Sid, 98
Bergman, Bernard, 177–78
Berlin, Irving, 91, 94, 245
Berlin, Mrs. Irving (see Mackay, Ellin)
Bernays, Edward L., 74
Bernstein, Walter, 269
Billingsley, Sherman, 257–58

Bishop, Morris, 143, 240
Blethen, Colonel, 145
Bliss, Tyler H., 36, 57–58, 75
Bohemian Club, 15–17
Bolitho, William, 208
Boothe, Clare, 212, 251–52
Bowen, Ray, 95
Boyle, Kay, 242
Brackett, Charles, 200
Brisbane, Arthur, 133
Brodie, Steve, 192
Bronx River, 149–50, 179
Broun, Heywood, 22, 39–40, 45, 53, 63, 120, 147, 198, 208, 215, 220, 222, 231, 254
Brown Jug, 238
Brown University, 22, 238
Brubaker, Howard, 59
Bryn Mawr, 139
Bull, Johann, 85
Burgess, Gelett, 47
Burke, Thomas, 45
Burrows, Edwin G., 36
Busch, Niven, Jr., 197
Butler, Nicholas Murray, 247
Butterick Publishers, 32–33
Bye, George T., 28, 223

Cain, James M., 230
Call and Post, San Francisco, 14, 17, 38
Cantwell, Robert, 240
Carpentier, Georges, 37
Carroll, Stewart, 33
Case, Frank, 39
Cerf, Bennett, 221–22, 257, 264–65
Chaplin, Charles, 152
Chasen, Dave, 223, 247
Chesterton, G. K., 45
Claxton, Oliver, 106–7
Coates, Robert, 243
Cobb, Irvin S., 43, 245
Cobean, Sam, 288
Cohn, Gene, 15
College Humor, 238
Collier's, 245
Columbus, Ohio, 155–59, 176
Connelly, Marc, 40, 43, 61–63, 71, 97, 120, 140–41, 201–2, 223, 231, 242, 255
"Conning Tower, The," 41, 150
Conrad, Joseph, 14
Conroy, Jack, 240
Cook, Joe, 223
Cooper, Fenimore, 14
Costello, Tim, 236
Covarrubias, 137
Crouse, Russel, 192, 234
Crowninshield, Frank, 45, 64, 208
Curley, Jack, 247

Darrow, Clarence, 245
Darrow, Whitney, Jr., 243
Day, Chon, 243
Day, Clarence, 234
Day, Robert, 228, 243
Decker, Richard, 243
Deerslayer, The, 14
de Kruif, Paul, 158
Dempsey, Jack, 37, 70, 233
De Vries, Peter, 280
Dick, Elsie, 99
Dictionary of Modern English Usage, 14, 118
Dietrich, Marlene, 291
Dietz, Howard, 255
Disinherited, The, 240
Disney, Walt, 288
Divine, Father, 253
Dorsey, George Amos, 158
Dos Passos, John, 45
Downey, Fairfax, 67
Downey, Morton, 233
Duer, Caroline, 163
Dunn, Alan, 136
Durante, Jimmy, 233
Duranty, Walter, 28, 34

Eighteenth Engineers, 17–20
Elie, Frances, 223
Eliot, Charles W., 245
Errol, Leon, 91
Erskine, John, 223

Fadiman, Clifton, 239–40
Farewell to Reform, 240
"Fawkes, Guy," 197
Ferber, Edna, 3, 40, 43, 63, 254–55
Fields, W. C., 91, 247
Finny, Sterling, 107, 180, 199
Fishback, Margaret, 240
Fiske, Mrs. Minnie Maddern, 53
Fitzgerald, F. Scott, 45, 47, 158
Flanner, Janet, 167–68, 270, 293
Fleischmann, Raoul, 55, 59–60, 63, 68–70, 72–74, 78, 85–86, 90, 101, 113, 167–69, 185, 207, 213–14, 254, 265, 274–75
Fleischmann, Ruth, 82, 100
Fleischmann's Yeast, 178–79
Folwell, A. H., 67
Ford, Corey, 67, 85–86, 208, 280
Ford, Henry, 197, 246
Fortune, 104, 213, 249–50
Foster, William Z., 247
Fowler, H. W., 14, 118
Fox, Fontaine, 91
F.P.A. (see Adams, Franklin P.)
Fraser, Phyllis, 257
Front Page, 134
Frueh, Al, 68, 131, 137
Fuller, Rosalind, 41

Gabriel, Gilbert, 67
Gallant, Barney, 124
Gatti-Casazza, Giulio, 67
Geraghty, James, 285
Gershwin, George, 91
Gibbs, Wolcott, 139, 162–65, 172, 183, 192–93, 200, 243, 249–56, 280, 296
Gibson, Charles Dana, 130, 208
Gide, André, 208
Gill, Brendan, 248
Gluck, Alma, 91
Glyn, Elinor, 116
God and My Father, 234
Grand Central Station, 294–95
Grant, Jane, 38–39, 41, 48–55, 70, 275
Graphic, New York, 198
Gray, Gilda, 81
Great Tradition, The, 240
Guinzburg, Harold, 221–22
Guiterman, Arthur, 67, 237, 240

Hadden, Briton, 86
Hahn, Emily, 241
Hale, Nancy, 243
Hale, Ruth, 38–40, 53
Hamburger, Philip, 248
Hamilton, Nancy, 284
Hamilton College, 49
Hammond, Percy, 208
Hanley, Frank, 238
Hanrahan, John, 69, 72, 90, 167, 213, 274
Harbord, James G., 30–31
Harper's Bazaar, 212
Harper's magazine, 245, 262
Harriman, E. H., 9
Harriman, Margaret Case, 39n, 184
Harriman, W. Averell, 9
Harris, Frank, 192
Hart, Moss, 242
Harvey, Alice, 133, 135–36
Hauptmann, Bruno, 255
Having Wonderful Time, 242
Hawley, Hudson, 20–22, 30, 33, 36
Hayes, Helen, 154
Hearst, W. R., 197, 246
Hearst's International, 245
Hecht, Ben, 120, 134
Held, John, Jr., 7, 48, 136
Hellman, Geoffrey T., 248
Hellman, Lillian, 193

Hemingway, Ernest, 192, 197, 291, 293
Herald, New York, 215
Herald Tribune, New York, 246
Herbst, Josephine, 240
Herford, Oliver, 47, 130
Hersey, John, 292
Hicks, Granville, 240
Hill, George Washington, 113–14
Hind Let Loose, A, 117
Hirschfeld, Al, 282
Ho Hum, 187
Hoff, Sydney, 243
Hokinson, Helen, 81–82, 132–35, 136, 202, 282–85, 292
Hokinson, Mary, 133
Holiday magazine, 147, 282
Home Sector, 36–38, 43–44, 54, 57
Hoover, Herbert, 227
House at Pooh Corner, The, 117
Howey, Walter, 134
Hoyt, Julia, 91
Hubbard, Ernest F., 67
Huggins, Miller, 89
Hyde, A. Fillmore, 76
Hyde, Fillmore, 76, 79, 139–40, 188
Hylan, Mayor, 87

Infantry Journal, 269
Ingersoll, Ralph, 76, 92, 97, 102–5, 123, 170, 172–75, 179, 180–84, 200, 213, 249–52, 263
Insull, Sam, 245
Is Sex Necessary?, 203–6, 235
It, 116

James, Henry, 155
James, Marquis, 12, 38, 49, 59, 70
James, Mrs. Marquis (see Rowland, Bess)
Jester, Columbia, 85, 297
Johnson, Spud, 109
Johnston, Alva, 11, 246–48, 253
Jolson, Al, 91
Joplin, Missouri, 29
Josephson, Matthew, 240
Journal, Atlanta, 87
Journal, Columbus, 158
Judge, 47–48, 53–54, 58–59, 65, 68, 75, 78, 85, 115, 125, 134, 140, 153, 209, 238, 249, 279–80
Jumble Shop, 76

Kahn, E. J., Jr., 248, 269–70, 293
Karloff, Boris, 287
Kaufman, George S., 40, 43, 63, 221
Kaye, Danny, 260
Kieran, John, 208
Kirk, Roy, 17, 36
Knapp, C., 67
Kober, Arthur, 193, 241–43, 280
Kopake, Camp, 242

Ladies' Home Journal, 245
Land of Plenty, 240
Lardner, David, 271
Lardner, John, 271–72
Lardner, Ring, 43, 72, 88, 120, 147, 232–33, 239, 272
Laughing Lion Society, 297
Leacock, Stephen, 47, 151, 183
Ledger, Newark, 88
Leibowitz, Samuel, 247
Leonard, Baird, 121
Levy, Newman, 43
Lewis, Sinclair, 45, 117, 206
Liebling, A. J., 248, 253, 270–71, 293
Life (humor), 47–48, 55, 58–59, 68, 75, 78, 85, 115, 121, 125–26, 130, 134, 137, 140, 151, 153, 208–9, 231, 249, 279
Life (picture), 296
Life with Father, 234
Lindbergh, Charles A., Sr., 27
Lindsay, Howard, 234
Lippmann, Walter, 208

Little Review, The, 194
Lobrano, Gustav, 261–62, 285–86, 289–90
Lockridge, Richard, 240
London, Jack, 15
Long, Lois, 82–84, 101, 124, 178, 200
Lord, Kate, 161
Lord, Pauline, 68
Lord, Russell, 143, 161
Lorentz, Pare, 209

MacArthur, Charles, 134
MacArthur, General, 270
Mackay, Clarence H., 92, 94
Mackay, Ellin, 92–95, 158
McAllister, Ward, 76, 250
McCall, John, 95
McGeehan, W. O., 37, 208
McGinley, Phyllis, 240
McGuinness, James Kevin, 59, 70, 130
McIntyre, O. O., 233, 245
McKee, Donald, 238
McKelway, St. Clair, 163, 248, 250–51, 253, 256–58
McKenney, Ruth, 279
McLaughlin, Robert, 273
McNamara, Ed, 220–22
Maloney, Russell, 248
Mankiewicz, Herman, 59, 82, 105–6
Manning, Bishop, 247
March, Alden, 75
March, Joseph Moncure, 75–76, 78–80, 82–83, 86–87, 91–92, 102, 106
Markey, Morris, 87–89, 109–10, 115, 117–18, 122, 197, 248
Marks, Percy, 238
Marquis, Don, 122–23, 147, 158, 280
Marx, Harpo, 246
Marx, Karl, 8
Marx brothers, 239, 245
Mason, Walt, 47
Masters, Edgar Lee, 133
Mears, Helen, 58
Mencken, H. L., 120, 240
Mendota, Illinois, 132–33
Microbe Hunters, 158
Miller, Alice Duer, 43, 63, 163
Milne, A. A., 117
Mirror, New York, 133–34
Mitchell, Joseph, 248, 292
Moffat, Donald, 243
Montgomery, Field Marshal, 104
More Yank Talk, 34
Mosher, John Chapin, 200, 243, 262
Mumford, Lewis, 225
My Life and Hard Times, 235

Nash, Ogden, 229–30, 240
Nast, Condé, 46
Nathan, George Jean, 46, 209
Nation, 239–40, 292
New Republic, 23
Newhouse, Edward, 273
Nicholson, Harold, 208
Nini's Restaurant, 28–29, 40
Novis, Donald, 233

Oglebay, Kate, 50
O'Hara, John, 193, 243, 290–91
Ottumwa, Iowa, 40
Oulahan, Richard, 28

Pain, O., 41
Palmer, Frederick, 6, 49
Panter-Downes, Mollie, 270, 293
Parker, Dorothy, 40, 43–44, 46, 61, 63, 66, 70–71, 79, 115–17, 120, 147, 197, 200, 208, 230–31
Parker, James Reid, 240
Parrott, Ursula, 223
Paul, Elliott, 158
Pearson, Edmund, 240
Pegler, Westbrook, 223

Pemberton, Murdock, 39, 200
Penn Station, 237
Perelman, S. J., 238–39, 280–82
Perkins, Frances, 39
Pershing, General, 25, 32
Petty, Mary, 136
Phi Gamma Delta, 143
Pisco John's, 15
Plastic Age, The, 238
Players, The, 122, 285
PM, 104, 263–64, 291
Poetry, 280
Post, New York, 159, 198
Powell, William, 50
Pratt, Theodore, 182–83
Press Club, San Francisco, 15–17
Price, Garrett, 136
Price, George, 243
Punch, 60, 63–65, 125–26, 129–30, 171–72

Rage to Live, A, 291
Rea, Gardner, 131, 137, 238
Republican, Springfield, Massachusetts, 22
Reynolds, Quentin, 238
Rice, Elmer, 192
Rice, Grantland, 28, 91
Richmond, Virginia, 88
Richter, Mischa, 243
Robber Barons, The, 240
Rogers, Ginger, 257
Rogers, Lela, 257
Romanoff, Mike, 247–48
Roosevelt, F. D., 226, 228
Roosevelt, Mrs. F. D., 228
Roosevelt, Theodore, Jr., 70
Root, Esther, 73
Rose, Carl, 136
Ross, Anthony, 296
Ross, George, 5, 80
Ross, Ida, 6, 80, 220–21
"Ross, Leonard Q.," 279
Ross, Lillian, 291, 293
Rosten, Leo C., 279
Rovere, Richard H., 292–93
Rubenstein, Helena, 113
Runyon, Damon, 233
Ryan, Bill, 12–13
Ryder, Bob, 158
Ryder, Melvin, 33

Sacramento, California, 10–13
Sainte Anne Hotel, 120
Saks-Fifth Avenue, 95, 113
Salt Lake City, 5–9, 11, 37, 80, 220
Sampson, Martin, 143
Samuels, Arthur, 90, 169–70
San Francisco, 14–18, 29
Saratoga Springs, 215
Saturday Evening Post, 52, 221, 245, 270
Saxton, Eugene, 203
Schindler, Ray, 212, 222
Schnitzler, Arthur, 45, 208
Schriftgeisser, Karl, 197
Season in the Sun, 296
Seattle, 145
Seldes, Gilbert, 119
Shaw, Irvin, 273
Shawn, William, 268–69, 289, 292–93
Sherwood, Robert E., 45–47, 63, 208
Shirer, William L., 158
Shuman, Ik, 265, 278, 290–91
Simon, Robert, 200
Simplicissimus, 60
Sitting Bull, 180
Smart Set, 46–47, 158, 194
Smith, Adam, 8
Smith, Al, 191, 237
Smith College Club, 133–34
Smith, "Hardboiled," 37
Smith, Rixey J. W., 36
Social Register, 40, 76, 78, 92–93
Society for the Suppression of Vice, 181–83, 253

Soglow, Otto, 131, 200–1
Spaeth, Sigmund, 91
Spencer, Herbert, 13, 16–17, 39
Spoon River Anthology, 133
Springfield, Massachusetts, 22
Stage, 213, 274
Stallings, Laurence, 63
Stamford, Connecticut, 223, 262–63, 294
Stars and Stripes, 3, 20–34, 31, 36, 57, 70, 198
Steig, William, 243
Steinberg, Saul, 288–89
Sterling, George, 15
Stevens, Willie, 154
Stewart, Donald Ogden, 43
Stone, Lucy, 39
Stork Club, 256–58
Strollers, The, 157
Strunk, William, Jr., 143
Stryker, Lloyd, 74
Sullivan, Frank, 71, 85, 147, 215–17, 231–32, 280, 297
Sun, Cornell, 143
"Sun Dial, The," 122, 147, 158

Tarkington, Booth, 117
Taylor, Deems, 91, 208, 223
Taylor, Joseph Russell, 156–57
Taylor, Richard, 243
Technique of the Love Affair, 117
Thanatopsis Literary and Inside Straight Club, 28, 40, 43, 50, 71, 221
Thoreau, Henry, 141
Thurber, James, 139, 141, 152–62, 176–79, 183–84, 186, 191–97, 215, 234–36, 297
"Tilley, Eustace," 85–86, 124, 291
Times, New York, 23, 28–29, 38, 42, 75, 94, 246–47, 263–65, 291
Times, Seattle, 145
Tony's, 172
Toohey, John Peter, 39, 41, 60, 68
Town and Country, 262
Townsend, F. H., 129
transition, 194
Tribune, Salt Lake City, 7
Truax, Hawley, 49, 52, 72, 74, 275, 285
Twain, Mark, 14–15, 118, 152–53

Ulric, Lenore, 68
Union, Sacramento, 10–13
United Press, 144

Vallee, Rudy, 81
Van Anda, Carr, 42, 70
Vanderbilt, Sanderson, 248
Vanity Fair, 43–47, 64, 82–85, 92, 128, 208, 212, 279
Viskniskki, Guy T., 21, 23–28, 30–31
Vogue, 46, 92, 279
Von Blon, Philip, 30, 36

Walker, Jimmy, 91
Wallgren, Albian A., 21, 25, 28, 30, 33–34
Walpole, Hugh, 45
Walsh, Christy, 247
Watson, Mark, 31
Watts, Richard, Jr., 251, 258
West, Rebecca, 270
Whalen, Grover, 247
Whitaker, Rogers, 240
White, Andrew D., 143
White, E. B., 139–55, 158–59, 161–62, 165, 169–70, 175–76, 179, 180–83, 186–91, 193, 202–6, 225–26, 236–37, 259, 261–62, 273–74, 280, 294
White, Katharine (see *also* Angell, Katharine), 139, 207, 243, 250, 254, 259, 261–62, 289
Why We Behave Like Human Beings, 158
Williams College, 113

Williams, Gluyas, 137
Williams, R. Norris, 30
Wilson, Edmund, 208
Winchell, Walter, 100, 198, 208, 255–58, 264
Winkler, John K., 197
Winney, Harold, 264–65
Winslow, Thyra Samter, 47, 194, 243
Winterich, John T., 22, 24, 26, 31, 33, 35–36, 54, 212
Wismet, Helen, 260
Wolheim, Louis, 68
Wons, Tony, 233
Woollcott, Alexander, 3, 22–23, 26–30, 33–34, 36–37, 39–41, 43, 45, 49–54, 60, 63, 70, 89–90, 97–98, 147, 154, 164, 198–200, 208, 231, 245–46, 253–55
World, New York, 41, 68, 71, 87, 147, 159, 192, 198, 215–17
Wylie, Hugh, 48
Wylie, Philip, 58, 61, 80–82, 92, 105, 127–28, 132

Yale Record, 20
Yank Magazine, 31
Yank Talk, 33, 36, 266
Yates, Haydie Eames, 180–81
Youth's Companion, 137